T0293704

PRAISE FOR *THE 10 RULES OF HIGHLY EFFECTIVE PRICING*

'Company marketers spend a lot of time on promotion and take pricing for granted. Zatta's new book *The 10 Rules of Highly Effective Pricing* will help wake up company marketers to the profit coming from creative pricing.'
— **Philip Kotler**, S. C. Johnson Distinguished Professor of International Marketing, Kellogg School of Management, Northwestern University

'Success in the luxury industry is all about a controlled balance between value and price. The book of Danilo Zatta is an unmissable tool to unlock the hidden value for customers in your company and transform it in profitability.'
— **Stephan Winkelmann**, Chairman and CEO, Automobili Lamborghini

'Unlock the true potential of your business with this exceptional pricing book that demystifies the art and science of pricing. Dan Zatta, one of the world's leading pricing minds, equips you with the knowledge and tools needed to achieve superior competitive advantage and enhance your bottom line.'
— **Financial Times**

'This book is a game changer: it will help you increase profitability through 10 concrete rules on how to manage pricing. Dan Zatta, leading strategy and monetization thought leader, brings new perspectives, relevant for every company.'
— **Peter Brabeck-Letmathe** Chairman Emeritus Nestlé SA, Vice-Chairman of the Foundation Board of the World Economic Forum, Chairman Emeritus, Formula One Group

'This book is a must-read for anyone who wants to increase profits via optimized prices: It offers several concrete ideas and tangible insights on a subject that is fundamental to corporate success.'
— **Thomas Ingelfinger** Board Member Beiersdorf AG a.d. Board Member at several corporations, Investor

'As a CEO, I believe that a strategic approach to pricing is an excellent lever, sometimes little considered in a structured way, to increase corporate profit. *The 10 Rules of Highly Effective Pricing* is an excellent read, full of insights, very concrete, written by Danilo Zatta, whom I have the pleasure to know personally as a great expert on pricing and revenue models worldwide.'
— **Giovanni B. Vacchi**, Group CEO, Colombini Group (Colombini, Febal Casa, Bontempi, Rossana Cucine)

'Danilo Zatta's new book is a solid guide for everyone leading the organization towards pricing excellence. He gives actionable insights in the enablers for your success and a roadmap to make highly effective pricing really happen in your organization. Take benefit of Danilo Zatta's rich experience and lead the transformation journey in your organization with confidence.'
—**Pol Vanaerde** – President – EPP – Pricing & RGM Platform

'Zatta's book will give you and your team a great foundation for the strategies and tactics needed to increase your pricing acumen and your company's performance. Make sure to take advantage of his insights to learn what to do, and perhaps even more importantly, what not to do when planning your strategies and tactics.'
—**Kevin Mitchell**, President, Professional Pricing Society

'The kind of pricing Danilo talks about in this book is the best way I have found of crystallising -and testing- the real value your products and services create in highly competitive markets. It supports growth even in declining, mature industries. Danilo is a true practitioner, one of those rare consultants that gets involved and is curious enough to work with you from where you are, without off the shelf answers. Working with him has been invaluable for our businesses…and a real pleasure.'
—**Carlos Barrasa Ruiz**, Executive Vice President Commercial & Clean Energies and Member of the Management Committee, Cepsa

'Danilo's inspiring book on pricing reminds us once again that only management attention, a clear plan supported by a long-term strategy and a convincing narrative can take us "to the port we want to reach", transforming value into price and making our companies' profitability journey a success.'
—**Marcella Montelatici**, Managing Director Sales & Services, TRUMPF Werkzeugmaschinen

'The numerous case studies and industry examples make *The 10 Rules of Highly Effective Pricing* a very valuable guide to a state of the art pricing.'
—**Markus Mildner**, CEO Siemens eMobility

After the best seller *The Pricing Model Revolution*, this new book by Dan Zatta deep dives new key topline topics, proposing to CxOs simple but effective rules to lead the *Pricing Transformation*. With the support of several concrete cases Dan also shows how in this journey C-level pricing attention is a key factor of success to reach above average profitability.'
—**Luigi Colavolpe**, General Manager & CFO UniCredit International Bank (Luxembourg)

'Danilo Zatta, one of the world's most authoritative pricing experts, offers readers an essential guide for companies (and others) in an increasingly fluid and complex world, an indispensable compass to navigate the turbulent ocean of pricing.'
—**Il Sole 24 Ore**, leading Italian business newspaper

'Companies understand the context and improve their proposition to generate value. Also pricing is linked to context and needs to be strategically elevated to the same level as the proposition. *The 10 Rules of Highly Effective Pricing* provides guidance on how to do so and the respective businesses cases are a proof point how contextualizing pricing can lead to maximization of value.'
—**Alessandro Piccinini**, CEO Nespresso Germany

THE 10 RULES OF HIGHLY EFFECTIVE PRICING

HOW TO TRANSFORM YOUR PRICE MANAGEMENT TO BOOST PROFITS

DANILO ZATTA

WILEY

This edition first published 2024

Danilo Zatta©2024

All rights reserved. No part of this publication may be reproduced, stored in a retrieval system, or transmitted, in any form or by any means, electronic, mechanical, photocopying, recording or otherwise, except as permitted by law. Advice on how to obtain permission to reuse material from this title is available at http://www.wiley.com/go/permissions.

The right of Danilo Zatta to be identified as the authors of this work has been asserted in accordance with law.

Registered Office(s)
John Wiley & Sons, Inc., 111 River Street, Hoboken, NJ 07030, USA
John Wiley & Sons Ltd, The Atrium, Southern Gate, Chichester, West Sussex, PO19 8SQ, UK

Editorial Office
The Atrium, Southern Gate, Chichester, West Sussex, PO19 8SQ, UK

For details of our global editorial offices, customer services, and more information about Wiley products visit us at www.wiley.com.

Wiley also publishes its books in a variety of electronic formats and by print-on-demand. Some content that appears in standard print versions of this book may not be available in other formats. Designations used by companies to distinguish their products are often claimed as trademarks. All brand names and product names used in this book are trade names, service marks, trademarks or registered trademarks of their respective owners. The publisher is not associated with any product or vendor mentioned in this book.

Limit of Liability/Disclaimer of Warranty
While the publisher and authors have used their best efforts in preparing this work, they make no representations or warranties with respect to the accuracy or completeness of the contents of this work and specifically disclaim all warranties, including without limitation any implied warranties of merchantability or fitness for a particular purpose. No warranty may be created or extended by sales representatives, written sales materials or promotional statements for this work. The fact that an organization, website, or product is referred to in this work as a citation and/or potential source of further information does not mean that the publisher and authors endorse the information or services the organization, website, or product may provide or recommendations it may make. This work is sold with the understanding that the publisher is not engaged in rendering professional services. The advice and strategies contained herein may not be suitable for your situation. You should consult with a specialist where appropriate. Further, readers should be aware that websites listed in this work may have changed or disappeared between when this work was written and when it is read. Neither the publisher nor authors shall be liable for any loss of profit or any other commercial damages, including but not limited to special, incidental, consequential, or other damages.

Library of Congress Cataloging-in-Publication Data is Available:

ISBN 9781394195763 (Cloth)
ISBN 9781119901150 (ePub)
ISBN 9781119901167 (ePDF)

Cover Design: Wiley
Cover Images: © Varavin88/Shutterstock, © belozu/Shutterstock
Author Photo: Courtesy of the Author

SKY10057301_101023

To my wife Babette and my children Natalie, Sebastian, and Marilena who charge me with energy every day.

In memory of my mother Annemarie and my father Renzo – I will hold you forever in my heart.

CONTENTS

PREFACE

Several years of constant work and research gave birth to *The 10 Rules of Highly Effective Pricing.*

I wanted to write a different pricing book with no mathematical formulas, no academic theories, nor complex graphs. Instead I wanted it full of case studies, examples, and anecdotes from C-Levels and practitioners who reveal the secrets of their above-average success achieved via TopLine transformations, that is, their magic potion.

I therefore started gathering key success factors of such commercial transformations that help companies unlock profitable growth, identifying 10 decisive elements. The result is a book for executives and managers not familiar with TopLine excellence but also for pricing practitioners who want to be inspired and see how best in class companies use this lever to succeed. The 10 actionable rules can be introduced to any company to boost profitability.

In the past more than 20 years I have had the privilege of working as a management advisor on thousands of TopLine Transformations across geographies and industries. My intention was also to capture the learnings of all those assignments in a concrete guide that readers could benefit from. Indeed, companies following these 10 rules achieve above-average profitability. This is what the application of the rules has demonstrated in corporate daily life.

The goal of the book is thus to illustrate each of the 10 rules and provide a concrete guide on how to increase your company's profitability with several examples and best practices taken from various industries and geographies.

Each chapter starts with an introduction to provide context, followed by a main part that deep dives the core of the material and closes with a summary to capture the essence of what was shared.

If you have read and enjoyed *The Pricing Model Revolution*, then hopefully this new book will provide you with further insights and food for thought from a different perspective. If the key topic of my last book was the *Pricing Revolution* as a new source for a competitive advantage, the key topic of this book is the *Pricing Transformation* that helps you become a pricing champion with above average margins from your company. As this is a book written for top executives, managers, and practitioners, I chose a storytelling approach, with several anecdotes, examples, and cases: it intends to serve as a source of inspiration. This is a business book, with lots of references and also quotes from philosophy, history, science, and from movies as parallels to pricing can be drawn from many sources, bringing fresh perspectives.

Please let me know how you liked this book and reach out to me to share your thoughts. I also would love to hear your opinion on the 10 rules as well as your own pricing experiences.

Keep in touch,

—Dan
Rome/Munich, November 2023
zatta.danilo@gmail.com
www.linkedin.com/in/danilo-zatta

PART I
INEFFECTIVE PRICING RULES

WHY PRICING IS KEY BUT SELDOM EFFECTIVE

'Give me a lever long enough and a fulcrum on which to place it, and I shall move the world.'

Archimedes, mathematician

Introduction

We push ourselves to the limits of what is possible to excel. We delve into the depths where the shadow still lingers of the things, of the objects, that will one day tell those who come after us who we have been and what we have done, attempted to do, with the time that has been granted to us to transform the present for a better future.

'Excellence' and 'transformation' are two key terms that you will find expressed in the various chapters of this book. They represent what we know about life and growth.

The socio-economic context is increasingly complex.

Navigating by a compass – regardless of the target market – is becoming increasingly difficult, as is trying to do our best within the context we have chosen, or happened to find ourselves in, to play the 'game' that is our working life.

But what does the word 'work' mean today?

What are the characteristics that society and technology impose on us?

Where is the market pushing us: do we need to be more flexible or find new ways of interpreting the world?

Many are starting to talk about a *paradigm shift*, in the era of the energy transition that is shaping the new geography of the present. The world that will be: tomorrow.

In order to recognize what we sometimes fail to see, we must be able to anticipate trends – the *filter bubble*, tendencies, social media, the new rules of communication that state that 'if you're not online, you don't exist' – and implement fast and fluid thinking that takes into consideration the new geopolitical order, crises, wars, and uncertainties that reach us daily through radio, TV, and streaming. We live in a constantly connected world. We are potential victims of overload (too much of everything) and fakeness (everything is true, nothing is true anymore).

That is why we are like speleologists; our task is to find a way out, tunnels of air and light for our activity. To succeed, we venture out to explore the rough seas of the market, withstanding fluctuations, and learning to face the profound unknown of what we call 'society' – a word with dual meaning: specifically, our companies, our ventures; and, more generally, the sum of individuals who make up and shape the daily relationships in which we are immersed.

To each object, a recognized value.

To each good or service, a price.

'Give me a lever long enough and a fulcrum on which to place it, and I shall move the world', said Archimedes, or words to that effect.

That is why understanding the leverage of price is an essential tool to implement the necessary transformation required by the changes imposed on us today.

Give me a lever, and I will lift the world. Give me the pricing lever, and I will lift the fortunes of your company.

Enjoy reading.

Short-sightedness in Pricing

In many companies, there is a noticeable imbalance.

On the one hand, a lot of time, money, and attention are dedicated to research and development of new products (followed by production, distribution, and marketing efforts). However, when it comes to determining the 'fair reward' for the effort put into bringing the new offering to the market, the commitment diminishes significantly.

As a result, decisions regarding how to monetize products or services risk becoming arbitrary. 'We have always set prices this way' is the answer I never want to hear when I ask how the price was determined. Unfortunately, it is what I hear most often.

This approach lacks vision and is both incorrect and arbitrary.

The importance and impact of pricing leverage are greatly underestimated.

'Myopia', or short-sightedness, reigns in pricing.

This short-sightedness is obvious in all the companies that fail to see the direct and immediate relationship between prices and profits.

It is precisely this direct relationship that makes pricing the most powerful and immediate lever available to companies.

Let us take the case of a company operating in retail with a profit margin of 3% (a percentage that is typical in its industry as well as in several others): to contextualize this, consider that Walmart, the world's largest retail chain, in the year 2022 recorded a margin of 1.9%, which is even lower.

Returning to the company with a 3% margin, for every dollar of revenue, the profit amounts to 3 cents. If this company could optimize its pricing and increase prices by just 1%, charging, for example, $1.01 instead of $1.00, the profit per transaction would increase by one cent. Therefore, instead of earning 3 cents per dollar, it would now earn 4 cents. Thus, a mere 1 cent increase means increasing profits by over 33%, or 1 cent more for every 3 cents of profit.

Now, what if we hypothesize that demand remains constant when we increase the list prices by 1 cent?

It becomes a magic trick. In reality, there would be no need to even increase list prices by 1%; we could simply reduce the average discount by 1%. The effect would be the same: 1 cent more.

In both cases, we would achieve the same result. The purpose of this example is to understand how to pull the rabbit out of the hat, demonstrating that a small price variation has a significant beneficial impact on profits.

At companies like Walmart, with a profit margin lower than 3%, the increase of profits coming from the additional cent would be even higher than 33%.

The relationship between prices and profits is direct, strong, immediate, and entirely evident.

However, it is important to note that increasing prices does not mean generating inflated and undeserved revenues to be ashamed of. Rather, it means monetizing the value provided.

It is the essence of pricing power, the ability to capture the value delivered to the client.

In fact, the best compliment a customer can give is paying a higher price because the customer perceives the value of our product or service as superior to that of others.

With well-established pricing we can exercise our pricing power capturing the value we deserve without wasting a single penny of the stakes on the table.

Pricing – Main Lever of Profit

Over the past 20 years, I have worked with numerous companies operating in different sectors, from B2B to B2C, and in all continents of *our* planet.

Based on my experience as a management consultant, I can testify that companies that have given the 'right' importance to monetizing the generated value have stood out with above-average profits. At the same time, they have realized that pricing is the strongest and most immediate profit lever.

Well-implemented pricing generates the profits needed to invest in the future of the company.

A pricing transformation pays off in a short period of time.

Thus, pricing can become the foundation for profitable and lasting growth.

After my latest book, *The Pricing Model Revolution*, was published, I had the pleasure of receiving feedback from scholars such as Professor Philip Kotler and leaders from various industries, who all emphasized the essential nature of this lever. Among them is my friend Peter Brabeck-Letmathe, who served as the Group CEO of Nestlé for 20 years, making him the most successful individual in the history of the company. He is currently a board member of several companies and institutes. Peter told me, 'Pricing has always been the primary lever to increase profits in the companies I have led. Price management will become increasingly important, thanks to new technologies. That's why I dedicate my time also to companies that develop new solutions to digitise and innovate pricing.'[1]

Similar conclusions have been reached through empirical analysis and by many professors and scholars.

However, most companies still do not give proper attention to managing the price lever. In fact, they often neglect pricing, lack dedicated pricing managers at the organizational level, use outdated approaches, miss potential opportunities, and, above all, lose profit. Other initiatives, such as supply chain management, lean manufacturing, risk management, Six Sigma, have enjoyed significant attention for decades, attracting investments, resources and top management support.

However, their benefits are significantly inferior and more drawn out over time compared to the price lever.

So, why does this pricing myopia prevail?

There is probably no single answer to this question.

One reason could be the difficulty companies face in establishing the right price. Limited experience, the dispersion of price management responsibility among functions and geographical areas without clear oversight, or incentives favouring sales volumes over margins – all these factors hinder ideal monetization.

Therefore, it is understandable that myopia has spread in pricing.

Monetization remains ineffective, and companies continue to operate without transforming price management. What then? How do most companies act when they intend to monetize the value they offer to customers?

Many simply react.

They react to competitors' moves.

They react to the management's demand to generate a certain margin by adding it to the cost.

By doing so, they miss the opportunity to make pricing a real lever for generating profits.

What can be done to overcome all these issues, and transform pricing to capture greater profits?

10 Rules for Highly Effective Pricing

To transform pricing and use it as a lever to maximize profits, it is necessary to understand and internalize 10 fundamental rules.

Each rule guides every individual in the company on how to excel on the commercial front, setting the stage for sustainable and profitable growth.

1. MAKE PRICING A CEO PRIORITY Pricing should be one of the top priorities on every CEO's agenda. Innovative pricing models are revolutionising monetization in many sectors and becoming a new source of competitive advantage. CEOs play a crucial role in elevating pricing from an operational burden to a company priority. They must set the strategic direction and make it clear to everyone in the organization how immediate and direct the link is between pricing and company profits.

2. DISSEMINATE THE CULTURE OF PROFIT To promote profit generation, it is important to foster a profit culture. According to Peter Drucker, culture is the most difficult factor to control and change. It is this contradiction between its importance and its resistance to change that makes it so unique.

   The three guidelines for spreading a profit culture are: 1) *avoid spoiling customers* by refraining from excessive concessions; 2) *direct the use of discounts* by granting them only when strictly necessary; and 3) *communicate the value of products*, as a strong perception of value is the foundation for sustaining a certain price level. Everyone in the company, especially salespeople, should be aware of the value, so that a certain price level can be maintained.

3. UNDERSTAND AND SELL VALUE To capture and sell value through value pricing, five steps should be followed: 1) *understand needs and create value*: knowing what customers need is the starting point, followed by aligning the company's offer and prices accordingly; 2) *analyse the competition*: their offerings evolve, and new competitors with alternative solutions enter the market: this will influence the perceived value of our own offer; 3) *quantify the value*: having identified and analysed

the sources of value in the competitive context, the value must be quantified (that is the difference between customer perception and the value of what is offered); 4) *price on the basis of value*: consider the quantification of value drivers for each customer; and 5) *communicate the value effectively*: have a compelling value narrative to support the price argument.

4. DIFFERENTIATE PRICES In many cases, it is fairer to discriminate prices for the same product or service rather than applying a uniform price. This pricing paradox benefits customers, businesses, and society. To support differentiated prices, it is important to be able to justify the differences transparently and explicitly.

5. CONSOLIDATE PROFITS BY INCREASING PRICES There are many possibilities and ample room for creativity when it comes to raising prices. Six established paths include: 1) *increasing value and prices* by providing more value to the customer; 2) *increasing prices while offering less value*, which is the opposite of the first approach; 3) *applying surcharges* by evaluating which products or services, currently provided free of charge, should be charged for in the future without changing the existing price list; 4) *pricing by segments* to monetize the perceived value from different customer groups effectively; 5) *incrementally raising prices up to the next threshold* to increase profits without losing volume; and 6) *adjusting the pricing model to increase revenues*.

6. AVOID PRICE WARS Price wars can harm an entire industry and can have a devastating and lasting impact. Therefore, successful companies consciously avoid price wars for three reasons. First, customers expect lower prices to be the new reference prices going forward. Second, gaining market share becomes challenging as, in a competitive environment, competitors quickly respond to price cuts. Third, everyone loses in a price war.

Chapter 7 analyses the causes and characteristics of price wars, as well as the intentions of the involved competitors.

7. CULTIVATE YOUR PRICE IMAGE Price image is the customer's perception of a company's positioning. It is an essential element that needs to be defined, managed, and monitored because it doesn't always reflect the actual price level but rather the conscious or subconscious sensation of where the price level stands in the customer's mind.

   One typical approach to influence price image is through the presentation of the 'price point'.

8. EMPLOY TECHNOLOGIES, DIRECTING ALGORITHMS Modern technologies allow for effective pricing management.

   Successfully introducing a suitable solution for a company follows a structured path, including analysing the business context and needs. This chapter covers options for realising the technological solution, its implementation, and the solution itself.

9. SET THE PRICING GOVERNANCE Pricing governance is the system of rules, practices, processes, and organization through which pricing is managed within a company. It should be a priority for any company aiming to increase its profitability. If the pricing function positions itself as a strategic partner for other functions, it becomes the key to success.

10. DEBUNK THE MYTHS OF PRICING There are seven myths that undermine the potential of pricing as a lever. Companies that have debunked these myths achieve higher-than-average profitability.

In summary, while my previous book focused on the *Pricing Revolution* related to revenue models, with this new text we will tackle together the market's new challenges with what we will call the *Pricing Transformation*!

PART II
THE 10 RULES OF HIGHLY EFFECTIVE PRICING

RULE 1
MAKE PRICING A CEO PRIORITY

'Cutting prices or putting things on sale is not a sustainable business strategy.

'The other side of it is that you can't cut enough costs to save your way to prosperity.'

Howard Schultz, Starbucks CEO

What can we say of this constant, relentless need for self-improvement? As if we were never good enough. And time is a non-secondary variable of what we call illusion. Modern times, to say it with Charlie Chaplin words, have forced us into increasingly narrow margins; we live in the interstices, often sacrificing more than we gain. Success, money, we expend energy and resources – which we don't have, so we must 'fish' for them from other places: a holiday, an impossible love, a passion elsewhere, friends – we engage ourselves on multiple fronts. Just to say 'it was worth it'.

The great explorers of the nineteenth and early twentieth centuries knew they would depart. The endeavour was stronger, more pressing than the comfort of staying. *Staying* not simply in the sense of remaining on familiar ground, but also resting on the comfortable certainties of our preconceptions.

But we know that the world is much bigger than we thought it was. Just step beyond the borders, which don't even exist in nature;

we invented them as we invent the partitioning of knowledge: as if it were possible to divide a human being into the many pieces they are made of, my aptitude for numbers like my love for *pasta all'amatriciana*, my passion for golf separated from my university studies; as if it were possible not to love someone just because you love someone else, a child, the place we call home, Argos, the faithful dog of Odysseus, who allows himself to die only after seeing his human friend return. To bid him farewell one last time.

The idea of this second book on pricing has a lot to do with *going* instead and specifically with the mountain. Here, the mountain is meant in its archetype of climbing, of challenge to the vertical sea. First, which mountain will we climb? How much weight can we carry? These are the starting conditions. But still, what will be the best path to reach the summit, and this applies as much to business as it does to life.

After years of corporate races and mountain trails, I have understood that the difference lies in the approach.

A mountain is climbed first with the mind, and then with the body.

We prepare ourselves, put on a good pair of technical boots, decide whether to pack food or water in our backpacks, and what to leave behind. Every day, we are constantly called upon to make choices. Like in the novel *Into the Wild* by Jon Krakauer, based on the dramatic story of Christopher McCandless, which Sean Penn adapted into a poignant film.

If there's one thing you learn by going into the woods, it's to breathe deeply: we realized this during the pandemic, the sense of freedom, reclaiming space. That period, although terrible, in some ways meant reordering our priorities.

Heading straight for the goal is a matter of legs but even more of endurance.

When fatigue sets in – a business deal gone wrong, disillusionment, a low blow from someone we believed to be a friend, lack of results – that's when we must draw upon all our resources.

The path to navigate in the market *jungle* is long and treacherous.

Therefore, this handbook aims to be a support for the upcoming climbs, a reflective manual full of examples and passion, that gets straight to the point.

It was designed to share as much small but important knowledge as possible (since culture is the only good that increases, when divided among many, instead of diminishing). It is important to know the levers that make *the climb* possible, especially *pricing*.

In this regard, the metaphor of the mountain has a double meaning: on the one hand, it means that we must be able to reach the summit, navigate the (treacherous) currents of the market, and aim high; on the other hand, the snow-capped peak represents the head of the rock giant; and, by a similar token, for us, the summit, the apex to which this manual is addressed, is the mind of the company, those who have a global vision: managers, senior executives, owners, CEOs, in short, the captains of the enterprise!

Pricing as a Top Priority for CEOs

One of the most famous quotes from the legendary investor Warren Buffett, who is now one of the richest men on the planet, is: 'The single most important decision in evaluating a business is pricing power. If you've got the power to raise prices without losing business to a competitor, you've got a very good business. And if you have to have a prayer session before raising the price by 10 percent, then you've got a terrible business.'[1]

Buffett refers to *pricing power* as the ability to provide significant value to the market on the one hand and to extract that value through appropriate pricing on the other. For him, pricing is the sum of a broader project that should receive the utmost attention from top-level executives.

Among all the profit levers, pricing not only stands as the strongest but also the quickest, as demonstrated by various studies and publications;[2] crises, wars, pandemics. Price is a lever, and, without invoking Archimedes, it is the essence that allows us to interpret the present and future of our activities.

However, the majority of top-level executives focus their attention on other issues such as costs, market share, or engagements in mergers and acquisitions. This imbalance is confirmed by managers themselves, as in the case of Jeff Immelt, former CEO of General Electric (GE), who said: 'Not long ago, a guy here named Dave McCalpin did an analysis of our pricing in appliances and found out that about $5 billion of it is discretionary. Given all the decisions that sales reps can make on their own, that's how much is in play. It was the most astounding number I'd ever heard – and that's just in appliances. Extrapolating across our businesses, there may be $50 billion that few people are tracking or accountable for. We would never allow something like that on the cost side. When it comes to the prices we pay, we study them, we map them, we work them. But with the prices we charge, we're too sloppy.'[3]

Recent studies indicate that only one in five companies has a dedicated pricing team within their management department.[4] Specifically, only 22% of the largest US companies listed on the Fortune

500 have a dedicated pricing department. This implies that approximately 80% do not allocate a specific function to this lever within their company. In turn, this means that there is a lack of a systematic and structured approach that enables efficient monetization or, to put it more accurately, they are unable to climb the impossible, simply because they don't see it.

Thus, what prevails is a less evolved pricing approach based on the principle of *cost plus*, with manual or Microsoft Excel support, and with responsibilities shared across multiple functions and regions.

The pricing approach is a mindset, as mentioned at the beginning, a mental space that allows us to look at our enterprises (in both the sense of adventures and business) through a dedicated special filter. Pricing is a rope, a harness that allows us to lift the weight of our company and reach the goals we have set for ourselves, safely, and leveraging our abilities.

Why is it not like this yet?

Because while it is true that to revolutionize the whole world is impossible, we can start by revolutionizing our way of thinking about the world. As in the cult movie *Matrix*, where the child tells the protagonist Neo: 'Do not try and bend the spoon. That's impossible. Instead . . . only try to realize the truth.' 'What truth?' 'There is no spoon.' 'There is no spoon?' 'Then you'll see that it is not the spoon that bends, it is only yourself.'

Currently, among the 22% of companies claiming to be structured around pricing, there are at most one or two dedicated full-time resources. We do not envy at all those who have to deal with different levels of pricing, in situations where revenues are in the region of billions of dollars, with the equivalent of only a spoon!

But why do so many companies neglect price management when the importance of this lever is so evident?

Several elements explain this phenomenon.

Firstly, top-level executives themselves believe in various myths (more on this in Chapter 10), such as the idea that 'market share and profits are correlated', or that 'the price of a commodity cannot be increased', or that 'cost is the basis of price', 'customers want low prices'. Within many corporate leadership teams, the belief that pricing is a strategic issue is not universally shared. Instead, many consider it a tactical task carried out – as and when – by workers lower down in the company hierarchy.

In reality, an increasing number of companies operating in various sectors and geographical locations have found in innovative pricing models the source of their competitive advantage, revolutionizing the way they monetize in multiple sectors and triggering a pricing revolution, as I illustrated in my book *The Pricing Model Revolution* (2022).

At the same time, there is a lack of training in pricing. Only in recent years, and only in a few universities across the world, have price management courses been validated: in the vast majority of universities, there is no offer to study pricing as in-depth as it should be done. Today's top executives, who studied 20 or more years ago, have never dealt with this issue. Probably even the pricing managers who have been in charge of the department for several years are not clear about the case studies, best practices, or levels of other companies, valuable comparisons that could bring some evidence to the attention of top management, convincing them of the benefits that a transformation in this area can generate.

But this is quite normal: if you have been working in a specific business reality for a long time, exposure to external influences is severely limited.

Only by travelling do you get to know the world. You will be able to see not only the different horizons but, more importantly, the features and rhythm of the daily life in other realities. And this is significant, in an increasingly global and interconnected world.

We are not an Absolute Truth. We are open worlds or, to put it in the Hollywood New Wave terms, we are 'multiverses': multiple and diverse realities.

That said, as indicated by GE, price management is often ignored or considered a non-priority by top corporate executives. Supposition and approximation take over in managing this lever. So, rather than investing to improve pricing, they focus on other goals, say, more within reach.

Again, the line between *possible* and *impossible*. What a shame to treat the main profit lever like this!

On the other hand, a conscious management of the price lever leads to extraordinary results.

When top executives dedicate time and attention to pricing, performance surpasses that of companies where it is lacking. Various studies attest to superior performance. In companies with top management overseeing pricing, the following are observed:

- a margin higher by 1–2 percentage points,
- a success rate of over 23% in price increase campaigns, and

- active price management through a dedicated department or function supports the reduction of discounts in favour of value-based selling.

Results like these are achieved where executives consider pricing as one of the key strategic competencies that enable profitable growth. It can be said, as in the case of Wendelin Wiedeking, who headed the German automaker Porsche from 1993 to 2009, that they are almost 'obsessed with pricing', not wanting to miss any critical decisions.

Unfortunately, there are not many who make such considerations. Fortunately for me as a management advisor, it must be said, the work of a profit culture is still to be built. But I will never tire of saying it.

A sound income generation becomes a solid foundation for future growth.

A conscious and targeted price management is not something optional – a nice-to-have – but rather an essential competence to develop and invest in.

The Role of the CEO

Too often, it is mistakenly believed that pricing is merely an operational task. When that is the case, there is a risk that the prophecy self-fulfils (we know from Homer onwards that oracles, just like those who 'hear voices,' never end well), and pricing remains a secondary function.

In this sense, the role of the CEO is decisive in elevating pricing from an operational task to a priority for the company. It is the CEO who must make it clear to everyone in the organization how immediate and direct the link between pricing and company profits is.

The CEO sets the strategic direction.

A key aspect is price positioning and the associated *price image* that the company wants to convey. Our 'perception' in the market.

When setting price positioning, there are several possibilities: at the two extremes, we find premium followed by luxury, and on the opposite side, low cost up to ultra-low cost.

Positioning oneself, the values of one's company, in terms of price is one of the most critical and strategically relevant choices, also because once made, they are very difficult to change.

In addition to setting the strategic direction, the CEO must also establish cultural aspects that influence how the company creates, communicates, and captures value.

This cultural aspect has multiple implications, influencing, for example, how the company sets revenue models to monetize value, how it negotiates, what pricing discipline and quality are expected from the image we project externally, what type of talent we will hire, whether we prefer value-oriented or volume-oriented salespeople, and which distribution partners we will ally with for product sales. In other words, the CEO ensures alignment between price positioning and corporate culture.

One frequently cited CEO who prioritized pricing is Wendelin Wiedeking. He lifted Porsche out of a crisis and transformed it into one of the most profitable vehicle manufacturers in the world, with a revenue of €34.6 billion in 2022 and a 16.5% increase in operating profit to €6.4 compared to the previous year.[5]

One of the secrets to this success was the priority given to price management.

Wiedeking insisted on being involved in all major pricing decisions, such as launching a new model. He saw his role as a catalyst for in-depth analysis and discussions, examining all aspects related to the value and price of vehicles without encroaching on the operational decisions of the team. In this way, he demonstrated great competence while respecting the roles and work of others.

Regarding pricing, Wendelin was always on top of things and knowledgeable about the details. Even during periods of high pressure, he staunchly defended the concept of value and price level over volumes. One of his famous quotes was, 'When demand declines, we don't lower prices; we reduce production quantities.'

Wendelin wanted to maintain the value of both new and used cars by ensuring a higher demand than supply, which allowed for sustained prices. He was able to sell entire limited editions within a few days, such as the legendary 997, of which only 250 units were produced at high prices, without succumbing to the temptation of pushing sales with low prices.[6]

The value-oriented culture of Porsche was one of the most important legacies left by Wendelin in the company.

Pricing excellence became part of Porsche's DNA. One of his mantras was to build the product around the price – that is, understanding the target price and target cost during the development phase.

Even today, Porsche continues to invest in improving performance and investigating customer-perceived sources of value (and those that are not) to best capture purchase willingness. While not many companies have the brand and products of Porsche, this approach is replicable in any type of company, regardless of industry and geography.

We mentioned the case of GE, which realized it had neglected the pricing lever. Once aware of the situation, the company implemented a series of measures to give pricing the right priority.

One initial result was the introduction of the Chief Pricing Officer role in different business units, reporting directly to the leader of the respective division. These new positions also had the task of supporting negotiation preparations to defend the value better. The term *black belt* from the Six Sigma methodology, which designates highly skilled individuals and team leaders within a cost-reduction project in GE, was extended to pricing. The concept of 'price discipline' was also introduced, referring to adherence to and defence of target prices. The result was a significant increase in profitability, thanks to a higher achievement of target prices, as confirmed by CEO Jeff Immelt: pricing discipline bore fruit, surpassing even expectations.

However, you still have to be careful not to go down the wrong path, even with good intentions!

This is what happened to the CEO of a machinery manufacturer who, despite wanting to increase profitability, ended up reducing it instead.

His reasoning seemed logical: overwhelmed by many customer requests, he couldn't dedicate his attention to every bidding process. Therefore, he established a minimum gross margin of 25% to be achieved on each new order. Up until that point, the average gross margin had been 27.5%, so with 25%, he wanted to allow for some additional flexibility in negotiations. Any offer below 25% would require his approval.

So far, everything seemed reasonable.

When I met this CEO in person during the new fiscal year, I asked him with interest about the outcome of his initiative. 'The approval requests have been drastically reduced', he replied with satisfaction. When I inquired about the development of the gross margin, the answer was less satisfactory: 'The average margin is now 25.2%.' More than a 2 percentage point decrease in margin! What a disaster!

How can this decrease be explained?

Simple: if the CEO indicates that prices can go as low as 25%, why would a salesperson risk losing customers by asking for a higher price? It's better to lower the prices and secure the sale. Consequently, even if there were some cases in the past where sales were made with margins of 30% or 31%, these instances became more unique and rare.

Another worst-case scenario, listed under 'behaviours to avoid', occurs when top management interferes in price negotiations that should be handled by others. While there may be some cases where this overlap makes sense, in general, I would say that damage can be done when there is a lack of alignment.

The CEO of a major consumer goods manufacturer had a habit, every December, of informally visiting the management teams of their clients, mainly distributors and retailers, to personally extend holiday greetings. Since it was the end of the year, commercial negotiations between sales and purchasing departments were also in full swing. During these visits, the CEOs of the visited companies often brought up the topic of pricing. In the end, the CEO of the consumer goods manufacturer always ended up granting some form of concession or *ad hoc* discount, undermining the hard work and value defence of their sales team.

My clear recommendation was to cease the visits and instead send a good book as a gift for the holidays. After putting an end to the ritual of annual visits, there were no more margin reductions due to the CEO, and everyone returned to celebrating, as they say, happy and content.

The Pricing Tasks of the CEO

Just as every expedition has an 'expedition leader', there are several pricing tasks that can fall under the responsibility of the CEO, including: assuming price leadership, sending price signals, and, finally, avoiding price wars.

One of the primary tasks that any CEO in leading companies within their industry should undertake is to consciously assume price leadership.

When we are at the helm of a leading company in our sector, we must be the first to increase prices when, for example, the costs of raw materials rise. We cannot expect, the followers, our competitors, to make the first move. This is what we could define as 'price leadership'.

This phenomenon can be observed in various contexts. In the US automotive industry, for decades, General Motors (GM) was the price leader. When it held a market share of around 50%, GM directed the entire market: it raised prices annually, and competitors followed suit.

If GM had not increased prices, competitors would not have dared to raise them first. By doing so, the pricing leader company allowed all industry players to prosper.

There are sectors where the opposite has happened, such as the tyre industry in Spain or the beer industry in Italy. In both cases, there was no company capable of positioning itself as a leader, and thus, in the respective markets, we witnessed full-fledged price wars.

With constant discounts, promotions, and special offers, the price level only knew one direction for a long period: downward. Customers were educated not to buy at full price but always to take advantage of some form of discount or promotion.

A strong example of price leadership can be found in the retail sector in Germany: the Aldi brand is the undisputed price leader in several product categories. In a newspaper article published some time ago, the role of price leadership was explained as follows: 'Aldi is significantly increasing prices. The market is oriented towards Aldi. It is expected that other retailers will follow Aldi by raising prices.'[7]

The American Express company is another example of a company that positions itself as a pricing leader. It has a strong position in the credit card industry and is able to impose higher fees than most of its competitors.

A similar scenario is documented in the US beer industry, where following price increases, a logic of this kind followed: 'AB InBev regularly increases beer prices, and MillerCoors follows this path.'[8]

A second task is to mitigate the risks associated with price changes.

Price changes always carry a risk: when we increase prices, our competitors may not follow suit, causing us to lose market share due to the larger price difference. When we temporarily lower prices, we may be misunderstood as hostile and unintentionally trigger a price war. In both cases, we jeopardize our profitability.

To avoid such risks, it is possible to send price signals, known as price signalling. How does it work?

Before changing prices, signals are sent to the market. These signals can be, for example, statements or interviews given by the CEO to the press. Then, we listen and wait for the reaction of competitors, customers, and investors before deciding how to proceed.

An example in this regard is provided by Rene Obermann, as the CEO of Deutsche Telekom. In a context of declining prices in all market segments of fixed-line, mobile, and DSL telephony, Rene Obermann intervened by delivering a clear message to competitors: 'As long as we have a 50% market share in all new DSL connections, we will keep prices stable. Otherwise, we will do everything possible to regain this market share.' The message to competitors was unambiguous: if you dare to lower prices to take away market share, we will react strongly. However, if you accept the current market balance, we can coexist peacefully. Competitors understood the message and kept prices stable, resulting in prices remaining around €30/month for many years.

A similar signal was sent by Mr. Im, head of international operations at the Korean car maker Hyundai: 'If Japanese car makers become aggressive in increasing incentives and the red light comes on regarding our sales target, we will consider increasing incentives [for buyers].'[9] The message to competitors was that Hyundai would quickly react to price cuts and not remain passive.

In the same vein, Søren Skou, CEO of the shipping company Maersk Line, moved when he announced in newspapers after a ruinous price war: 'In terms of size and market share, we are positioned where we want to be. That is why our strategy is changing from "growing faster than the market" to "growing in line with the market." We hope that our competitors are also satisfied with their positions. If not, we will defend ours by all means necessary.' In this case too, the signal was strong and received. The price war ended, and a few months later, Skou revised his statements, saying, 'We are seeing the first signs that our industry is returning to rational behaviour. Once again, it is discovered that competing on prices to gain more market share is rarely a smart move.'

Price signalling is not inherently illegal as long as the communication is directed to all market participants, from competitors to customers and investors. What should be avoided is the possibility that such statements could lead to 'agreements' or 'cartels' that would undermine free competition, such as stating that prices will be increased if a competitor raises theirs.

With price signalling, it is possible to legally influence the market. Moreover, if the CEO personally does it, they will have not only greater credibility and influence but also an effective and credible position.

The third task of the CEO, finally, is to avoid price wars.

These are the most effective ways to destroy the profits of an entire industry in a lasting manner, much to the delight of customers.

Often, in this regard, the phrase is mentioned: 'In a war, the atomic bomb and price have the same limitation: they can be used only once.' The reason is that they lead to complete devastation.

But how can the CEO avoid price wars? It's not an easy question to answer because assuming pricing leadership also means understanding which limits can be broken and which cannot.

What a CEO can do is establish a culture and strategy in such a way as to avoid warlike attitudes. In fact, there are corporate executives ready to do anything to sweep away competitors. This is what Tesla did in the automotive sector in 2023 when it lowered the prices of its cars.[10] It's what happens in the oil industry after another true bloody war, following Russia's invasion of Ukraine.[11] Amazon, Microsoft, and Google have also fought battles by slashing prices to secure cloud services by as much as 85%.[12]

In a Board of Directors meeting to which I was summoned some time ago, it was mentioned that a foreign competitor had entered the national market. The reactions were immediately harsh: 'We must send them home at any cost.' When top executives spread such an attitude, it is no wonder that they are then perceived as aggressive in the market. I immediately tried to calm things down.

In such cases, it is important for the CEO to take appropriate measures and targeted communications to avoid or immediately put an end to hostilities. The President of Toyota, Hiroshi Okuda, made such an intervention by indicating to journalists that 'the Japanese automotive industry must give Detroit time and space to catch its breath.'[13] What he meant was, 'Toyota will raise prices in the United States', which it indeed did. This increased their profits while also giving US manufacturers the opportunity to achieve higher sales volumes.

The communication from the CEO in this regard must be clear and unambiguous, avoiding any possibility of being misunderstood as an intention to attack competitors or become aggressive in any form, inadvertently triggering a zero-sum battle where no one wins. This happened to a consumer electronics manufacturer: the company had developed a product which, 6 months after its launch in the market, was no longer generating sales. With warehouses full and knowing that the obsolescence of this product would make it unsellable shortly, the company's executives decided to heavily cut the prices to get rid of it and then discontinue production.

However, this sudden and drastic price cut was misunderstood by the competition as a declaration of war aimed at capturing new market share. The response was a series of price cuts on similar products, creating a downward spiral of prices.

In the communication related to that promotion, the explicit mention that the price cut was limited to a single product and until the stock was depleted for a product that would soon be out of production was omitted. It was already too late: the price level for the entire product category was compromised. If any CEO had communicated, in a credible manner, that it was a circumscribed action, the reaction would have been completely different.

From all this, we can deduce that the actions of corporate executives help to avoid price wars that annihilate profits, thanks to a strategy aimed at not provoking uncontrollable reactions from competitors.

How to Make Change Happen

If price management has been neglected so far, to demonstrate to the organization that top management has finally given it priority, it is advisable to promote three initiatives:

1. Analyse the current maturity in pricing within the company.

2. Define a transformation roadmap.

3. Mobilize the team.

The first initiative to be launched in the company helps in understanding the state of pricing management. Also known as *pricing health check*, it ideally investigates four main areas: pricing strategy, price determination, price implementation, and price control. It also sheds light on everything that supports price management, such as processes, organization, IT systems, and skills.

Depending on the scope of products, customers, and countries involved, such an analysis typically lasts between 1 and 2 months when carried out by a dedicated team. The collected information, which will then be processed, comes from interviews with experts and data analysis, providing the initial evidence of opportunities along with their respective quantifications.

This activity provides a comprehensive picture that allows an understanding of the starting point and, above all, where one wants to go.

These insights form the basis for the next initiative, which is defining the state to aim for, also known as the target picture. It is a prefiguration, an imaginary framework that will guide all subsequent choices. With this goal in mind, a transformation journey can be set up, which will last from 1 to 3 years, depending on the size of the company.

Ideally, there will be a series of short-term benefits to be achieved, the so-called quick wins, followed by medium- or long-term improvements that will all contribute to increasing the company's profitability.

An aspect not to be overlooked in this transformation is the technological aspect.

Developments in this area over the past 10 years have enabled companies to access everything they need to make pricing management even more effective. New solutions, some of which are based on the cloud and equipped with artificial intelligence, enable higher monetization efficiency, and accelerate result generation. Implementing pilot projects generates evidence regarding the expected benefits.

In any case, this process could also be started with a limited scope and then expand the application to the rest of the company.

Finally, we will mobilize the entire organization to embark on the transformation journey. This typically involves multiple initiatives, from creating a team to communication and organization.

First and foremost, the team that will drive the entire process at the operational level needs to be identified. To this end, we look for individuals within the organization who are already involved in pricing and focus on which aspect of pricing they work on. Many organizational chart analyses reveal that there are numerous people dealing with pricing across different business units, functions, and geographies. From this pool, the future pricing champions are selected to lead the initiative.

Communication is another aspect of this mobilization phase. How to communicate the new orientation towards profitability, even if it implies lower market share or a vision related to a certain price positioning, such as medium to high, and cease everything that goes against this strategy (such as heavy discounts and promotions).

Another aspect that has proven to be very useful is to organize regular committees, perhaps monthly, to review the progress of the transformation from a pricing perspective.

This also demonstrates that price management now enjoys the attention of top management. During these meetings, the pricing champions report back on the achieved results, potential obstacles, and the next steps of the transformation in front of top executives and leaders of the various business units involved.

Summary

Pricing is undoubtedly one of the topics that should be on the agenda of every CEO. The pricing lever is the strongest and most immediate lever of profitability and is too important to be ignored by top management.

At the same time, innovative pricing models that are revolutionizing the way monetization is done in many sectors and triggering a pricing revolution are the new source of competitive advantage.

In business practice, often the perspective on pricing differs. When there is no support from the top management, the company loses its pricing power, which is so important that it guides the choices of the Oracle of Omaha, Warren Buffet.

It is essential for pricing to become one of the priorities of top management.

Companies where top management has elevated pricing as a priority show significantly better results compared to similar companies where this does not happen. When the CEO declares profitable growth as one of the cornerstones of the company, it paves the way for greater profitability. This implies having a stranglehold on the topic, such as a pricing team or function, being aware of the sources of value for customers, and practicing value-based pricing.

The role of the CEO is crucial in elevating pricing from an operational burden to a priority.

It is their responsibility to make it clear to everyone in the organization how immediate and direct the link between pricing and company profits is. The CEO sets the strategic direction.

Another important aspect is price positioning and the price image the company wants to convey.

There are several pricing tasks that can fall under the CEO's purview: 1) assuming price leadership when leading the market-reference company, 2) sending price signals to prepare for pricing changes, and 3) avoiding price wars that heavily damage the profitability of entire sectors.

If price management has been neglected so far, to demonstrate to the organization that top management has finally given it priority, it is advisable to promote three initiatives: 1) analyse the current level of maturity in pricing within the company to understand the point of departure; 2) define a transformation roadmap to achieve the desired state; and 3) mobilize the team to embark on the long journey towards transformation.

RULE 2
DISSEMINATE
THE CULTURE OF PROFIT

'The first ethical responsibility of a business leader is to make a profit.'

Nitin Nohria, Dean of Harvard Business School

Introduction

The words *purchase* and *sale* are conceptually not separate. The Indo-European root **dō* means both 'to give' and 'to take'. Similarly, in Sanskrit, the term for 'purchase' is *vasna*, and in Latin it is *uēnum*, which also mean 'to sell'. Remarkably, this demonstrates that etymologically the act of selling is interconnected to that of purchasing and illustrates a fundamental tenet of any transaction and trade.

Our ancestors – certainly less tired and stressed than we are – made another clear distinction: the act of paying, which concludes the purchase, is separate from the process of agreeing to the price. These word roots show how, across the millennia, the economic process has been linked to a culture of exchange, and to the idea that goods are exchanged for money.

It should be noted that purchase and sale on the one hand, and trade on the other, are different things. In the past, the exchange of goods was linked to surplus, which we now call profit. The term *pretium* 'price', which in recent years has experienced significant fluctuations due to pandemics and wars, could derive from *merx, mercor, mercator*, meaning 'object of trade'. Thus, *negōtium* (literally translated as 'what one does in the absence of leisure') is a term that has dominated the development of all economic terms since Roman times.

These terms, which may initially seem distant from our contemporary age, actually encompass an essential factor: TIME.

Time that never seems to be enough, and that remains a crucial factor in all exchanges, transactions, and investments. 'Time is money', as they say, but why?

Once again, the origin of words comes to our aid. It is no coincidence that *negōtium* is the translation of the Greek term *askholía*, which means 'being short of time'. This *occupation* – being active hence short of time – is mentioned by Plato, Socrates, and even Pindar, and had a positive connotation. It is where modern terms such as 'negotiate' and 'take care of business' come from, all concepts that are related to *prâgma*, being pragmatic when it comes to business. So, the next time someone reproaches you for your determination in business, remind them that being pragmatic is typical of those who connect people and things, and in a sense, facilitates an exchange in both space and time.

The frenetic rhythms of contemporary life often make us *busy*, which is where the abstract term *business* originates.

Those who do not have leisure time 'cast the first stone' (although that's another story) because the economy involves exchange activities. The terms of wealth, as well as operations such as purchase, sale, lending, and finance, have always been the essence of economic relations among human beings.

Similarly, when we say that in business, gut feeling is as important as intellect, we are once again confirming the multifaceted nature of the term *ratio*, which means 'to count' or broadly 'to calculate'. If we were to conduct some semantic research, we would find one of the terms that most significantly impacts our daily lives: the word 'strategy'. This lemma originates from the Greek term *stratēgós*, which means 'leader of the army' and refers to someone capable of leading and preceding the army.

On the other hand, lŭ-*crum* refers to what we call profit, benefit, quid or simply the 'something extra' that an activity can generate as a result: surplus (in the dual sense of an unexpected outcome or, rather, the result of our managers' strategy). It is noteworthy that the word 'money' derives from *solde*, *soldat*, which means 'paid with a coin', from the Latin word *solidum*, which indicates a gold coin. Similarly, 'salary' in its Latin formation, *salarium*, means 'the money given to soldiers to buy salt', while 'pay' comes from the Latin word *pacare*, meaning 'to satisfy' or 'to calm' by distributing money.

Where are we going with this discussion on the relation between words and a business? We mean to show that the connection between exchange value and profits, between human beings and transactions, between research and comparison, is part of the history of humanity. In fact, goods themselves can be seen as information. In the days before the Internet or television, goods that were shipped from one part of the world to another, say onboard ships, carried more than their material value: they carried the colours and news of the distant worlds they came from. Goods are information, and products are a vehicle for narrating the philosophy of a company, because a company needs to sell its image and its activities to its customers, who must trust the enterprise. Because the world is an adventure, and we are all travellers on this vast sea.

The Culture of Profit

We are often told that to set up a business it is sufficient to have a clear idea about what the customer needs are that we want to satisfy, and then gather the resources to start our entrepreneurial activity. In other words, 'so far, so good', as in the anecdote of the person falling from the 50th floor, who repeats the phrase like a mantra. However, we all know that 'the problem is not the fall, but the landing' (this is the first scene of the movie *La Haine*, directed by Matthieu Kassovitz and featuring a very young Vincent Cassel, which won the Best Director award at the Cannes Film Festival in 1995, and was filmed just before the outbreak of the banlieue riots in France).

The issue becomes more complex when we must ensure the long-term profitability of the company. If we look at the stark numbers, 90% of newly founded companies fail within a few years, a worst-case scenario confirmed by *Forbes*.[1]

Not only that, but 20% of start-ups go bankrupt in the first year, and 50% within the first three years.[2] In the end, only 1 in 10 highlanders survives. What does this depend on?

One of the main reasons for failure is the inability to generate profits, which initially leads to a lack of necessary liquidity and eventually results in the slow but certain death of the company when costs exceed revenues.

As we have seen (also from a linguistic perspective), profits are the essential foundation of every company. The world we see is defined and given meaning by the words we choose (as Ludwig Wittgenstein said). In our case, without profits, the fundamental basis of the business is compromised, and eventually, at the first shock, the entire structure collapses upon itself.

A company thrives solely thanks to profits, and its existence is exclusively ensured by its ability to generate and regenerate that condition.

To promote profit generation, it is important to instil a culture of profit, which entails creating a context that supports price management aimed at generating earnings, thereby achieving sustainable and balanced growth.

According to Peter Drucker, one of the world's foremost *management thinkers*, culture is the heart and essence of every company. Organizational culture encompasses the company ethos and the dedication to achieving objectives, as well as the underlying values, shared at all levels. It is the synthesis of the beliefs and values that guide the activities of everyone who works within the company. That is why it is so important.

Pricing is a core issue for every business, and it should be treated as an aspect of the company culture, as it involves a wide range of functions.

Top-level management determine the revenue model and, accordingly, establishes the monetization approach and pricing model.[3]

Strategists work on the positioning and price image of the products.

The pricing function determines the price level.

The marketing department is responsible for managing promotions.

The sales department, on the other hand, develops negotiation strategies and offers discounts.

The finance function evaluates promotional financing models, such as zero-interest rates.

The accounting department monitors product and customer margins and profitability.

Research and development create new products by assessing both target costing and target pricing aspects.

And these are not all of the divisions involved. However, since the company is a complex and integrated organism in which each part is related to the other functions, everyone must have full awareness of how their work impacts price management and, consequently, profit.

According to Drucker, the most challenging factor to control and change in a company is its culture, and the evident contradiction between the importance of and resistance to change is a singular phenomenon. Therefore, clear guidelines are needed to promote the diffusion of a profit-oriented culture and to spread it with specific enablers. In this chapter, we delve into the three guidelines and three enablers that help the company grow profitably (see Table 2.1).

Table 2.1: A culture of profit: guidelines and enablers.

Guidelines	Enablers
1. Do not spoil your customers	1. Incentivize profit margins, as well as sales volumes
2. Tailor your discount	2. Share your pricing experiences
3. Communicate clearly the value of your product	3. Monitor the relative value

Guidelines to Disseminate a Culture of Profit

1. Do not spoil your customers

'Marketing means seeing the entire business through the eyes of the customer' is one of Drucker's most famous quotes.[4] Being able to do this allows us to understand, and sometimes anticipate, the needs of customers and respond to their wants in the best possible way. However, we must be careful not to go too far, for example, by indulging the customer excessively, especially when it comes to pricing.

Recently, I met with the CEO of a well-known industrial group that operates through five business units, and he told me, 'Our largest business unit has customer satisfaction rates well above the industry average, as we offer excellent services and high quality at particularly affordable prices. The thing I don't understand is why we are incurring losses.' In cases like this, while we may be very strong in terms of delivering value to the customer – the so-called *value delivery* – we fail to obtain adequate compensation in return, or *value extraction*. Are we doing something wrong? Perhaps we are not earning enough, and in the worst-case scenario, we are, or will soon be, incurring losses. These queries arise if we formulate the right questions. 'There are no answers, only questions', as the philosopher Hans-Georg Gadamer argued. It is therefore essential to understand when to stop indulging customers by sacrificing their satisfaction for the sake of our profits. In other words, we need to cash in every point that improves our margin of self-worth, which is essentially the only thing that allows us to thrive in an increasingly competitive market. How can we do that? For example, by ensuring that we receive fair return for the value provided.

But first, let's analyse the most common ways in which we may unintentionally 'indulge' our customers. A classic example is offering discounts and price reductions. Here's a personal example.

My adult daughter asked me some time ago to help her book a car for her and her three friends for 5 days during the New Year period. Being a loving father and passionate about pricing, I couldn't help but gladly accept the request and offer my assistance. I immediately took action and called a well-known car rental company. After requesting a quote from the call centre agent, who quoted me a staggering $597, I started listing all the possible discounts I could access: from the discount for members of the national motorists club to the one for Star Alliance airline members, from the promotional code I found on the website, to the one on a flyer. Each discount category corresponded to a different price. The result? First victory: a remarkable reduction to $490 thanks to the Star Alliance member discount, which also included winter tyres at no extra charge (in addition to the possibility of receiving a free upgrade to a higher car class based on availability). Far from stopping there, I mentioned the promotion for those who join the car rental loyalty programme, which, according to the website, allowed for an additional 20% savings, equivalent to $98, bringing the total to $392 – second victory! Furthermore, I managed to have the student discount applied, another $25 to deduct, bringing it down to $367 – third victory! Finally, I secured a second named driver, advertised at $9 per day, at no additional cost: another significant saving – fourth victory! In the end, after my efforts to squeeze everything I could out of the car rental call centre, we achieved a total discount of $230, in addition to the aforementioned $9 per day, winter tyres included at no extra charge, and the upgrade. All this during a peak season!

Apart from my obsession with price, I ask you: is it really necessary to indulge customers by granting all these reductions? Wouldn't it make sense to limit some discounts during the high season or, let's say, make them non-cumulative? I certainly would have paid a higher price just to find a car for my daughter. As they say in France,

Le prix s'oublie, la qualité reste – the slight disappointment caused by a high price is quickly forgotten, while the pleasure of a high-quality product or service remains. Perhaps it would have been better to charge me a higher rental price, which I would have gladly overlooked, seeing my daughter enjoy the trip with her friends, and creating beautiful memories.

2. Tailor your discount

Discounting is an important tool to close a deal or finalize a sale. However, as soon as we activate this lever, we lose profits. That's why it's crucial to instruct the sales team on when to offer discounts and when not to.

There can be various situations where applying a discount makes a lot of sense. For example, if we are selling the same product available at a neighbouring store at a lower price, offering a discount serves to align our price and secure the sale. However, value differs even for completely comparable products. This is where the salesperson's expertise comes into play. They should be able to grasp the value that specific product holds for that particular customer – that's the magic touch. Let's explore this with another example.

> When I used to take my three young children to the beach during the summer, they would inundate us with constant requests, wanting to buy everything (much to the delight of the shopkeepers!): from a new bucket to an alligator-shaped float, from ice cream to chewing gum. I was often amazed at how easy it was to receive discounts on these items. For instance, at the newsstand that also sold buckets and shovels for playing in the sand during the summer, simply mentioning the price of the same product seen at a discount store two kilometres away would instantly bring down its price to the same level. On the

other hand, I remember the lesson taught to me by a sales-person at a home products store. We entered his shop next to the beach with my son who absolutely wanted one of the kites on display. He had been asking for it for days, every time we passed by on our way to the beach. It was a persistent request. When I asked for a discount on the rather expensive kite, with evidence that I had found the same product at a lower price online, the salesperson responded, 'You are free to purchase the product online. We do not offer discounts, and the fact that you haven't bought it elsewhere shows that there's a rea-son you came to my store.' The response was spot-on. Buying the product from him had several advantages for me, such as being able to have it immediately and satisfy my child's relent-less pleas. It also meant having someone, the salesperson, who could tell us how to fly the kite since we had never had one before and didn't know how to use it. The mere thought of my son's disappointment if I failed to launch the new kite scared me (I could envision Charlie Brown's frustrating and endless failed attempts). Therefore, I purchased the kite at full price, and received valuable guidance on how to fly it.

The sales team, with appropriate distinctions, should operate like the kite seller (the famous debut novel *The Kite Runner* by the Afghan-American writer Khaled Hosseini): even when faced with identical products, a higher price can be sustained if one is able to capture the perceived value and monetize the benefits of their offer.

Another case where a discount makes sense is when it helps with upselling. For example, if I sell small appliances and a customer comes in to purchase a Bosch toaster, the offer of a discount on a high-end Smeg toaster will allow me to sell a product with a higher margin. In this case, despite the discount, the upselling will have helped generate an overall higher margin compared to selling the Bosch brand without a discount.

In negotiations, discounts also serve the purpose of acquiring new customers, perhaps by luring them away from the competition. If the initial sale in the customer's lifecycle is not very profitable due to the initial discount, having a new customer who will continue to make regular purchases from us can be considered a valid reason to offer discounts.

To guide the use of discounts, it is good to keep these three considerations in mind: 1) offer discounts in kind, not on price,[5] 2) limit the scope of discounts, and 3) avoid incurring losses. Let's examine them in more detail.

Some concessions can be made in the form of price discounts, which involve a reduction in the price, or in the form of in-kind discounts, also known as merchandise discounts. In-kind discounts have several advantages: they maintain the nominal price level and are more profitable, in terms of the same percentages, compared to price discounts. Additionally, they generate higher volumes and often result in economies of scale.

Let's illustrate this with the case of leisure products priced at around $10,000 each. When deciding to offer a discount, the manufacturer provides their retailers with one free product for every five purchased. Since the retailer receives six products but only pays for five, the discount amounts to 16.7%. Based on a price of $10,000, the calculation is as follows: total revenue of $50,000, six units sold, and a margin of $14,000.

If, however, the manufacturer were to offer a direct discount of 16.7% on the price, the calculation would be as follows: total revenue of $41,650, five units sold, and a margin of $11,650.

Therefore, in-kind discounts allow for both higher volumes, generating economies of scale, and a higher margin. In-kind discounts are also explicitly proposed as a limited-time action and can be withdrawn more easily compared to a price discount, which automatically weakens the price list.

The second consideration states that each discount should be specific to a customer and limited (to a product or a time frame). Ideally, it should also be tied to a counter-performance by the customer, such as an upfront payment, or the purchase of another product with an interesting margin, or an excellent review that highlights the quality of the product. If the discount were not limited and it became public knowledge, all other customers would want a similar treatment. This would unleash chaos, resulting in a haemorrhage of profits.

Finally, it is important to ensure that the average selling price is higher than the average cost, to avoid operating at a loss. The average selling price results from the weighted average of all prices based on sales quantities. The average cost, on the other hand, includes all costs (raw materials, production costs, human resources, etc.). Costs higher than prices can occur, for example, with so-called loss leader products in large-scale retail, but the situation is limited to a few items and, above all, for a set time only. However, if everyone offers discounts below the average cost, the unfortunate end of business activities will be just around the corner.

3. Communicate clearly the value of your product

The Latin term for price is *pretium*. A deeper investigation reveals that *pretium* also means 'value'. The ancient Romans used the same word for both: pretium = value = price, to indicate what is at the centre of every transaction.

Therefore, value is the most important aspect of price management and pricing strategy or, more precisely, the value perceived by the customer. The willingness of customers to pay and the price set by the company always reflect the perceived value, or the benefits of the consultation and service provided.

By giving the same word to both sides of the transaction, the ancient Romans understood the fundamental connection between price and value. Interestingly, Latin also provides us with a second linguistic meaning that goes in the same direction. *Pretium facere* (literally, 'fixing the price') also meant asking a price (from the buyer) and offering a price (to the seller).

Behind a substantial price, we find a perception of high value from the customer. To sustain a certain price level, it is necessary for everyone in the company, especially the salespeople, to be aware of the value – the *allure*, as the French would say – and understand how it is conveyed.

If the value, as we have highlighted, is not clear to those who need to sell the product, imagine how difficult it will be to convey it to the customer. This is why knowing how to communicate value externally to the customer and internally within the company becomes essential.

An old popular saying goes 'those who despise buy'. Certainly, buyers will always want to deny any form of value and emphasize how similar our offer is compared to that of our competitor, so that the decisive criterion for purchase is only the lowest price. This is precisely where we need to stand firm, look the customer in the eye, and stress all the sources of value that our offer contains.

The sources of value can be multiple. They are related to the product when they refer to the quality or performance of the offer. They are related to the service when they refer to availability or after-sales services. Apple provides a classic example of value generation: whether it's an iPhone, iPad, AirPods, or other products, the sources of value – the design, interconnectivity, ease of use, brand, and quality – support particularly high prices. This has allowed Apple to generate stellar profits with revenue of $394 billion in 2022, effectively quadrupling its revenue over the past 10 years.[6]

The value of a product can also become the key to avoiding discounts and generating additional profits. An example of value communication is Johnnie Walker with its Scotch whiskies (for the different, further diversities of whiskey|whisky|Rye and why they are spelled differently, we recommend reading online about their connection to Ireland rather than Scotland, malt, barley, or the United States, as in the case of Bourbon). In any case, to simplify, let's say that the different labels express different values. So, the red label represents the base product at $35, the black label is positioned at a higher level at $47; but there's also the green label at $75 and the platinum label at $119. Not to mention the flagship: the blue label at $243.[7]

When someone asks for a discount on the black label, they are offered the red label at a lower price without a discount. Loyal customers are instead offered the most prestigious offer, the blue label, with significantly higher margins.

Various brands, from the watch industry like Rolex to car manufacturers like Audi, communicate products in the same way. They develop more affordable products, for example, for younger and less-affluent customers, as entry-level products to then build customer loyalty and sell higher-value products with higher margins.

All these examples demonstrate that once the value of a company is created, the aspect of communicating that value becomes a priority as it influences its perception externally. As a customer, it is fundamental to understand what a product or service offers and, based on that, determine how much one is willing to pay.

Profit Culture Enablers

1. Incentivize profit margins as well as sale volumes

One of the pillars to achieving excellence in sales is rewarding behaviours that align with the company's sales policy. In price setting, the sales team plays a central role, particularly when the selling process takes place at the customer's location, where sales go hand in hand with the ability to negotiate prices or offer discounts.

A company that incentivizes its salespeople based on sales revenue should not be surprised if the salespeople are willing to sacrifice margins in order to secure additional volumes. 'Sales excellence' means giving multiple objectives to salespeople, not only rewarding them for achieving sales revenue but also, and more importantly, if they can offer smaller discounts while maintaining good levels of profitability.

We often observe significant heterogeneity among salespeople in terms of sales revenue and contribution margin. When I was asked to evaluate the performance of the sales team in a metal-mechanical company, among the various sales managers, there were two specific individuals: the saleswoman we will call Mary Wilson had achieved the second-highest sales revenue among all 40 salespeople, amounting to $1.7 million with a margin of 5.3%. On the other hand, her colleague Elisabeth White, with only $350,000 in sales revenue, had obtained a margin well above average, at 26%. In our example, both Wilson and White have (almost) equal absolute contribution margins, amounting to $90,100 and $91,000, respectively.

An incentive limited to rewarding volumes would have penalized Elisabeth White, who, with lower sales revenue but higher-value sales, had made a greater contribution to the company's profitability.

Incentivizing the sales force proves crucial for a 'goal-oriented pricing', which means that the incentivization process, from the configuration of the incentive system to its actual implementation, is consistently aligned with the company's strategic objectives. It takes into account the long-term perspective and vision. Once again, strategy comes into play.

In practice, however, commission based on sales revenue is quite common. However, this form of commission doesn't make sense if it remains tied to the pricing decision-making authority. Instead, it should be accompanied by an incentive based on profit or, in other words, contribution margin. However, this form also encounters problems in practice. On the one hand, providing salespeople with information about profits or contribution margins carries the risk of that information ending up in the hands of customers (which is usually not desirable). On the other hand, it is difficult to provide information about the contribution margin of individual customers, as is done with sales revenue data, because it requires highly developed information systems that many companies do not possess.

To avoid these difficulties, an incentive system can be applied that avoids the undesired effects of commission based on sales revenue and instead focuses on contribution margin. In this case, the variable compensation is still based on generated sales revenue, but there is an additional 'bonus' for the price that can compensate for the price reduction made by the individual salesperson, precisely because it relates the price level achieved to the target price level.

Salespeople who achieve sales revenue while maintaining strong price discipline are in a much better position compared to 'discount givers'.

Our experiences show that such systems contribute to a lasting improvement in price quality. The commission percentage depends on the discount granted: the greater the discount granted, the lower the commission rate, which is also based on sales revenue (i.e. an 'anti-discount commission').

To strengthen the incentive effect, the commission achieved is displayed on the salesperson's PC or tablet, allowing them to immediately see how their bonus changes when the discount increases from 5% to 10%. The impact of this practice on profit has been significant in our experience. This new incentive system was introduced in the metal-mechanical company mentioned above. Within two months, the average discount granted decreased from 18% to 16% without any loss of customers or quantity. This represents a 2 full percentage point increase in margin and a 2% price increase.

However, incentive systems for the sales teams to be effective, they must satisfy three basic conditions: a) simplicity, b) fairness, and c) equality.

Simplicity ensures that the logic and effect of the incentives are understood by the salespeople. Fairness means that salespeople actually receive the monetary reward when they act in the agreed-upon manner. Equality means that comparable performances are remunerated equally.

Alongside monetary incentives, non-monetary stimuli also play a prominent role in sales and can be used for pricing management. Sales force incentives can include prizes for the best sales teams (such as incentive trips). In one company, the company car policy for salespeople was also based on the margins generated: those who met their objectives by generating margins in line with or above expectations had the right to upgrade to a higher model car, while the opposite occurred for those who failed to meet their objectives, resulting in a punitive effect.

Some companies award the title of 'pricing champion of the month' to those who achieve maximum prices, minimal discount concessions or the highest contribution margin.

Internal communication is also capable of creating or reinforcing non-monetary incentives. Sales meetings regularly discuss market price developments, current pricing issues, necessary price increases, and pricing strategies. These opportunities could be used purposefully to propose incentives aimed at a better overall pricing policy.

The introduction of an incentive system promotes the dissemination of a profit culture and represents one of the most effective methods for rapidly improving profitability levels.

2. Share your pricing experiences

Never like in recent years have we witnessed such dynamic markets and fluctuating customer preferences. In a rapidly changing context, sharing best practices, experiences, and significant actions that have led to the best results in price management becomes crucial.

The daily interaction with customers allows for the accumulation of valuable lessons. For example, learning how to communicate value, increase prices, or sell without granting discounts. What one salesperson has learned can be treasured by another, allowing them to replicate their successes.

In several companies, we have initiated regular exchanges on pricing best practices, structuring the interaction. A session of this kind, held once a month for 45 minutes with the sales team, can cover specific topics and facilitate a discussion on keywords. First, price management and the arguments used to implement price increases can be explored, identifying which strategies have worked better than others. Second, the theme of value can be discussed to understand how to defend the value of our offering. It is highly beneficial to share feedback from customers explaining why they prefer our products. These points can be taken up and reiterated in future negotiations.

Sharing insights about competitors is a third aspect that helps determine if and how to react based on the previous points. Additionally, involving representatives from various functions involved in price management allows for first-hand testimonies from the front lines, where daily actions are taken to improve and refine price management. Ideally, this also presents an opportunity to celebrate pricing champions, recognizing those who have excelled in pricing and selling the perceived value of the company to customers.

3. Monitor the relative value

The perception of value (economic, financial, and image-related) by customers is also influenced by the alternatives they have in terms of purchasing our products. When discussing value, it is important to analyse what makes competitors' products appealing, their price positioning, and specific product attributes. With a clear understanding of the competitive context, it becomes easier to refine the value proposition and determine the best monetization approach.

This is how Miele, a manufacturer of high-end appliances, operates. Markus Miele, the descendant of the founder Carl and current head of the company, explained their strategy in an interview: 'We have positioned ourselves in the premium segment. Our products are built to last 20 years. In terms of technology and ecology, we are among the best on the market. Customers are willing to pay higher prices for this promise.'[8] Indeed, Miele's prices are, on average, 30% higher than the competition. However, the company keeps an eye on relative value compared to competitors: 'Certainly, Miele also needs to ensure that the price difference compared to the main competitors is not excessive. That's why we constantly work on reducing the cost structure. We never forget our philosophy: forever better. We cannot win a battle by claiming the lowest price, but we will win when it comes to having the best product.'[9]

Monitoring the competition, therefore, becomes part of the value proposition process because it sheds light on the context in which we operate and allows us to emphasize those aspects that generate more value compared to competitors. In this sense, typical information is gathered, such as technical characteristics of current products, plans for launching new products and services, prices, promotions, applied discounts, customer base, announced strategies, and even reasons why we succeeded in making a sale or, conversely, when we lost a customer to a competitor.

It is important to encourage all teams to be proactive, collecting and documenting all relevant information, which will be useful in the next pricing determination phase at the latest.

Summary

To promote profit generation, it is important to foster a profit culture, which supports price management that generates earnings and achieves profitable growth.

According to Peter Drucker, culture is the most difficult factor to control and change in a company. The contradiction between the centrality of culture and its resistance to change is a singular phenomenon.

The three guidelines to promote the dissemination of a culture of profit are:

Do not spoil your customers: Avoid excessive concessions. Every concession that is not strictly necessary results in an immediate loss of profitability.

Direct the use of discounts/apply a clear rationale to your discount policy: Grant discounts only when strictly necessary, such as to align the price and make the sale, facilitate upselling, or win a new customer. It is always advisable to direct the use of discounts towards non-price aspects, circumscribe the scope of these discounts, and, above all, avoid sacrificing profitability.

Communicate clearly the value of your products: To justify a substantial price there must be a matching value perceived by the customer. To support a certain price level, it is necessary for everyone in the company, especially the salespeople, to be aware of that value, how it was formed, what it represents, and what it symbolizes/provides in the exchange. If this is not clear to those who sell the product, it will be difficult for them to convey the value to the customer.

To spread a value culture, specific enablers can be employed:

1. *Incentivize profit margins as well as sales volumes*: An organization that rewards its salespeople solely based on achieving revenue should not be surprised if they are willing to sacrifice margins to achieve higher volumes. 'Sales excellence' means having multiple goals for salespeople (for example, granting low discounts while achieving margin objectives).

2. *Share your pricing experiences*: In a continuously changing environment, sharing best practices, experiences, and actions helps build a team based on the best results achieved.

3. *Monitor the relative value*: A customer's perception of value is also influenced by the alternatives they have regarding the purchase of our products. That's why we need to understand what makes our offering appealing. With a clear understanding of the context, it becomes easier to refine the value proposition or even create it and determine the best monetization approach.

RULE 3
UNDERSTAND AND SELL VALUE

'The greatest of all gifts is the power to estimate things at their true worth.'

François de la Rochefoucauld, writer

Introduction

How much is a glass of water worth? It depends.

If I am sitting comfortably at home, watching the Champions League final on TV with friends, it will have a value of diffuse sociability. Drinking water will be a momentary necessity, easily satisfied. I will drink it absentmindedly, while doing something else, perhaps not even aware of whether it's sparkling or still.

But what if that glass of water is the reward I expect after a long run – I hate running! – or while hiking in the mountains, when water is in short supply and must be rationed along the way? Or, and I am letting my imagination run wild here, if that water is the coveted prize after a long period of 'nil by mouth' in hospital; or, picturing a more adventurous scenario, after a ride on camelback, after a night spent in the desert – a fascinating experience, of course, but certainly a situation where water is not so accessible and guaranteed.

Freshwater: one of the 'wars of tomorrow' according to some analysts, if the prediction that global warming will raise sea levels by 2100 is true. How valuable will the opportunity to drink fresh water be in that case, in that *Underworld*, as depicted in the science fiction movie from a few years ago starring a very young Kevin Costner?

Furthermore, what would I be willing to exchange that glass of water for? In the case of the football match on TV, maybe some juice, or a beer, as is popular in Germany. But the exchange value would not be the same if the valuation is done the moment I return home after a hot afternoon outdoors in the scorching sun, say, in Ibiza. And the evaluation of that glass of water would be off the scale, if water were a precious and scarce commodity, if we were in the midst of one of the water wars mentioned earlier (for those interested in the topic of water grabbing when water is a rare and therefore valuable resource, I recommend visiting the website https://www.watergrabbing.com/).

The focus of this chapter will be on value, in its double meaning of attribution of characteristics (more or less rare, more or less valuable) to a given good or service, and of putting it in relation to other goods or services. Is everything comparable? Can I compare apples and oranges? The answer is obviously yes in our gold standard system, where gold, the currency, can set an absolute price compared to a good, and an 'exchange value' in relation to everything present on the market. For example, when I think of $20, I immediately make the correlation: how many books can I buy with that? Two if they're cheap, or one if I buy Cormac McCarthy's latest. For someone else, like my daughter who loves chocolate, those $20 will be equivalent to three to four high-quality chocolate bars. Therefore, the same value – $20 – will be a book for me or four chocolate bars for my daughter. Will we be able to exchange our fulfilled needs? Probably, if I have just finished reading that book and my daughter has already eaten two chocolate bars.

What we are realising, therefore, is: how much are we willing to pay to obtain something – in absolute terms (chocolate, which is finished once eaten) or relative terms (a book, once read, can be put on a coffee table, and later resold or placed in the home library)? Furthermore, how much is the immateriality of a pair of shoes with a famous basketball player's logo worth, compared to the same pair of shoes with three diagonal stripes? It is a fact that the same objects cost more depending on the perception we have of their uniqueness. This brings us directly to the question of how much the fulfilment of a need is worth, or in other words, how much are we willing to pay to see our own – albeit small and ephemeral – desire fulfilled (desire comes from the Latin expression *de sidera* 'to sense the lack of stars, that is, of auspicious signs'), desire being 'that feeling or emotion which is directed to the attainment or possession of some object from which pleasure or satisfaction is expected' – as the *Oxford English Dictionary* puts it.

Let us now shift the meaning of the term 'value', as we have framed it so far, towards what is in fact the primary relationship for any company operating in the market, namely the customer. We will do this by analysing what, in my opinion, can be considered the five steps required to 'grasp' the value of products and successfully sell them in a mutually beneficial exchange:

1. understand needs and create value;
2. analyse the competition;
3. quantify the value;
4. set price based on value; and
5. communicate the value.

Understand Needs and Create Value

The customer is at the centre of everything: everything revolves around the customers and the satisfaction of their needs.

As distinguished Professor Theodore Levitt stated in his famous article on marketing myopia, published in 1960 in the *Harvard Business Review*, companies must focus on the needs of their customers, their expectations, and the value they seek and appreciate, rather than solely on the production and sale of products.

In essence, Levitt urged companies to concentrate their efforts on finding ways to exceed customer expectations in a broader perspective compared to the competition – both current and potential. Once again, this raises the question of the medium to long term versus the short term, the relationship between 'right' immediate gains and a wider strategic perspective. We must always ask ourselves: what is the ultimate goal, the horizon we are moving towards while concerning ourselves with staying afloat, navigating the monstrous sea that is the market?

Understanding customer needs, if we think about it, is a sort of superpower – as described in the novel *Pattern Recognition* by science fiction author and inventor of the cyberpunk genre (think *The Matrix* film) William Gibson, where the protagonist is a trend forecaster by profession, thanks to her special empathy. Understanding customer needs is the basis for developing and offering solutions that meet those needs. This should be the starting point for shaping one's offering and pricing, for example, by creating a unique selling proposition (USP), also known as an 'exclusive selling argument', which filters and organizes a series of considerations presented as reasons why a product or service is different or better than that offered by the competition.

To satisfy customer needs, in other words, to satisfy 'the other' – and this applies to both life and the market – and to draw a satisfactory return for both parties, it is necessary to establish a relationship and a dialogue. The more tangible and unique the value created by a company, the easier it will be to ask the customer for a price that is 'in line' with the value offered, because the customer recognises it as not arbitrarily imposed.

You may agree with Oscar Wilde, then, and wonder: 'What is a cynic? A man who knows the price of everything and the value of nothing.'

But what is meant by 'value'? In the context of this book, value refers to the qualities of a particular product or service from an aesthetic, functional, or undisputable quality-to-price ratio perspective.

'Value' depends greatly on subjective perception and varies depending on the number of people involved. In general, we can standardise its meaning in economic or status terms, and yet we have also seen that the same person will perceive a different value – even for the same product – depending on the context.

Identifying and quantifying the value-adding characteristics of a product is the greatest challenge in value-based pricing. Going into detail, we can say that there are three types of functionalities that customers associate with products and services:

1. *Hygiene factors*: these are the necessary conditions for considering a purchase.

2. *Preference drivers*: they determine whether a customer will purchase our product or another.

3. *Value sources* or *value drivers*: what motivate customers to pay a higher price.

What does all this mean in practical terms?

Let's try to give a concrete example of a customer looking to buy a jacket.

The available range of sizes is a *hygiene factor*, for example, because the aspect 'size' must be obtainable in the specific measurements that fit the customer for the purchase of the jacket even to be considered. In the absence of a suitable size, interest in the purchase fades: a product that lacks hygiene factors will be excluded straight away by the customer. In other words, if the jacket is not available in the requested size, the customer will not buy it, regardless of its price.

Preference drivers also determine which product the customer will buy based on personal preferences. An example is the colour of the jacket.

When it comes to monetizing value, *value drivers* come into play. In the example of the jacket, a value driver is the perceived high-quality material, such as leather or the special craftsmanship of the garment. It is the 'something' for which customers are willing to pay more. The value driver is what companies should focus on as it justifies higher prices and generates willingness to pay. It is important to understand the value sources that customers perceive in the products or services we offer.

To identify where we can create value, it is necessary to understand the competition in our area.

Specifically, are there direct competitors, or does the competition come solely from alternative solutions? Are we faster, more efficient, reliable? Do we offer better conditions? We will delve into the analysis of competition in the next section.

To determine which characteristics of the product offered are value drivers, there are various market research methods available. One can start by asking customers, as well as all internal departments that interact with customers, what they consider the value drivers to be.

Rather than just having a brief conversation, it will be necessary to go into detail and conduct in-depth interviews to understand our customers' activities, processes, and especially the usage of our product within those processes.

It will be useful to identify the different stages along the value chain and recognise where we differ from the competition: in a 'complex value chain', we may even create value for our customers' customers.

Value drivers can be intangible or emotional – think of brand, design, the perception of lower risk, the implicit reassurance that objects provide.

Value drivers can also be tangible, of an economic nature, allowing for increased productivity and revenue or process efficiency, cost reduction, thereby increasing profits – aspects that are particularly important for business customers.

The value drivers can be varied, and the first step in identifying them is to categorize them. In Table 3.1, we find some examples, certainly not exhaustive.

What is listed should be taken as a guideline and adapted to our own products, taking into account what the entire organization can offer – beyond the product – such as after-sales services, warranties, responsiveness, etc.

Table 3.1: Categories and examples of value drivers.

Value driver category	Examples of value drivers
Reputation	Brand, references, company history, credibility, innovation, product range, international presence, culture, flexibility, positioning, certifications, etc.
Product	Quality, usefulness, robustness, design, size, weight, shape, compatibility with other products, ecological sustainability, colour, reliability, durability, resale value, utility, etc.
Service	Availability, responsiveness, reliability, accessibility, geographic coverage, languages spoken, flexibility, expertise, friendliness, etc.
Interaction	Trust, transparency, problem-solving, accessibility, relationship management approach, interpersonal rapport, etc.

Each of the value drivers listed in Table 3.1 will result in specific benefits for the customer depending on the context and situation they find themselves in. For example, credibility or brand have intangible or emotional benefits that drive the customer to prefer a specific offer, while responsiveness in service delivery, such as promptly repairing a production line in a factory, brings tangible benefits that are quantifiable in monetary terms.

Each source of value contributes to creating a competitive advantage, which can be utilized by the sales teams during negotiations with the customer, by the marketing team when preparing arguments to promote the products, or by product managers as a basis for evaluating the product portfolio and planning new offers.

Analyse the Competition

As we enter the third millennium, we can clearly see that the competitive landscape is becoming increasingly dynamic. What used to take 2 years to happen now occurs in 2 days. We became aware of this with the Covid 19 pandemic. We experience it directly by observing the constant updates and new releases in the technology sector.

Competitors' offers evolve, and new contenders enter the game with innovative solutions, which inevitably impacts on how the value of our own products is perceived.

We have seen this happen. The perception of value varies; value is not an absolute and stable entity, unless what we are selling is 'a disruptive innovation'. But it is highly unlikely that anyone wakes up every day with a paradigm-shifting new product in their hands!

It is important to understand what options are available to our customers by asking ourselves: 'What product would they purchase if mine were not available?'

The answer to this question, the reference product, also known as 'the next best alternative', becomes the benchmark, a useful point of comparison to help us calculate the differential value of our product compared to others. The analysis of the competition also helps us understand whether the value we are offering is still as it was – considering that the perception of value is not static – or if our competitors have released something that has changed or will change the playing field. How do we do this?

To understand this better the example that follows helps to put ourselves just for a moment in someone else's shoes. It is an exercise in empathy, a word derived from the Greek *empátheia*, composed of 'en-' meaning 'within' and 'pathos' meaning 'suffering or feeling', thus referring to the capacity to immerse oneself in the natural forms of sentiment (see also the related concept in German, *Einfühlung*).

Here is the example: let's suppose we are a television manufacturer, like Samsung. We are about to launch a new television and we need to set its price. It is a SMART TV, in the OLED category, with a 4k resolution, multi-view for up to two screens, and an 88-inch screen, making it the largest available on the market: 233 cm diagonally.

Let's assume that there is a benchmark competitor in the market, say Sony, who recently introduced a SMART TV, completely similar to ours except for the size, smaller at 75 inches, for $899. The two TVs have everything in common bar 13 inches: 88-inch screen against a 75-inch screen.

In this example, segmentation also comes into play: the whole debate only applies to a specific market segment, with matching needs and perception of value.

Samsung's target segment, in this case, consists of customers who purchase large-sized TVs. If the segments to consider were multiple, it would be advisable to set different prices for each segment.

Once the market segment has been identified, it is not sufficient to know who the main competitors are, what they offer, and at what price. It is more useful to have a general overview and ask questions such as: what strategies are they pursuing in the short and medium term? What is their financial strength? How are they positioned? What are their sources of value and how do they monetize them? In what phase of the product life cycle is their competing product?

In the past, people sought answers from the stars, from oracles – the most famous being the Oracle of Delphi, and Cassandra, Apollo's priestess. Nowadays, we have evolved: instead of reading coffee grounds or colourful tarot cards, which have made a strong comeback (someone would say we are short of a future), the answers to these questions are often found, much more prosaically, in financial statements and annual reports, in the case of publicly traded companies. Financial performance, strategies, positioning, new products, and growth ambitions are just some of the aspects that can be gleaned. Other indications can be obtained from statements made to the press by executives of these companies. For privately held companies, interviews given to local newspapers and websites can be examined, or the way they present themselves at trade fairs. All of this helps us to understand their tactics and strategies, which translates into the ability to anticipate their moves and understand how they might react to ours. In this case, it's not so much crystal ball gazing to predict the future, and more like a game of chess. After all, having complete transparency on competitors is impossible to achieve. However, by putting together various pieces of the puzzle, making assumptions where necessary, it is possible to create a framework to orient oneself.

Once the strategic direction of the competitors is understood, the next step is to analyse their sources of value and how they compare to ours. By comparing the different product features (in the case of a car: size, fuel consumption, price, top speed, options, seating capacity, space, etc.), it is possible to determine if an advantage exists, and where it is. In the case of the TV mentioned above, the size of the screen appears to be the key feature. Sometimes it is possible to find comparative studies conducted by agencies. Other times it is necessary to purchase the competitor's product, study and dissect it to evaluate it properly.

All of this serves to determine who provides the greatest value and what that implies for the pricing strategy. Once the value differentials have been identified – in terms of the features of one's own offering and that of the competition – the next step is to analyse the range of prices on the market.

When competitors' products have publicly available price lists, for example, in B2C products, it is relatively easy to find them on the Internet, at retail outlets or from distributors. Sometimes price lists are available even if the actual net prices applied are significantly different from those listed. In order to discover the 'true' level of transactional prices, market research companies can be engaged. There are various types of these companies, specializing in anything from individual spare parts to pharmaceutical products. Alternatively, simulated purchase negotiations, or mystery shopping, can be conducted to determine the extent to which the listed price can be reduced.

In the case of products that are not sold through public price lists, as is the case in B2B fields, there are many possible avenues to explore: interviewing distributors and agents, or even customers directly. This is where research and storytelling work becomes useful. This would entail approaching your own salespeople, who face the competition every day; analysing sales data such as statistics on won and lost bids, focusing on the reasons for losses, if documented; or verifying the existence of specific studies and databases. It is also possible to approach former employees of competitors and interview them, or as mentioned above, implement mystery shopping.[1]

This data-collection exercise is repeated regularly to capture the dynamic evolution of prices in the market. For example, a well-known automotive company collects information on competitors' spare part prices once a year to monitor their movements. While a lingerie manufacturer uses a web crawler that compares online prices in real time to track prices and promotions offered by the competition.

It is therefore essential to have in place a price-collection process, with someone in charge, that can produce information regularly and timely, as appropriate to the market context.

Quantify Value

After identifying the sources of value and analysing them in the competitive context, the next step is to quantify the value.

This involves understanding the value as perceived by the customer and calculating the value of what is offered. Therefore, the question is: how much is each individual driver worth to the customer?

The mapping of key value factors often reveals services linked to the product that add value for the customer but are not charged for, nor listed, because they do not generate additional costs. Instead of focusing on costs, we should ask ourselves what benefits the customer derives from having these services. What costs would the customer incur if this service did not exist? Finally, what is the starting point of the value that can be monetized?

Many companies struggle to quantify value, for example, when there are no cost differences between products. Let's take the example of the Volkswagen Group, which offers three vehicles with different brands and positions but built on the same production platform: Seat Leon, Volkswagen Golf , and Audi A3.

While the cars have different purchase prices – ranging from the Leon as the most economical model to the A3 as the most expensive model – the same spare parts used for the different models have the same price. However, customers loyal to the Audi brand would be willing to pay a premium for that car compared to Volkswagen, and even more so for Seat, so it can be assumed they would also be willing to pay a premium for spare parts.

Assuming a price index of 100 for the same spare part across the three vehicles: wouldn't it make sense to price Seat spare parts at 100, Volkswagen spare parts at 115, and Audi spare parts at 130?

This was the rationale followed by automobile manufacturers for identical spare parts, among brands or models positioned in different price ranges. It has been observed that by differentiating the prices of identical parts by brand or model, it is possible to monetize the higher willingness to pay of certain customer segments.

To evaluate the value of a product we offer to the customer, the sources of value must also be analysed separately, using a specific formula or calculation logic to quantify the amount in dollars. Usually, it is sufficient to select the main sources of value, up to a maximum of five or six value drivers.

In the case of the Samsung TV, for example, only one value driver was sufficient: the screen size. All the other features such as OLED category, 4K resolution, multi-view up to two screens, had already been taken into consideration in the price set by Sony.

Quantification requires some creativity in finding data and inputs for the calculation logic.

It is possible to rely on official sources or base the calculations on their own hypotheses or experiences within the company. Alternatively, market research can be conducted, such as conjoint analyses, to understand the value of the premium that our company offers compared to other market offerings. Another approach is to extract data from targeted customer surveys.

Table 3.2, presents sources of value and examples of calculations for machinery intended for business customers.

The exemplary quantification of the sources of value shown in Table 3.2 makes it possible to compare our advantages with those of competitors and ideally demonstrate that we provide superior value. However, it is important to remain realistic: we may be superior in

Table 3.2: Quantification of value sources with specific calculation criteria.

Source of value	Calculation criteria	Quantification
Increased productivity	Higher quantities produced resulting in additional revenue	100 units produced per day × $10 = $1,000 of additional revenue
Streamlined timelines	Saved work hours reducing costs	1.5 fewer hours of work for daily tasks × $90 = $135 cost reduction
Waste reduction	Reduced waste generates savings	30 fewer scraps × $10 = $300 savings
Immediate availability	Reduced waiting days for a spare part translates to the ability to restart stalled machinery	2 fewer waiting days × $5,000 of additional daily revenue = $10,000
Higher product quality	2% increase in market share	2 percentage points × $1,000,000 per point = $2,000,000 of additional revenue

certain aspects, while less competitive in others. It is unlikely that we will be the best at everything. That is why it is important to have a good understanding of competitors' offerings and highlight the advantages related to purchasing our products when engaging with customers.

Price Based on Value

Value-based pricing represents the most advanced way of capturing value compared to cost-based pricing or competition-oriented pricing.

A well-known example of value-based pricing is the iPhone: Apple customers are willing to pay much more for their device compared to similar products available on the market. Whether it is the design of the iPhone, the luxury purchasing experience in Apple stores, the brand or the sense of belonging to the Apple community, the higher price can be justified by the benefits that customers receive from purchasing and owning the product, without focusing too much on the actual production costs.

To determine the value-based price, we consider the sum of the quantification of the value drivers of our product for the customer. As a starting point, we can take a comparable product or service that customers would choose in the absence of our offering. When determining prices, it is still useful to keep profitability considerations in mind on the one hand, and consider competitors' moves on the other.

In the example of the aforementioned new Samsung TV, we should ask ourselves: how much would customers who purchase large-sized TVs be willing to pay for an additional 13 inches? (Can you hear echoes of Sergio Leone here? 'For a Few Inches More' could be a sequel of *For a Few Dollars More*. . . .)

Suppose we have discovered that the value of 13 inches is equivalent to $100. What we will do is add this amount to the price of $899 for Sony, which is the next best alternative, to arrive at a price of $999, which is the value-based price for Samsung.

The formula to calculate value-based pricing is the reference price plus the sum of the value sources. In other words: value-based price = reference price + $\sum$ value driver 1 up to n.

In the example shown in Figure 3.1, a reference price of $1,000 is taken, which is the price of a comparable product from a competitor, the next-best alternative. Sometimes the cost in the absence of comparable products is also used, to which the amounts related to four

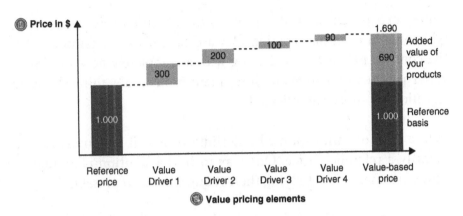

Figure 3.1 Value pricing elements – illustrative example.

value drivers that differentiate our product from the competition are added, totalling $690.

Our final price will be $1,690, thanks to the added value provided by the four value sources.

The reference price is the starting point and deserves further exploration: it is determined by the price the customer would pay for a product 'perceived' to be similar to ours, that is, the reference product. In the absence of value sources that can be added to our proposal, the two products will turn out to be alike, and it will not be possible for us to charge a higher price for ours.

For the reference product, the customer expects to pay a reference price based on their previous purchases of this product. Our task here will be to gather information regarding the reference price relevant for the customer. Sometimes finding the reference price is as simple as conducting online research through competitive analysis or leveraging the accessibility of price lists and offers from other market players to our sales force, or asking other customers. In other cases, however, customers may not share the reference price and simply expect our offer. It will be up to us to infer reference prices, which could even be a straightforward task if we are familiar with the context. But, if we are dealing with a completely new and innovative product or a large and infrequent project sale, things become significantly more complicated.

In the case of innovations, by definition, it will be impossible to identify a reference price. One way to find a solution is to analyse how customers are satisfying their requirements *at present*.

If that is not possible either, the offer can be tested with potential customers. Especially those who are not entirely satisfied by what is available now and will be keen to try our product – if it promises to deliver what others don't – as soon as it hits the market.

One final note: be careful not to become too greedy and retain the entire value created.

Our products still need to be attractive to the customer, so we will have to share part of this value with them. This is the 'price' to pay for transactions among equals.

Sharing the creation of value in a fair way is essential for maintaining long-term business relationships, which is why one should never overestimate or underestimate the value of offers.

Revising our approach to value pricing is also an ideal opportunity to review and optimize existing revenue models and eliminate any unnecessary features or ones that customers are not willing to pay for, reconstruct service packages, and create new value-based offerings to meet different customer needs.

A successful value-pricing approach creates a win–win situation for both the company and the customer.

Communicate Value

After identifying and quantifying the sources of value, we can use them to communicate the value to the customer and defend the substantial prices, in line with the value.

To argue the value and have an effective *value story*, it is advisable to refer to the customer's needs and articulate how the value sources of our solution allow us to satisfy those needs.

Value pricing should become the guiding principle within the company, the one that unites every department and function.

All efforts must also be channelled to identify, create, and monetize value: this often requires a drastic change in mindset that extends well beyond just the price.

The sales team plays a crucial role here: having the salespeople on board is decisive for materializing everything that has been developed so far. It will be up to them to sell the value, not the discount, to the customer, defending the price level because the value justifies the price being asked.

However, it is often during this final phase that value pricing fails. Selling value and communicating value are as important as the value itself created for the customer: if the customer does not perceive the value, it cannot be monetized.

However, it is not always the customer who is the most difficult to convince. The sales team is happy to sell improved products but may be more reluctant to change the way they sell them.

Transitioning from a transactional-sales approach to a value-based sales approach can be daunting. Operators who have been selling the same product to the same customers for over 10 years, for example, may fear losing customers if they feel obliged to change the way they sell.

Resistance to a value-based sales approach is often much greater internally because it involves changing a psychological mechanism.

The sales force needs to become familiar with the value of the offers and be prepared to sell and properly defend that value. This requires training, new sales scripts and supporting materials, training courses on how to implement this new approach and handle objections, and value-based sales exercises and simulations.

It is about changing the mindset of the sales force so that they can demonstrate to customers the true value they will receive when purchasing our products and services.

One way to approach value-based selling is to relate the sources of value to the customer's needs.

This will demonstrate that we understand the customer's requests and requirements.

Based on that, we can then explain how our solution can satisfy those needs.

By explicitly stating the value, we can also convince the customer that what they are buying and paying for is necessary and 'right'.

Communication should also be tailored to the specific context in which the customer is located, in terms of product, geographic area, economic context and so on.

As for the sources of value, it is advisable to limit the selection to a maximum of five to seven, prioritizing the elements with the greatest benefit for the customer; going beyond that number complicates the argumentation and makes it difficult for the customer to remember all the acquired information.

By explicitly stating the benefits, we become concrete and relevant, capturing the customer's attention.

The sum of the benefits provides tangible value: but simply citing numbers is not enough. Storytelling – the art of telling the story of the product and service – around these quantifications becomes essential. The logic behind the calculation should be explained, and made clear and understandable. Whole numbers should be indicated, without decimals, if possible, with strong and high-level messages, without getting lost in the details. All of this is to stay focused and not get distracted. In other cases, when it comes to non-business customers, numbers and quantification may not be necessary, but rather qualitative arguments. Emotional aspects of selling value should also be taken care of to create a positive relationship with the customer and earn their trust.

The introduction of value-based pricing can lead to higher and sustainable profitability. It not only ensures that customers are willing to pay for the value they receive but also creates new norms and practices associated with our offerings. It is a win–win situation for both the company and the customer, and this narrative must be communicated loud and clear, because it leads to success.

Value-based prices can completely transform our company and even change the rules of the game.

Summary

To capture and sell value through *value pricing*, five steps need to be followed:

1. Understand needs and create value

   - Understanding customer needs is the starting point for setting up our offer and pricing.

   - To satisfy needs and extract economic returns from the market, it is necessary to create value.

   - Identifying and quantifying the value-added features of a product is the greatest challenge in value-based pricing.

   - There are three types of features that customers associate with products and services: *hygiene factors*, which are the necessary condition to consider a purchase; *preference drivers*, which determine whether a customer will buy my product or another; *value drivers*, which motivate customers to pay a higher price.

   - *Value drivers* can be intangible or emotional (brand, design, lower risk, reassurance) or tangible and economic in nature. Each source of value contributes to creating a competitive advantage and provides the basis for quantifying value.

2. Analyse the competition

   Competitors' offerings evolve, new antagonists with new solutions come into play, influencing the perceived value of our offering. The perception of value varies: it is relative and not absolute, unless what we are selling constitutes a *disruptive innovation*. Therefore, it is important to monitor such developments to understand what options are available to customers. The reference product, the so-called *next best alternative*, becomes an important benchmark for calculating the differential value of a product compared to others. This holds true in cases of segmentation, that is to say for a specific market segment sharing needs and perception of value.

Once the strategic direction of competitors is understood, their sources of value are analysed and compared to ours, comparing the prices applied by competitors. The analysis of the competition provides important inputs for quantifying value.

3. Quantify the value

After identifying and analysing the sources of value in the competitive context, the next step is to quantify the value.

To assess the value of a product, the sources of value are analysed separately using a specific formula or calculation. Typically, selecting a maximum of five to six value drivers is sufficient. Quantification requires ingenuity in finding data and inputs. Official sources can be used, or calculations can be based on assumptions or experiences gained within the company. Market research such as conjoint analysis and surveys can also be conducted.

4. Price based on value

To determine the price based on value, we consider the sum of the quantification of the value drivers of our product for the customer. As a starting point, we can take a product or service comparable to ours. The formula for calculating the price based on value is the reference price plus the sum of the sources of value: (value-based price = reference price + Σ value drivers 1 to n). The price that is determined is what the customer would pay for a product perceived as similar to ours, or a *reference product*.

5. Communicate the value

- Selling and communicating value are as important as the value itself: if the customer does not perceive the value, it cannot be monetized.

- To argue the value and have an effective *value narrative*, it is advisable to refer to the customer's needs and indicate how the sources of value in our solution satisfy them.

- The sales team plays a crucial role: they will 'sell the value' and not the discount, defending the price level in front of the customer.

- The introduction of value-based pricing can lead to higher and sustainable profitability, create new norms and practices, and even change the rules of the game for the entire company.

RULE 4
DIFFERENTIATE PRICES

'Once an idea has taken hold of the brain it's almost impossible to eradicate.

'An idea that is fully formed – fully understood – that sticks; right in there somewhere'.

From *Inception* (2010) of Christopher Nolan, filmmaker

Introduction

Where does the world end if not in our minds? In the thoughts that we can formulate? In the place where we are able imagine all that is yet to come?

If we were to strip ourselves of our mental constructions, like shedding our clothes in the thick of a forest . . . The sun would rise through the trees.

What is left of me, of you, after a divorce, a loss, after the failure of a venture, beyond the money that has been dissipated? It is the idea of the passion we have invested, the time we have spent on trying to make it work, all of which has been wasted. What is left behind are objects, and all the stars we had imagined we would reach.

Sometimes, when confronted with the law of large numbers, the market, we feel inadequate, if not non-entities: think about how sad it would be to see a small quality bookstore, right in your neighbourhood, a place where you occasionally buy books, close down. Think of the owner, a guy who got a master's degree with distinction in Publishing, who then dedicated body and soul to his dream of opening a 'business' selling books, pouring all his passion for Eastern philosophy and motorcycles into it. Imagine his favourite book being *Zen and the Art of Motorcycle Maintenance* by Robert M. Pirsig:

> I think that if we are going to reform the world, and make it a better place to live in, the way to do it is not with talk about relationships of a political nature, which are inevitably dualistic, full of subjects and objects and their relationship to one another; or with programs full of things for other people to do. I think that kind of approach starts it at the end and presumes the end is the beginning. Programs of a political nature are important end products of social quality that can be effective only if the underlying structure of social values is right. The social values are right only if the individual values are right. The place to improve the world is first in one's own heart and head and hands, and then work outward from there. Other people can talk about how to expand the destiny of mankind. I just want to talk about how to fix a motorcycle. I believe that what I have to say has more lasting value.

That's what we are talking about: being able to change the essence of things. And thus change our own existence.

Everything is change. Everything is about encounters, wind blowing, a train whooshing in the distance. That day when we walked past the window of the small bookstore and met someone; the face of a girl on the other side of the street; the couple arguing while sitting outside a café last week, when I was in Paris for a conference, then back to the office, yet another business trip. And then? It's still raining. The ground is waterlogged. Entire communities will rise from the mud. Willpower and money, these are the two things that change the course of events, together with luck, which as we know, is a blind goddess. Meanwhile, the notes of a piano play through the forest, it's a Japanese animated film, my daughter would pay gold to have the DVD of that *anime*.

Things take on different contours depending on who observes them; we could say that they have a soul (precisely), but it's always us who give it to them: 'We take a handful of sand from the endless landscape of awareness around us and call that handful of sand the world', as the guy from the bookstore underlined on one of the pages of Pirsig's manual.

Sometimes what changes us is a movie, a book, a journey. A kiss. How much will the ticket to the concert where 'it' happened 'be worth' to us? Other times, a special friendship will be priceless: that someone who has been there for us from primary school, sharing a desk at the back of the classroom, through to university, and the course in Economics that we completed with minimal effort because, oh, we were so young! And immortal.

More often, things have a price. A toy for a child, and the same toy for an adult collector (I think of my children's Pokémon cards, there's a card valued at a million dollars!). And a trip to Indonesia for me, who always wanted to go there, compared to a colleague who only likes French champagne, Provence, lavender fields, and Mediterranean scents.

For each of us, the objects that surround us, a pair of motorcycle gloves, a jumper, an LP of contemporary classical music – Greg Haines' poignant work, *183 Times* – everything has its intrinsic and relative value. Why? It's how we human being function; we transfer onto objects the love we cannot put into words.

So, how much is the small bonsai on this desk worth to me, or the scent of undergrowth it releases after I've given it just the 'right' amount of water? How much is the tag from the first hat I bought years ago in New York worth, in the days before the pandemic struck and halted the world? What happened to the resolutions to live better that we had made during those days? How much are they worth today?

The Pricing Paradox

It is for all these reasons that charging different prices to two different customers for the same product, even when the production cost is the same, is not only fair but also more equitable than charging a single price for everyone!

What may seem like a paradox is, in many cases, standard practice already.

Think of the discounted prices offered to the elderly, children, or students. Or to members of certain organizations, clubs or loyalty programmes: in all these cases, the fact that benefits, discounts, and lower prices are granted to some but not others is widely accepted.

Let's consider the case of students: in several countries, their student ID card entitles them to special offers with (for example, in Milan, they get free public transport until the age of 14). They can get discounts on train tickets, cinema and entertainment, holiday stays, restaurants, or various products ranging from computers to clothing. The underlying assumption is that students, while studying, do not have substantial earnings and therefore have fewer economic opportunities and less disposable income.

The 'price discrimination' – a term coined in 1920 by Arthur Cecil Pigou in his book *The Economics of Welfare* – becomes, in this case, a beneficial practice, which we will call *the pricing paradox*.

But, as usual, let's question the terms.

The term 'discrimination' often carries a negative connotation, and it is usually associated with outright penalization. Therefore, those who do not wish to use this term sometimes speak of 'segmentation', or 'revenue management'.

In Pigou's hypothesis, however, it is not a matter of discriminating on the grounds of religion, race or ethnicity, but rather based on the subjective perception of value.

The civil aviation industry is the exemplary case that demonstrates how price discrimination brings benefits to customers, businesses, and society as a whole.

With the introduction of revenue management, airlines became capable of applying different prices to individual market segments, even differentiating prices for each passenger.[1] Robert Crandall, former CEO of American Airlines, said in this regard: 'If I had 2,000 passengers and 400 different prices on a particular route, I would obviously be 1,600 prices short': the goal shared by all actors was to implement a form of discrimination that would lead to personalized pricing.

Differentiating prices based on the time of the booking, refundability or the chosen class has, in a way, democratized air travel, providing access to the service for entire market segments that previously could not afford to fly.

Applying a uniform price to each passenger on a given route would not have exploited the full payment capability of the affluent customer segment, while it would have rendered flying prohibitive for a less-affluent customer segment.

The same applies to hotels:[2] if you look to book a single room at the Marriott Park Hotel in Rome, you can find it on Booking and Expedia for $236. On the Marriott website, the price is $230 at full price. For members of Bonvoy, the loyalty programme of the Marriott chain, the price is $225. On Trivago, the price is $197. Dollarsun offers it for $188. On Destinia, the price is $177. If you book through a multinational booking portal, you only pay $147. If the booking is non-refundable, the cost drops to $135. Searching the web for a mere 5 minutes, you can find offers for the same product ranging from $236 to $135. A price difference of 75%! The CEO of a well-known hotel chain told me: 'It is normal to offer up to 600 rates for hotel rooms based on room type, services, and conditions.'

To each his own: if I really want to go back to that very hotel in Venice where all those years ago I met ... well, maybe, as it happens, I won't even look at the price. Because the emotional value of recapturing that experience, for me, will always be greater, it will 'be worth' far beyond its mere numerical expression, and also because – if you think about it – you only live once (except if you are James Bond)!

As long as customers have some form of control over prices, they will accept price discrimination even when it sometimes leads to higher prices, as in the case of air travel. If I book a flight for tomorrow, I must accept the fact that I will pay a much higher price than the passenger sitting next to me who booked the same flight 6 months ago paying a fraction of what I am being charged now. In this case, I am the one who decides when to purchase, through which channel, and the type of ticket.

The moment this form of control is lost, there will be strong protests.

Coca-Cola, a true international giant and one of the Big Giants of modern and contemporary capitalism, had this experience.

Coca-Cola's intention was to vary prices based on temperature at the vending machines, on the principle that the hotter it is, the more willing people are to pay for a cold drink. This was the logic of then-CEO Doug Ivester: 'Coca Cola is a product whose worth varies from moment to moment', he claimed, explaining that as demand for a cold Coca-Cola rises when it is very hot, 'it is fair [it] should be more expensive' in certain conditions. For that reason, the company developed vending machines equipped with a thermostat and a software capable of raising prices when certain temperatures are reached, automating the price adjustment process.[3]

The reaction of strong protest and dissatisfaction from customers around the world to this plan was immediate. Temperature, after all, is a condition beyond our control.

The end result was that Coca-Cola shelved plans to alter prices based on temperatures.

What this example shows is that varying prices is easier said than done.

Price discrimination is acceptable as long as it is justified and fair. The challenge that many companies face when trying to differentiate prices is that the perception of price fairness varies greatly from customer to customer based on many factors, such as the type of product, geographical area, disposable income, and product usage.

Therefore, before differentiating prices, it is necessary to analyse the factors that influence the perception of fairness.

Every company evaluates what is fair or unfair in terms of prices based on norms, culture, and history. Only by keeping this composite value in mind can businesses seize the great opportunities offered by price differentiation while respecting the parameters of fairness. Explicit and transparent communication of the reasons for price variations greatly helps acceptance of these price changes. A typical reason could be membership of a loyalty programme, delivery costs, or conditions, services, and guarantees associated with the sale.

Price differentiation represents an important lever that must be used judiciously, enabling a company to benefit from varying prices while still being perceived as fair.

Companies that understand what drives their customers' perception of fairness can ensure they capture customers' willingness to pay.

In the next section, we will discuss six ways to differentiate prices.

1. Differentiation based on customers

A study published a few years ago in the *Times* caused a stir: the data revealed that women pay approximately 40% more than men for the same products.[4] Beyond what this says about the issue of gender gap and the permanence of an age-old patriarchal logic (something that is fortunately changing) this also demonstrates that it is possible to differentiate prices based on specific customer characteristics, that predict the price level they are willing to pay. Age, for example, becomes a criterion for modifying prices, suggesting the offer of discounted museum tickets for older people or of reduced-price admission tickets for children at theme parks.

If the customer to whom we are providing a service is a business, we should understand whether they are a multinational corporation or a small company, a government institution, or a non-profit organization. To find out their position, we will consider elements such as revenue or legal status, which can help us make assumptions on their ability and willingness to pay: this is likely to be higher for a rapidly growing pharmaceutical multinational company and lower for a small individual business operating only at local level, and with the same small, if steady, revenue over the years.

But let's go back to the so-called gender pricing that discriminates prices based on the gender of customers: Tesco, one of the main retail supermarket chains in the United Kingdom, charges double for pink disposable razors compared to blue ones. The difference, between the two, if truth be told, is 'just' the colour. In Argos, a well-known UK retailer, blue scooters cost £5 less than the exact same product in pink. Even women's Levi's 501 jeans cost on average 46% more than the men's version. Boots sells Chanel Allure spray deodorant for £30, while the same product for men costs only £24.

On Amazon, regular Bic ballpoint pens cost £2, while the branded 'for her' pens cost £3.[5] This is not just a UK phenomenon: similar examples can be found in many other countries. 'What a scandal this pricing policy is!' some thought following the publication of the study, and from an ethical standpoint, one could easily join the chorus condemning this pricing policy. On the other hand, some ventured the hypothesis that some women might have greater willingness – let's say – to pay compared to men, for reasons difficult to fathom (given that the very real gender pay gap often means that women, in equivalent positions, are still paid less than their male counterparts).

In reality, this is a legitimate *modus operandi* practiced for a long time by both manufacturers and retailers.

'Women's' products have an average margin 25% higher than 'blue' products, which implies the generation of huge additional profits. After all, sellers – and the sophisticated minds of marketing people before them – think that no woman is forced to buy the pink product: she freely chooses to! Recognizing this difference in willingness to pay and capitalizing on it can be both legitimate and justified.

Gender pricing relies on a hypothesis: women attribute a higher value to certain products than men do.

However, there are also cases where the female customer is favoured over the opposite sex: women, for example, are sometimes granted free entry to a nightclub, while men have to pay – you may have experienced this. Or, again, they get discount vouchers for drinks inside the venue, while men pay full price.

In short: we could say that there are many gender-based pricing tactics and, after all, what makes the world beautiful is the fact that it is diverse.

2. Temporal differentiation

One of the most common methods of differentiation is using the factor of time, a unit of measurement that can take various forms: seasonal prices and sales, pre-sales, product launch offers, last-minute prices, Cyber Monday, Black Friday, hourly price variations, and so on.

The basis of this differentiation is the fact that different customers have different willingness to pay based on *when* they make a purchase.

The willingness to pay for a hotel room in a city increases when the city hosts a trade fair. Hoteliers know well that in those days they have a unique opportunity to raise prices – regardless of whether from all other points of view that is officially 'low season' – and that if they don't do it, they lose profits. It's a cynical and ruthless logic, some may argue, and yes, it is. But not just that: it's also about balancing supply and demand.

Many products are initially launched at a high price, following what is known as a price-skimming strategy. There are customers willing to pay a premium to be among the first to have a certain product. Then, over time, prices go down to make the product accessible to customers with a lower willingness to pay.

Apple, for example, tends to lower the prices of older models after introducing a new one. The price of the iPhone 13 dropped by $130 when the iPhone 14 was launched in September 2022. The same happened with the price of the iPhone 12, which dropped by $100 when the iPhone 13 was launched in September 2021.[6] And so on, going back in time.

A particular case of temporal price discrimination is that of a well-known logistics company. When I met the CEO in mid-2023, he said, 'We offer different types of deliveries. The express delivery is scheduled for the next day by 12:00 pm, then there's the 2-day delivery, and finally the 3-day delivery. The 2-day and 3-day deliveries arrive at the warehouse at the same time as the express delivery, but we keep them in stock at a cost, albeit minimum, in order to justify a higher price on the express delivery.'

This company has educated customers to pay a premium for faster delivery, even if it generates costs by slowing down other delivery options. Nevertheless, applying such price discrimination, the overall profit is higher.

The publishing industry provides other examples in this regard: best-selling books by authors such as J.K. Rowling, Sarah Maas, or Holly Black are initially sold in hardcover for an average price of $30 and later in paperback for $10. The content is the same, and production costs vary only marginally. Yet, those who want the latest Harry Potter episode and are not willing to wait several months for the cheaper edition – or the even cheaper still electronic version – demonstrate their high willingness to pay by purchasing the first and more expensive hardcover edition. The publisher thus manages to bank a surplus of $20. Different prices for the same content are applied to different customers over time.

The same phenomenon is found in the fashion industry: those who want to wear the latest style by purchasing items sold at the beginning of the season will have to pay a high price. These are customers who highly appreciate being among the first to own the latest trendy items and therefore accept that they must pay the full price. Towards the end of the season, when the sales are on, even those who are interested in these items but are not willing to pay full price can buy them. These customers are happy to wait a little longer and purchase end of season items, or items from the previous year's collection, at a lower price.

For a series of music or sports events, where tickets are put on sale months before the event itself, the value increases over time. Given the long timespan for ticket purchases leading up to the event, last-minute purchases have a higher value. If my favourite team has made it to the football championship final, I will be willing to pay more to see the match. Thus, in the week before a New York Yankees base-ball game, the price of a ticket can even double from $119 to $274.[7] And on the day of the game, the price rises again. A classic case of dynamic pricing.

However, be careful not to lose out by differentiating prices!

Companies often make mistakes when attempting to differentiate prices based on the time factor.

In a project for a theme park for teenagers in Italy, we discovered that they offered a 30% discount on weekdays during certain time slots, but despite the attractive deal there was no increase in the number of tickets sold. We found a similar situation with a large multi-level underground parking operator in the city centre. During the week, the price for a single hour was €4. On Sundays, the price was reduced to €1 per hour, but despite the reduced cost of parking their car, the number of users did not increase.

In both cases, the problem was absence of demand. At the theme park, it made little sense to discount tickets for weekdays entry, as teenagers couldn't take advantage of the offer because they were in school; in the case of the car park, with shops and offices closed on Sundays, it was unlikely that there would be the same – or even a higher level of demand as during weekdays because of the reduced price alone.

In both cases, it was proposed to raise the lower prices, which allowed for increased profits without losing volume.

The lesson in this case is that it is not enough to consider the level of demand alone, but it is also important to look at the elasticity of demand in relation to price – that is, how customers respond to price changes over a certain period of time.

3. Differentiation based on location

The price of the same product can vary depending on where it is sold. For example, a can of Coca-Cola costs $0.89 at a discount supermarket, $2 at a beach kiosk, $2.99 at the airport, $5 at a 4-star hotel minibar, and $10 at a nightclub. Between the two extreme prices, namely the discount and the nightclub, the difference is more than 1,100%!

Therefore, where customers make their purchases is a good indicator of how much they are willing to pay. Different prices in different locations also reflect different purchasing power: prices in the centre of London will generally be higher than prices in a rural area. Different prices also express a different competitive context: if I sell pizza in the city centre where I have several fast-food restaurants and bars next to me, I will have to take that into account. On the other hand, being the only pizzeria within a 10-km radius might allow me to impose a much less competitive price (in extreme cases, even a 'monopolistic' price).

While Peroni Nastro Azzurro beer has a medium-low positioning in Italy, in the United Arab Emirates it is a premium product that costs up to four times more.

If you visit a Gucci store in the centre of Rome, near the Spanish Steps, you will find the current collection at full price. A luxury brand in an exclusive location would not contemplate offering discounts because it wants to maintain its positioning in the luxury segment. However, if you are willing to take a trip to an outlet store outside the city, where you may not necessarily find that specific item or size, you will definitely find much more attractive prices, which for fashion items means up to 30, 50, or 70% off the original price tag.

Many companies differentiate based on location precisely because distance is a deterrent.

If you become aware that a service station 50 km away sells petrol at a lower price than your local pump, for you to go to the trouble of going that far the difference must be substantial: if the saving on a full tank is negligible, you will probably conclude that it is worth your while filling up locally.

However, customer behaviour is often far from rational.

The irrational nature of customer behaviour was confirmed by a test, administered to participants divided into two groups.

In the first group, people were presented with a pair of shoes priced at $150, and were told that they could purchase the same shoes for $5 less in a shop less than half an hour away by car.

In the second group, people were presented with a pair of socks priced at $20, and were told that they could buy them for $15 in a shop a half an hour's drive away.

In both cases, the absolute savings amounted to $5. However, in the first group, only 24% of the customers expressed a willingness to drive half an hour to pay the lower price, while in the second group, the result was nearly three times higher: 71%!

Clearly, saving $5 out of $20, or a quarter of the price, is considered a good deal, while saving $5 out of $150 is seen as marginal.

Price considerations related to location are therefore relative and not absolute.

The concept of 'location' also includes the sales channel, which can be physical or virtual. For example, Dow Corning sells silicones directly at a fairly substantial price, and uses online platforms to sell the same products – with certain restrictions – at a much lower price.

However, caution must be exercised not to overdo it. If the price in one country exceeds a certain threshold, assuming that transport and customs costs are not excessive, distributors may decide to buy the product from countries where the price is lower, reimport it to countries where the price is higher, and pocket the difference.

Cases like this are defined as *grey markets* or parallel imports, meaning movement of products from one market to another across one or more borders, not controlled by the manufacturer. There are many examples of this phenomenon:[8] the beer from the AB InBev Group being more expensive in Belgium than in the Netherlands led to imports from the Netherlands to Belgium. The fashion brand Guess maintained higher prices in Western Europe compared to Eastern Europe, resulting in parallel imports from the latter.

In the United Kingdom, Tesco decided to stop purchasing Levi's products from UK wholesalers for retail sales and instead to import them directly from the United States, where they found them at much lower prices.[9] This allowed them to offer jeans at prices 45% lower than other British retailers.

Some companies have declared *grey market* exploitation as their main activity. Kohlpharma, which reimports medicines with price differentials, saving customers at least 10%,[10] generates $660 million in revenue.[11]

To avoid parallel imports, manufacturers are now taking different approaches.

One is to introduce 'price corridors' that establish minimum and maximum prices, limiting price dispersion in a specific region and making the *grey market* less profitable. Others restrict the quantities they send to places that sell at lower prices so that they are only enough to satisfy local demand, reducing the risk that quantities in excess are re-exported. Or they limit warranties or after-sales services to the region they are intended for, which can be monitored with codes on each product. This way, if a product intended for the Asian market re-emerges in Europe, it will not be covered by a warranty.

4. Differentiation through bundles

The creation of product groups, known as *price bundles*, is a common differentiation practice in multi-product companies. Multiple products are grouped together and sold at a price lower than the sum of the individual product prices. Classic examples include Microsoft Office packages (with programs like Word, Excel, PowerPoint), Burger King or McDonald's meal deals (with beverages, burgers, fries), and all-inclusive vacations (with accommodation, meals, transport).

From the seller's perspective, the main advantage of bundling is the ability to increase profits by effectively leveraging the spending propensity of potential customers. The bundle transfers the unexpressed spending propensity towards a particular product to another product within the company's offering.

Bundling also offers numerous benefits for customers, such as reduced transaction costs. Customers can find what they need from a single provider at prices that are overall more affordable. This leads to increased customer satisfaction, greater loyalty, reduced complexity, and enhanced clarity and transparency. However, bundling does not always prove to be a successful strategy.

In the many cases we have observed, 'flops' and 'failures' generally occur when companies do not adhere to four rules:

a) Meeting the needs of customers

A critical aspect for the success of price bundling strategies is the optimal design of the packages. From the company's perspective, combining attractive products with less sought-after items from the company's range to increase sales of the latter can be a good idea. Both Microsoft Office and McDonald's value meals reflect this principle. However, focusing only on the company's needs risks neglecting the needs of customers, which can easily result in a drop in sales. If the bundle contains too many unattractive products, customers will opt to purchase the products separately, ignoring the less appealing ones. Therefore, it is crucial to align customer needs with those of the company offering the bundle. To reconcile these two perspectives, it is necessary to clearly define the target customers. Different packages must be offered, each catering to a specific segment's preferences. Considering customer needs is vital for the success of a bundling strategy.

b) Aligning package pricing with business objectives

Optimal pricing is also fundamental to the success of a specific package. However, before decision-makers determine the price level to apply, they must determine the most suitable 'price structure'. Regarding the structure, two options can be pursued: a single pricing covering all components of the bundle or a building-block system where the price depends on the type and number of selected services. The preferred option for a particular company is determined by various factors such as business objectives, customer preferences, and legal aspects. After determining the price structure, it is possible to define the optimal price level. To incentivize the purchase of the package, this is generally offered at a lower price compared to the sum of the prices of the individual components. Experience shows that the optimal discount for a package typically falls within a range of 5% to 20%, depending on the number of components included in the package offered. Alternatively, instead of offering discounts, providing additional services can be an option. In any case, careful attention must be paid to price thresholds. Some empirical studies have shown how the choice to use *mixed bundling*, where both the complete package and individual components can be offered to the customer, can make more sense in terms of profit optimization, contrary to *pure bundling*, which only allows the purchase of the complete package.

c) Creating an organization that supports bundling

Very often, packages consist of products belonging to different profit centres or divisions within the company. Since the price of the package is generally lower than the sum of the component prices, this negative difference must be distributed among the different profit centres. This often leads to resistance and conflicts. Therefore, it is necessary to create an organizational structure that enables the bundling strategy to succeed despite the probable internal frictions. An organization structured on customer segments, for example, could help avoid this problem.

d) Controlling the bundling process

Bundling is a particularly complex topic. Experience shows that many companies lack the adequate skills for controlling this process (objectives, product selection, legal checks, identification of customer spending propensity and segment size, simulation and optimization of the most relevant combinations). Consequently, a control system is necessary to ensure customers are not discouraged from purchasing due to the presence of less interesting products within the bundle or due to an incorrect price structure. If managed correctly, the profit increments achievable through bundling range from +10% to +40%.

5. Differentiation based on quantity

Who doesn't know the saying 'the more you buy, the less you pay'? As the quantity purchased grows, the discount increases, and the price per unit decreases. A lower price represents a clear incentive to consume more.

There are many options for differentiation based on quantity. One example is a percentage promotion: 'Buy two products and get a 50% discount on the second one.' A 50% discount on the second product sounds more appealing than a 25% discount on both products. Even more enticing is 'Buy one get one free.' In this case, the discount for the second product is doubled to 100%.

The German DIY chain Praktiker went even further by extending the discount to almost the entire assortment with the slogan '20% off everything except pet food'. It managed to position itself as a discount store. However, it went bust in 2013 (probably because it had gone overboard with the discounts!).

Other quantity-based discounts can also be used to reward customer loyalty. Near my house, there are several barbershops. There is one, for example, that distributes simple paper cards: they stamp the card after each haircut, and when you reach 10 stamps, you get a free haircut. Although I don't have much hair to cut, I regularly go to the barber, and I must admit that this card I keep in my wallet motivates me to always go back to the same barber despite the alternatives available.

Another similar example is the BahnCard, a card that can be purchased from Deutsche Bahn, the largest European train operator based in Germany, which offers various card options with different discount rates. The BahnCard 25 is the least expensive one, costing €35.90, and it offers a 25% discount on second-class travel for 1 year. To offset the cost of the card, the cardholder will need to spend at least €43.60.[12] Beyond this amount, they will benefit from additional discounts, which represents a strong incentive to prefer trains over other means of transport, such as cars or planes.

Discounts can also be granted in the form of free services, such as delivery costs. Amazon offers promotions with zero delivery costs to incentivize sales. In other cases, to obtain free delivery, a minimum spend is required, for example, $50.

To boost sales, price reductions can also be proposed under certain conditions. By combining prepayment tied to certain conditions with a discount, the sale of certain quantities within a specific period is facilitated. For example, cruise ship operators like MSC Cruises offer discounts to those who book well in advance.[13]

Wholesale discounts are also common between companies. A manufacturer establishes a 10% discount for orders over 10,000 units of a product and a 12% discount for orders over 15,000 units, encouraging the distributor to purchase more.

Trade-in credits are another tool to incentivize sales, encouraging customers to return their old products to benefit from a discount when purchasing a new one. Apple offers a $75 discount for the purchase of a new product if an iPhone 8 is traded in.[14] The same applies to cars: those interested in buying a new Audi, Alfa Romeo, or BMW can trade in their old car. The seller receives a product that can be resold or partly recycled, demonstrating commitment to both the circular economy and ecological sustainability, as well as economic sustainability.

6. Differentiation through incentives

When conducting market research to understand customers' willingness to pay for a good or service, respondents are rarely asked directly whether they are willing to pay a certain price.

That is because the answers would not reveal the value they perceive in that good or service, and how much they are willing to pay for it.

A more refined way to capture the true willingness to pay is to provide incentives to purchase that require a specific action from the customer. An example of an incentive is offered by several supermarkets: during certain time slots, customers can access a promotion. For example, Agorà supermarkets in Italy offer a 10% discount on non-discounted items between 8.00 and 10.00 pm. Other supermarkets in the United States or Singapore offer the same 10% discount as an early bird promotion for those who shop between 6.00 and 9.00 am on a Sunday. But who is willing to go to the supermarket so late or so early instead of more normal and convenient hours? The price-sensitive customer!

Some time ago, I accompanied a friend to a large women's clothing store near Rimini. At the checkout, I immediately noticed a particular promotion: 'Donate your dress'. A 25% discount was applied to those who spent at least $400 on a new dress and donated an old one. Intrigued, I asked the cashier what they did with the old dresses. She responded, 'We donate them to refugees or people in need.' But who is willing to bother bringing an old dress when they go shopping? The price-sensitive customer!

Another typical incentive is the best price guarantee: companies like Dell,[15] MediaWorld,[16] or Iberia[17] assure that they offer the lowest price. However, if the customer finds a lower-priced offer for the same product, they will receive a refund for the difference. For these companies, there is the advantage of being able to boast about offering very competitive prices, improving their price image, and at the same time, attracting price-conscious customers by discreetly offering them discounts. But who is willing to spend time comparing prices, producing evidence, and claiming the difference? The price-sensitive customer!

Another tool is vouchers or coupons, which are tickets or documents that provide a discount on the purchase of a product. They can be found in flyers, newspapers, magazines, or on the Internet, on sites such as Groupon. This is how price reductions can be obtained in all stores affiliated with the Douglas perfumery chain,[18] or for sports items like those from Nike,[19] or supplies as is the case with Shell.[20] But who goes to the trouble of searching, cutting out, verifying, and redeeming vouchers? The price-sensitive customer!

Summary

Discriminating prices for the same product or service is often more just and fairer than applying a uniform price for everyone. This pricing paradox brings benefits to customers, businesses, and society.

To support differentiated prices, it is important to be able to justify the differences in a transparent and explicit manner. There are many ways to differentiate prices, here are six of them:

1. *Differentiation based on customers*

   Private (e.g. age or gender) or business-related (e.g. revenue or legal status) characteristics allow the application of different prices for the same product. In the case of gender pricing, the differences can even be up to 40% and can be sustained, as they are linked to a different willingness to pay.

2. *Temporal differentiation*

   The price varies depending on *when* a purchase is made. Thus, a higher price can be charged at the beginning of a product's life cycle and then reduced in the subsequent phase, following a market-skimming strategy. Those who want a new product immediately will be willing to pay a higher price compared to those willing to wait to benefit from an economic advantage.

THE 10 RULES OF HIGHLY EFFECTIVE PRICING

3. *Differentiation based on location*

The price varies depending on *where* a purchase is made. An example is online sales being less costly than offline sales. However, be careful not to exaggerate and create a 'grey market' where it is retailers, rather than the company, that benefit from price differences.

4. *Differentiation through bundles*

Charging different prices for individual products and for product bundles allows for differentiation of prices. By resorting to bundling, demand heterogeneity is reduced, and customers' spending propensity is leveraged in favour of the company. Bundling can be applied in pure or mixed form. To succeed, the following four rules should be observed: a) satisfy customer needs, b) align the pricing of packages offered with business objectives, c) create an organization that supports bundling, and d) control the bundling process.

5. *Differentiation based on quantity*

Price reductions are granted in order to sell larger quantities. Discounts are offered in various forms to generate sales volumes, for example, as a percentage of the full price, in the form of loyalty rewards or of free services (e.g. shipping), subject to conditions (e.g. early payment), to wholesale buyers, or as trade-in credits.

6. *Differentiation through incentives*

A sophisticated way to capture the true willingness to pay is by providing purchase incentives that require a specific action from the customer. These incentives can take different forms – promotions, price guarantees, vouchers, loyalty programmes – allowing the identification of customers with specific spending propensities so that targeted offers can be proposed them.

RULE 5
CONSOLIDATE PROFITS BY INCREASING PRICES

'Low prices and high profits rarely go together'

Peter Drucker, economist

Introduction

Sagacity, or wicked game. It is an evil game we play in the era of financial and technological capitalism: as soon as you are not effective, you lose; as soon as you are not efficient and up to date, you lose. And there are no second chances. That's the market, baby!

I read some time ago that in the Middle Ages, those who were unable to pay their debts or 'failed' in their enterprise, were forcibly made to wear a donkey hat, and thus were exposed to public shame, walking around with the horrible hat, subjected to the mockery of fellow citizens. The good name they had worked for, year after year, sometimes sacrificing everything else, shattered forever.

Fortunately, those times are behind us. Today, this type of behaviour would be seen as an affront to human dignity, and considered discriminatory towards the individual. Thankfully, we can say that we have left behind the dark centuries. Well, at least those practices that violated the fundamental rights of men and women, rights earned over the centuries.

If in the old days people faced black knights, dense forests, and dark cobbled streets, today the hostile climate of competition presents us with two opposing attitudes: abandoning the game or exposing the weaknesses of our structure – this is, for example, what happened to many excellent companies that, due to the pandemic first and the subsequent socio-financial crisis later, did not manage to maintain their market position.

What we are trying to do (which, at this point of the book, should have become clear) is to provide concrete help to those who have to make decisions every day in a market that is increasingly integrated and global. We hope that, after reading this book, they will be able to embark on their own 'price path', without doing anything that does not accord with their own nature, but rather using that as their point of departure, which is what Marco Polo, the thirteenth century Venetian merchant, did with his travels to the Orient: not only did he manage to adapt to the changes he encountered on his journey to the East, but he turned the experience into a bestseller, *The Travels of Marco Polo*. He travelled on foot and on horseback, mostly along the Silk Road that connected the Mediterranean to China, passing through Central Asia. Such a journey, at that time, meant being away from home for months, facing the elements, and being robbed by bandits. Those were times when you knew when you left but didn't know when or *if* you would return.

In the following pages, we will first see how to set price increases and what assumptions to keep in mind, and then how to concretely increase prices. In short, we will try to put ourselves in the shoes of the most famous young Italian traveller in the world, who, together with his father and uncle, not only obtained a safe passage through all the lands controlled by the Mongols – which extended from the Far East to the borders of Europe – but practically secured the opportunity to operate free trade on all the prices of goods that passed through the lands governed by Genghis Khan's grandson, Kublai.

Have a good journey.

Prerequisites to Increasing Prices

'Caterpillar's sales jump 17% on higher equipment prices', the *Wall Street Journal* headlined at the end of April 2023.[1] This is how the US company, a global leader in construction machinery, managed to exceed expectations in terms of both revenue and profit.

In the post-pandemic period, costs have risen significantly in most parts of the world and in many industries. It's not about bandits and gold coins anymore. With rising raw material costs, with inflation, with the new environmental regulations that finally consider the negative impact of, amongst others, air and noise pollution (although compliance with norms is subject to a preliminary period of 'mindset adjustment'), with the disruptions to supply chains (not to mention the war following Putin's Russian invasion of Ukraine), there have been plenty of reasons to raise prices.

However, only one in five companies, including Caterpillar, has managed to raise prices to the level desired. Why is that? What were the base principles on which the company rebuilt its pricing strategy? And furthermore: when did they raise prices, by how much, where, and why does increasing prices become one of the most important decisions for a company?

It is because increasing prices allows the value transmitted to customers to be captured and thereby to consolidate profits. At the same time, it is one of the riskiest and most complex decisions in the life of a business entity: in the worst-case scenario, it leads to the loss of customers, revenue, and profitability.

The difference between the 20% of companies that succeed in increasing prices as planned and the 80% that fail to meet the objective lies entirely in the approach to the move.

To prepare and implement successful price increases, five prerequisites need to be kept in mind, which, once fulfilled, will likely place us among the 20% of winning companies. These are:

1. IMPACT: Understand the implications of price increases.

2. POWER: Assess the relationship with the customer.

3. NEGOTIATION: Set 'price points'.

4. COMMUNICATION: Explain the price increases.

5. SALESPEOPLE: Involve the sales force.

1. Impact

What would have happened if Marco Polo, upon returning home, had not shared with others what he had seen? The smell of the air, the spaces and horizons he had ridden through, the archery and falconry, the magnificent Mongolian horses, short and sturdy, agile and strong, wild like only certain spring days can be; April can be the cruellest of months.

Increasing prices means increasing others' perceptions of that object. Every product, good, or service *exists* before it is sold; it is produced and packaged. It constitutes information that becomes a transaction. From fountain pens to falcon feathers personally collected by Sir Polo along the roads back from the 'marvellous' lands of Cathay.

Every price is the synthesis of an idea. We assign more value to an object – a good or a service – based not only on its solidity or beauty but also on the suggestion it evokes, the possibilities it reveals to us. *Aletheia*, the Greeks used to say: truth means unveiling, and price is no exception.

A price reveals how much we are willing to pay. It tells us what 'value' we are willing to assign, under what conditions, based on what narrative. So, do we truly believe that buying an electric Ford Mustang (my dream!) will make us as fast as one of those wild horses galloping beneath the Ural Mountains? Or will we recognize that it is 'just' a car? The best answer probably lies somewhere in between! To some extent, we know that we will always remain 'just' ourselves. Yet, when we sit behind the wheel of that car – wow! – we would feel different, at least for a moment. We would go back to being children, a time when everything was possible. So, what price would you give to that sensation? If you bought another, let's say, 'ordinary' car, would the sensation be the same?

Obviously not.

Therefore, understanding the implications of price increases is the first prerequisite for success, from a company's perspective.

Price is the mirror of value. That's why analysing the relationship between the value perceived by the customer and the price is crucial.

Possible positive impacts (like feeling like a child again) or negative impacts (beyond the exhilaration of driving, the speeding fines we would have to pay!) should be anticipated, and the best strategy should be evaluated.

In many contexts, changing prices is easy, immediate, and has limited or no cost. Supermarkets and retailers with electronic price displays, online retailers, fuel pumps, and airlines are some of the businesses that change prices in a fraction of a second, sometimes multiple times a day.

Many managers fall into the temptation of changing prices just as quickly. But be careful not to rush! Making the right pricing decision requires careful consideration.

The most common misconception is wanting to increase prices in line with cost increases, on the assumption that existing customers will continue to make purchases. However, in an inflationary context, as we can see in recent years, customers expect generalized price increases. Based on contextual analysis (sometimes simply by sniffing the air, sensing 'which way the wind blows'), they will evaluate what they can afford and what they no longer can.

The elasticity of demand in relation to price must be studied carefully, and typically sustainable price variations are lower than cost variations.

Faced with a flurry of high prices, some purchases may need to be cut or reduced.

My classic annual one-week ski vacation in the Alps, for example, has been reduced to six days because my favourite hotel has significantly increased prices. Even though competitors are doing the same – it's an upward adjustment of prices based on the purchasing power of families – it doesn't mean that customers can afford or are willing to pay more.

Elasticities need to be studied, and customer reactions should be anticipated.

Furthermore, if it is expected that a cost increase will be temporary, it is advisable to think twice before raising prices, only to lower them again as soon as costs or demand decrease.

A higher-than-expected price remains imprinted in the customers' minds. They might be able to pay it once, but if they later perceive that the price positioning is too high or that the experience wasn't worth the money spent, customers won't even consider us anymore.

A company is also the good reputation it carries.

In a situation like the one described above, 'our' price image would be tarnished, especially if we deal with products that, in the collective imagination, should remain constant in terms of price. This brings us back to the theme of 'perceived value' and how much it can justify a certain increase in the price of that product or service offered.

On the other hand, companies that remain strongly aware of their 'legitimate' value even when the prices of their products go up discover hidden profit potentials, while maintaining the same sales volumes.

Last but not least, the competitive context must be kept in mind.

Is Marco Polo the only one who can provide us with a fountain pen built around a peregrine falcon feather (which can dive at nearly 400 km/h!) or is there also one Sir Zatta who can provide me with a pen that is very similar in terms of value? And, most importantly, does it matter that the former is 'the one', meaning that in my mind it is irreplaceable? Or can I accept a substitute product that is virtually the same? Take the example of two cars of the same make but in different colours (we see this in the car industry, where dealers offer white cars at prices lower than other colours, despite model, engine size, and optional equipment being the same). And if Sir Polo and I had the exact same pen, can we raise the price because falcon feathers are running out, and I can't pluck all the local falcons to make pens? Especially because after a while there wouldn't be any feathers left, and in the long term, I would have to consider changing my job or at least the product I make ...

We know that if competitors are increasing prices, it will be easier for us to do the same. On the other hand, if no competitor (the Sir Polo of our example from history) increases prices, despite inflation or a sudden shortage of feathers, it will be more difficult for us to remain competitive if we raise our prices, even if our fixed costs have risen (electricity, water, gas bills – I am sure this rings a bell).

Lastly, if we were the undisputed leaders in the market for Mongolian falcon pens, we would be the ones who *will have to* increase prices at some point if we deemed it necessary. This is based on a very simple concept: as Joseph A. Schumpeter put it, the responsibility we have regarding prices (which is the sum of the value of the exchanged item plus the perceived value by the customer) is never taken by the *swarm of entrepreneurs* but always by the leader!

2. Power

The relationship with the customer directly influences the success or failure of a price increase. Therefore, it is necessary to analyse the 'balance of power' between the company and the customer in order to identify our strengths in relation to the broader pool of users.

For example, if the customer has no real alternatives to our offer in terms of availability and features, if they are loyal and have trust in our company, our identity, and our brand, if they benefit from our offer – which is perceived as the 'unique' source of satisfaction for their needs – then the balance of negotiating power will tilt in our favour, and the price increase will be feasible.

On the other hand, if we are one of many suppliers, similar to each other in terms of service or product provision, or if the customer does not consider the relationship with our company to be a prime concern– a behaviour that translates into being less loyal and highly price-sensitive – we will struggle to increase prices. The balance, the centre of gravity in the sale, tilts against us because we have to ensure a certain volume of sales, while the customer is satisfied with getting the lowest price (as was the case with online book sales before the user discount percentages were limited).

Continuing with the automotive example, shedding light on the 'power' facilitates the planning and calibration of the price increase. A series of questions must be asked: How successful were past price increases? What were the main challenges, and how were they overcome? What are the success stories, and what can be learned from them?

For example, if Sir Zatta had a contract with his customer, I would advise including a clause that allows for regular price increases and monitoring the commercial conditions granted to the customer because while other traders set off for the East, our Sir Zatta could adjust the discount conditions to his advantage.

3. Negotiation

The success of negotiations for price increases requires clear objectives and guidelines.

Before initiating any price negotiation, it is important to clearly define the starting *price points* in the discussion, the target price to be achieved, and the minimum price below which the deal will not be closed.

The room for manoeuvre, framework, and rules of engagement must be established, along with determining a time frame for when to stop.

As even Scrooge McDuck knows, having a 'bargaining chip' before the negotiation can support closing the deal successfully. Knowing in advance a list of potential concessions, in kind or price, based on our counterpart – these not only need to be structured, but they also need to be prioritized according to the value the customer represents for our company. Different customers correspond to different scenarios, different treatments, but also different points of agreement and concessions.

Finally, it is always necessary to consider the different buyers who may be involved in the negotiation. By mapping the scenarios in a 'decision tree', we will be able to identify the different negotiation techniques to use with different negotiating partners.

4. Communication

Many companies increase prices without informing customers. One of the main reasons for failed price increases lies in what we could define as a lack of tact, rather than just information: the fact that specific reasons are not provided to the customer.

Below a certain threshold, roughly an increase ranging from 1–3%, we can get away with it without extensive explanations. However, for more substantial increases or for products sold through subscriptions, leasing, or contracts where the customer is accustomed to paying the same amount every month, increasing prices 'under the customer's radar' does not work. In these cases, the company must communicate that prices have increased, to what extent in percentage terms, and for what reasons (ideally achieving an *inception* in the customer's mind, so that they say, 'Of course, it's only fair that it's like this') before the next billing cycle.

This is a task riddled with pitfalls.

If poorly executed, communication can lead to unwanted results such as complaints, outrage on social media, or, worse, having to backtrack on price increases, and in extreme cases, losing customers altogether.

There are plenty of examples of bad practices, of 'absolute don'ts' when trying to increase prices. For example, Deutsche Bahn, the main European railway operator, at one point decided to introduce a surcharge of €2.5 for ticket purchases made at the counter instead of the automatic machines, announcing the increase without any justifications.[2] The reaction was a genuine mass protest: the media calculated that the real increase would be 25% per 100 km.[3] Deutsche Bahn were therefore forced to backtrack because they were unable to communicate and justify the price increase properly. What an embarrassing defeat!

Another embarrassing defeat hit one of Germany's largest saving banks in 2023. Ralf Fleischer, CEO of Stadtsparkasse München, and his team worked intensively on a new pricing scheme with different price options and features. Finally, the day of the official announcement arrived in July 2023 where the new offering was presented. What happened next however was exactly the opposite of what the bank expected. The new pricing scheme got strongly criticized in local and national media. Users and media considered it complex, untransparent, and unfair. It was a complete flop. In just few days, a violent shit storm ruined the reputation and credibility the bank had been building for years. Even the mayor of Munich, where the bank had its headquarters, urged the bank to change the proposed pricing.

The influential *Verbraucherzentrale*, that is, the Consumers' Advice Centre, even advocated SSKM clients to quit the bank and search for a fair financial institution unlike SSKM. The CEO therefore decided to change the proposed pricing.[4] Evidently the bank did not test the pricing schemes and did not work on a customer-focused and coherent story. The impact of this mistake will hurt the bank for a long time.

To make any increase (even of a penny) acceptable, a motivation supported by data must be provided as to 'why' prices are increasing. People must be involved in our decision-making processes. Customers are more willing to accept paying more when they understand why they are being asked to do so. In addition to data, it can be emphasized, for example, how much time has passed since the last price increase and highlight how the prices of our customers' own products have also increased over time.

The most effective communications are always customer-centric. A coherent, concise, and specific story and narrative must be provided – the famous storytelling, the 'magical' power of stories, from cave paintings to Nike – that highlights the main benefits. A vivid story will always prove successful. This is what happened, for example, when United Airlines increased the membership prices for its service called the United Club. The company provided the following explanation: 'To offer a more productive and relaxing experience, we are investing over $100 million in renovating existing lounges and building new spaces with expanded seating areas, more power outlets, and enhanced Wi-Fi. We are also investing in a brand-new complimentary food menu that you can now find in most of our lounges in the United States and will soon be available in all our locations.'

United Airlines' communication was concise but provided a credible explanation.

The customer was placed at the centre of the story, and the price increase was immediately linked to a substantial increase in value for the customer. A value narrative can be effective even when price increases are due to rising costs. In this case, communicating that the brand can continue to provide the current benefits only if it increases the price, choosing to do so rather than compromising the product's quality, is a powerful argument, as it reinforces the brand's value for the customer.

Companies must communicate a price increase to customers with the same attention to detail and to customers themselves as when launching new products or making investments to strengthen the brand.

Such commitment will be rewarded with a price increase that is sustainable on the one hand, and with customers who feel engaged in a process that considers their interests on the other.

5. Salespeople

When it comes to increasing prices, in the end, it is the sales staff who have to interact with customers and address their objections. That's why the sales department must always be involved in the pricing strategy.

Salespeople need to be provided with concrete support by establishing the goals of the price increase, building trust through training, and closely monitoring negotiation trends.

Additionally, the teams should be equipped with materials that support value-based selling: negotiation scripts, topic-specific guidelines, value-selling training courses.

In my consulting work, when I help my clients increase prices, we start with less critical and smaller customer segments.

Raising the price level here is easier and less risky compared to so-called 'major clients'. Once the sales force sees the successful price increases we have achieved, they approach larger and more critical customers with greater determination and conviction, securing further victories. In other words, we start small, then negotiate, achieve a result, and sell the product or service by leveraging the story that brought us there and why we are selling at that increased price. For example, emphasizing the challenges we overcame to climb the mountain that seemed to be in front of us, and how we changed our attitude and simply started climbing, one step at a time.

Proceeding in phases based on customer criticality is a solid approach to increasing prices while reducing risks and capitalizing on accumulated experiences. Lastly, and no less important, the management must take a clear position regarding the sales strategy and expectations towards the sales force. Consistent communication from the top is essential to avoid conflicts between price and volume objectives.

The sales team should also be incentivized to promote sales quality: it is better to have lower sales volume at higher prices and margins than high volumes at discounted prices and non-existent margins. This should be reflected in the incentive system.

It is, once again, a matter of shifting the mindset from volume to value.

Those who bring in higher margins should be rewarded and celebrated. Those who increase prices and profits become *pricing champions*, something that is appreciated and recognized when returning home after a long journey, the journey that all goods take to reach us!

How to Increase Prices

There are many options, facets, and ample room for creativity when it comes to raising prices. There are even companies, like the discount retailer Aldi, that present price increases as if they were actually beneficial and advantageous for the customer. For example, when milk prices rise, Aldi purchases entire newspaper pages to communicate that, despite a general 8% increase in milk prices, they have managed to limit the increase to only 4%, thanks to various synergies, cost reductions, and margins. Hooray: an increase that is only half of what one would expect! And how do customers react? They are enthusiastic because the price increase is more limited than they feared. Thus, a well-communicated price rise is celebrated by customers and becomes a competitive advantage for Aldi.

Following the thread of pricing, let's look at the six most established routes in price communication strategy, namely:

1. increase value and prices together;
2. increase prices while providing less value;
3. apply surcharges;
4. increase prices for certain segments;
5. move prices up to the threshold value; and
6. calibrate the pricing model to increase revenue.

1. Increase value and prices together

One way to increase prices is to provide more value to the customer. Certain customers will be willing to pay a premium for additional services or better quality. For example, if the warranty of a car (my beloved Mustang!) is extended from 3 to 4 years, customers who perceive value in the extra 12 months of warranty will be willing to accept a higher price. A concrete example, apart from my wild and free aspirations, is Gillette, which has consistently improved its razors over the years by introducing features such as anti-friction technology, increasing the number of blades from one to five 'for a better shave', or adding micro-fins to the razor that smooth and simultaneously prepare the skin for a close shave. By doing so, Gillette has been able to more than quadruple its price over the years.

In fact, Gillette was acquired by Procter & Gamble in 2005 and is now the most profitable division of the group,[5] holding over 50% market share in the US razor market, which is worth about $3 billion.

Companies that pursue aggressive pricing take a different approach: they offer more value at the same price or a reduced price. This often happens in the technology field, especially in the computer sector. Just think of Microsoft, Sony, or Nintendo and how they have competed for the video game market over the years. And they continue to do so!

2. Increase prices while providing less value

This is the opposite approach to the first solution: increasing prices while providing less value. At first glance, this may seem contradictory. Let's see what it means.

This is a well-known phenomenon in the fast-moving consumer goods sector, where, despite the unchanged package size of items like detergents, food products, or cosmetics, the manufacturer reduces the quantity without changing the price. Although the list price remains the same, the products offered to consumers are downsized, effectively inflating the price per gram or centilitre. This is known as *shrinkflation*, a term coined from the combination of 'shrink' and 'inflation'.

For example, the chocolate industry has been notorious for this, such as the case of Toblerone from the Mondelez group, which reduced its weight from 200 g to 170 g in 2010, and then further to 150 g in 2016, marking a significant −25% reduction in quantity compared to the original.[6] Another example is Nestlé's Smarties snacks: same price but reduced packaging from 150 g to 130 g, effectively increasing the price by 15%.[7] Other examples include Burger King's chicken nuggets, reduced from 10 to 8, Gatorade drinks reduced by 14%, and Coca-Cola reduced their 2-litre bottle to 1.75 litres.[8]

To avoid customer complaints, it is important to be prepared to justify the reduced quantities. Kellogg's, for example, justified the reduction in weight of Coco Pops by claiming a decrease in sugar content, while Unilever, the owner of the Magnum brand, mentioned the need to lower the calorie intake of ice creams. And with the 'bikini season' approaching, who can blame them!

Another option in this regard is to outsource part of the service to customers. IKEA, for instance, allows customers to assemble the furniture themselves, many supermarkets reduce staff by implementing self-checkout systems, and some airlines like Lufthansa have customers perform self-check-in procedures.

3. Apply surcharges

Without changing the price list, some companies can evaluate which part of their products or services currently provided for free will need to be paid for in the future, effectively generating an increase in average price and higher revenues and profits for the company.

The beauty of this approach is that it leverages customer elasticity on accessory elements of the offer, which is typically lower than the elasticity of the main product, and it does not negatively impact the price image.

The main product or service can be a flight from Rome to Berlin, which has a certain price and elasticity. The surcharge can be applied to checked baggage or window seat reservation.

Other examples of surcharges include:

- $5 for paper delivery of bank statements instead of electronic format at various banks;
- $8 at hotels like the Meininger chain for luggage storage on the day of departure;[9]
- $20 from Ryanair for reprinting the boarding pass at the airport;[10]
- $50 at Europcar car rental if cancellation is made within 48 hours of the rental;[11]
- 1.5% up to a maximum of $70 at Emirates for credit card payment.[12]

For this to work, it is important to have transparency in communicating the surcharges. Without such information, customers may perceive it as a violation of fair play against them.

Therefore, I advise my clients to start by listing on the invoice or on their website all the services they are providing for free, without asking for any payment. Once the services are familiar to customers and a price point of zero has been established, it will be easier in the future to replace the zero with a number and request compensation when the customer purchases a smaller quantity or during peak seasons, and so forth.

The advantage of this approach is that, on one hand, it carries a low risk of losing customers since the price of the main product or service remains unchanged, and on the other hand, it avoids subsidizing customers who use additional (costly) services by directly charging those who do not use them.

4. Increase prices for certain segments

Undifferentiated prices, that is, the same for everyone, do not allow for the optimal monetization of perceived value by customers.

Every market consists of multiple segments, and price elasticity varies from segment to segment.

If we can identify segments with lower price elasticity, we can increase prices sustainably.

Customers are accustomed to higher costs during peak periods.

The likelihood of price increases in this segment being relatively uncontentious is higher than with customers who make purchases outside the peak period and are less willing to pay higher prices. Examples of sectors where it is easy to distinguish these two segments are:

- holiday rentals, with demand peaks during school holidays;
- restaurants, with differentiated prices for lunches and dinners;
- hotels, with high and low seasons;
- airline or railway, with peak time slots such as Monday mornings and Thursday afternoons; and
- electricity, with peaks during hot months due to, for example, air conditioning.

For example, Austrian Airlines has decided to increase prices by an average of 29% compared to 2022 in the summer high season of 2023, and Lufthansa even by 41%.[13] All this less than a year after the end of the pandemic.

However, Lufthansa's CEO, Carsten Spohr, expects increasing demand and considering the limitation of supply, especially during the high season, he intends to continue with further price increases.[14]

Here's another example of a specific price increase for a segment: in a project at an industrial client, we discovered a segment of small and less critical customers for the company. Furthermore, most of them were marginally negative customers, meaning they placed small and sporadic orders, which resulted in a lot of administrative work. Once logistics costs and administrative efforts were factored in, the entire segment had a negative margin. The only way to solve the problem in this case was a substantial price increase. Surprisingly, only a minimal portion of customers in this segment was lost. Many customers remained despite the rather 'steep' price increase, indicating that the perceived value justified the higher price.

5. Moving prices up to the threshold value

A well-known chewing gum manufacturer needed to increase prices to recover margins. Starting from a price of 90 cents for the best-selling package, they had hypothesized a 3–4% increase.

However, market research revealed that there was an important price threshold at $1: once that threshold was exceeded, demand dropped significantly. Below the threshold, demand would have remained stable. Our team's recommendation was clear: increase the price by 10% without significant risks of losing volume. The price was then increased to 99 cents, more than double what the company had initially considered, and the impact was immediate: an additional 9 cents per package in revenue, which was 'pure profit' since the costs hadn't changed, all multiplied by millions of transactions!

Over the following 12 months, the increased profits translated into millions of dollars. Increasing prices up to the price threshold is an effective way to increase prices and profits without losing volume. Examples of rounding could be:

- from $9 to $9.99;
- from $19.50 to $19.99;
- from $90 to $99; and
- from $990 to $999.

These rounding strategies can work depending on the type of product, customer reactions, and competitive context. It is not always possible or advisable to go from $17 to $19.99 (below $20). Again, the discussion about perceived value and elasticity analysis applies here.

I would advise more structured companies to verify new prices through market research before implementing them.

For smaller companies that cannot invest in market research, I would recommend testing prices in specific points or sales channels before changing the price list. If the price threshold is confirmed, it represents a quick win pricing opportunity that the company can immediately seize.

6. Calibrating the pricing model to increase revenue

Innovative pricing models represent the new source of competitive advantage.[15] By calibrating our pricing model, we can increase both prices and revenue. How?

By setting the price model in such a way that, for example, the use of our solution by customers increases their revenue.

In Marco Polo's *The Travels of Marco Polo* the author spoke of coloured fabrics, dyes, purple goods, perfumes, and incense from the other side of the world. That's what he sold. Not the goods themselves, but the distant worlds they evoked, the possibility of owning them, even just conceptually, for a limited time (but what else is life, after all, if not a limited time to use a body, a mind, a system of thoughts capable of adapting, changing, transforming).

Similarly, if we anticipate that the usage of our product or service by customers will intensify, it makes sense to introduce a pricing model that focuses on usage. For example, printer manufacturers like HP tend to offer an 'attractive' price for the printer but then increase the price of ink, which, with a lock-in effect, generates more revenue during the product's life cycle with the customer. A similar case is Sun Microsystems, which anticipates its users' needs in terms of medium-sized PC memory capacity, selling computers at affordable prices and increasing the price of memory extensions, thus increasing revenue.

While customers try to anticipate the future use of the solutions they purchase, they rarely have the same knowledge and familiarity as the manufacturers and retailers.

This better understanding of usage dynamics, as in the case of Sun Microsystems, allows for optimal calibration of the pricing model. Another example is users of monthly capped phone and data plans: often, users believe they will stay within the monthly limits, but as soon as additional data is needed, the extra price to pay is significant, almost always.

Summary

The line between the East – the rising of the sun, and of prices – and the cardinal point of failure, where the sun sets and companies fail to meet their objectives, is determined by the approach to decision making!

We have seen that there are five prerequisites that help achieve price increase objectives:

1. IMPACT: Understanding the implications of price increases is the first prerequisite for success. Price reflects value: analysing the relationship between the value perceived by the customer and the price requested is essential. Potential positive or negative impacts should be anticipated, and the appropriate strategy should be evaluated.

2. POWER: The relationship with the customer influences the success of the price increase. Therefore, the balance of power between the company and the customer should be analysed.

3. NEGOTIATION: Successful negotiations require clear objectives and guidelines. Before entering price negotiations, it is important to define the starting points, the target price to be achieved, and the minimum price below which you are not willing to go.

4. COMMUNICATION: To get price increases accepted, a narrative supported by data and information on why prices are increasing needs to be provided. Customers are more willing to accept price increases when they understand why they are being asked to pay more. The most effective communications for price increases are customer-focused, providing a coherent, concise, and specific story.

5. SALESPEOPLE: Ultimately, it is the sales teams that interact with customers. Salespeople need to be provided with objectives, training, and materials to support value-based selling and ultimately succeed in price increases.

To raise the price level, there are many possibilities, various facets, and ample room for creativity. The six established strategies we have seen are:

1. INCREASE VALUE, AND THEREFORE PRICES, BY PROVIDING MORE VALUE TO THE CUSTOMER. Some customers will be willing to pay a premium for additional services or better quality.

2. INCREASE PRICES BY PROVIDING LESS VALUE. This is a phenomenon known in the consumer goods sector, where the producer reduces the quantity without changing the price.

3. APPLY SURCHARGES. Without changing the price list, companies can evaluate which parts of their products or services currently provided for free will need to be paid for in the future, effectively generating an average price increase, higher revenue, and profits. In this case, the elasticity of the accessory elements of the offer is exploited compared to the elasticity of the main product, without negatively affecting the price image.

4. RAISE PRICES FOR CERTAIN SEGMENTS. Every market consists of multiple segments, and price elasticity varies from segment to segment. If we can identify the least price-sensitive segments, we can increase prices sustainably.

5. MOVE PRICES UP TO THE THRESHOLD VALUE: This is an effective way to increase prices and profits without losing volume. If the price threshold is confirmed, the company can seize an immediate benefit.

6. **CALIBRATE THE PRICING MODEL TO INCREASE REV-ENUE**: In this case, the pricing model is set in such a way that the use of the company's solution by customers also increases revenue.

RULE 6
AVOID PRICE WARS

'To win one hundred victories in one hundred battles is not the acme of skill.

To subdue the enemy without fighting is the acme of skill.'

Sun Tzu, *The Art of War*[1]

Introduction

It's dawn. The samurai leaves his house, walks along the path, passes through the bamboo gate that opens gently. He climbs the hill, the dragon teeth mountains behind him. It's the path of the warrior. In front of him, the sun is rising, crimson and orange. His long black hair flutters in the gentle morning rays. He closes his eyes. His skin absorbs the dry warmth on his cheekbones, and with closed eyes, he begins to imagine the upcoming battle. He breathes in, as the day breaks. It's the east. Before it dies. He softens his shoulders, then; there is a slight scent in the air, the fragrance of cherry blossoms. This year the blossoming hasn't happened yet. Perhaps the weather, the rains, but he knows – the samurai – that everything has its course. In nature there is no good or evil, only the moment and the opportunity to unfold truths.

Drums in the air. The enemy is approaching. His chest swells with love for all the life he has encountered on his path. The small wooden house on the hill. The woman who touched his eyes, kissed his thoughts, the two children with whom he learned the art of play, and the delicate run among the petals of the past. No one knows what day will be their last. Now he breathes in the wind. And he moves, like a wave along with the first rays that, down below, beyond the horizon, illuminate the fields, the blades of grass, the humpbacked profile of the terraces.

Now that I am blind, I see more, is the teaching of his master.

That's how you learn to fight. Sensing the life that moves, all around you.

He shifts his foot, it's a short and essential circle. His hands move to the dance of shadows. He doesn't know if he will die today, and yet, it doesn't matter. He roots his legs to the ground, feeling the telluric movement of the army approaching. He's not afraid for himself, the man. He fears for the women and children, that's why he bid them farewell the night before. By the fires in the night, under the quilt of stars: 'Don't leave', the youngest asked him; the eldest, who hasn't seen even 10 winters yet, handed him something.

He tousled their hair and smiled gently. He knelt in front of those children, the purity of the Immortals. Little deities of the forest. He took their hands and led them to the altar in the thicket, they walked the path together. His woman, her hand in his hand, no words spoken. Only the beat of sandals on the wooden bridge, the clogs like the drum of the heart beating in his chest. The samurai knows that the day will bring the truth.

The enemy's cry now rises high from the other side of the hill.

And it is there, and now, that he opens his eyes. At the same moment, the sun rises a few steps away from its infinite distance. He feels its slow vibration between his shoulders, the point where his wife touched him the night before, her hands sliding on his skin, breathing through her nose as she undressed him, cleansing every part of his body, ready for battle. She didn't ask him the echo of which war will take him away from her, the woman, she only thought it, yet he knows.

Silence and dignity. Nothing else matters.

The unspoken words that will still bring us into the world.

The drum is near now.

The samurai unsheathes his sword. The silk of his kimono falls to the ground, the fabric rustling as his feet make circular movements on the gritty, dewy earth that he knows well. He worked on it, together with his children whom he will see again one day, regardless of whether he dies. Under this sky intoxicated with life, the man thinks, as the light spreads, and it is there that the samurai sees the horizon ready to invade his land: the fields and the bonfire, red sparks that have ascended the path toward the stars, the wishes that his children will see, the tomorrow without fear, the caress that his wife gave him last night after they made love, the only tear, while now the samurai straightens his back and takes the sword with two hands by the hilt, and behind him, the others appear. Green armour and dragon scales, flame red, yellow and metal, black armour against the arrows that will soon darken the sky, devouring the space that still separates them from destiny.

He feels no fear now.

Because on the path he feels gratitude. Legs together, he touches the blade, and it is then that he sees it.

The cherry in bloom. Pale pink blossoming in the moment that is the absolute.

Because it is not the end that the man knows.

The cry of his companions rises high behind him. Horses snort, the mist will envelop them as they engage in battle.

Because to love is to protect. Now he knows. As he puts on his helmet, his second in command tightens his armour for him. The sword held high. He looks at the cherry blossom. And he only thinks. *Perfect.*

Whether he means the tree or the moment that is about to happen, no one knows.

The enemy arrives. The samurai stomp their feet. The embankment resounds. The scent of cherry blossoms, *sakura*, spreads everywhere. The breeze is pink, and hope ignites. The man breathes. Breathe, now, he tells himself. And he begins to run, the strength flowing through his bones and muscles, the fierceness of poetry that will keep him alive. Even tomorrow. As the sun rises and the valley fills with war cries. For his opponents, it would have been better never to fight.

Causes and Impact of Price Wars

'Tesla's price war' is one of the headlines that appeared in 2023 in all newspapers, and that summarizes the new direction taken by the California-based car manufacturer, which aims to achieve a new record of units sold by cutting prices.[2] This move has caused a stir in an industry – the automotive industry – that had never until that moment experienced any pricing wars or such equally unusual acceleration in price dynamism.

What Tesla did was initially increase prices, until the end of the year 2022, and then, at the start of 2023, it drastically cuts the price of its cars, up to 20%.[3] At that point, other manufacturers like Ford and Toyota accepted the challenge and lowered the prices of their vehicles accordingly, generating a dynamic never seen before, at least not on such a scale.

But what makes a company decide to start a price war?

If it invests in new technologies that significantly lower production costs and allow higher returns even at lower retail prices, whilst competitors are unable to do the same, then this path leading to a potential price war is practicable, because it will generate profit. Or, to put it in the words of the legendary treatise *The Art of War* by Sun Tzu, it will turn out to be a *sustainable strategy*.

In fact, nothing is enduring or absolute.

The clash of swords and the cry of battle. The samurai now move towards the enemy.

Drums in the valley.

However, as the great Chinese strategist who lived in the period called the 'Spring and Autumn' (722–481 BCE) advised, a war is a state of exception.

Therefore, it is necessary for us to evaluate the context and prepare ourselves for the 'true' lesson.

The only way to win a war is not to fight it.

We will succeed only if we can transform a disadvantage into a competitive advantage and, above all, if we are able to switch perspective.

The rule states that most companies that find themselves accidentally caught in the middle of a price war are mostly victims of misinterpretations and short-term tactical moves by overreacting competitors.

Several contexts favour price wars.

If an industry is characterized by high transparency, with a small number of players monitoring their respective prices, if it is saturated (not *sakura*) with low or flat growth, or worse, under pressure, or in a recession, then an explosive mixture is formed.

All battles start this way, with the flutter of a butterfly's wings.

Then come the drums. And the clatter of hooves.

That's how destruction begins.

It is equally likely that a price war will break out when product differentiation is minimal, or if the costs to change from one supplier to another are low or negligible, or customer price awareness is high, or there is an excess of production capacity. If any of that is the case, it will be necessary to maintain steady nerves and high sales volumes to reduce average fixed costs per unit. It is when new players enter the scene, the sun has risen, and rival factions face each other in the shadow of mountains – the very roots of the market, the penetration strategies – that price becomes our way of the samurai, the sword, the main parameter of choice.

Several studies have also revealed that companies often believe that it is their competitors who initiate bellicose activities. Thus, in the belief that they are responding rationally to aggression from rivals, they simply retort with price cuts.

The problem is that competitors often believe the same thing.

And it is impossible to know where the truth lies.

A slight change in perspective would have been sufficient. Putting oneself in the shoes of the other and understand that a war leaves dead and wounded on the battlefield.

Price wars have a devastating, and lasting, impact.

Not only will the village need to be rebuilt, but how many lives will have been shattered, and what values and traditions that had stratified over time, what gestures, everything that embodies what we call *home*.

Those who believe that aggressively reducing prices to gain market share and increase profits is a valid strategic option do not know what they are getting themselves into. The most successful companies consciously avoid price wars for three reasons.

First: as soon as a price war breaks out and the ordinary price level is abandoned in favour of lower prices, customers expect these lower prices to be the new reference point from now on. Now and in the future.

It will then be very difficult, if not impossible, to return to the pre-price-war levels. Rebuilding. What? And how? Ruins. That's what will remain, in any case.

Second: gaining market share is not easy because, in a competitive environment, responses to price cuts are not slow. Customers won over with the first price cut, by the way, are the most sensitive ones: as soon as the competition reacts with similar or more attractive price cuts, they will abandon us as quickly as they came.

Third: in a price war, everyone loses. War, as we see everywhere, is a zero-sum game. Even if a company has a strong cost advantage over its competitors (at least 30% lower), a price reduction will trigger unpredictable reactions. Competitors are unlikely to witness the loss of customers, sales volumes, and market share without taking action. The result will be a drastic reduction in profits for all market players: regardless of who wins, almost everyone will be worse off than before the conflict.

A famous example in this regard is the price war that occurred in 1992 in the US airline industry. Northwest Airlines, American Airlines, and other market players repeatedly lowered prices in response to multiple cuts by competitors. The result was a record number of travellers and record losses for all airlines. Some even argue that the total losses in 1992 exceeded the cumulative profits since the birth of the US civil aviation industry!

Another famous case was the war in the Italian civil transport sector with the debut of Italo – from *Ntv Nuovo Trasporto Viaggiatori* – in long-distance rail travel. Trenitalia, which up to that point was the only significant player in the sector, felt compelled to react by cutting fares for its *Frecciarossa* trains. Thus began a downward spiral of prices that also affected the airline Alitalia, which in turn reduced prices, starting with some regular routes like Rome–Milan. The result was a 15% increase in passengers, against a 30% decrease in average prices.[4]

Stop Wars before They Start

Clearly the best thing is to avoid price wars altogether. There are several ways to prevent them from breaking out, and they all entail actions implemented within the company, rather than directly affecting competitors or not linked to price.

Actions that can be put in place in-house to prevent price wars include promoting a culture of value, rather than one centred on volume or price.

If competitors focus their strategy on quantity, and are therefore keen to keep prices low, our company will have the opportunity to differentiate itself by offering superior quality and value; or – if our product is similar to our competitors' – by including additional services or value-added packages. A business playbook that provides guidance on how to react to competitors' price moves is another internal tool that helps us respond to, and curb, price wars from the onset.

An action aimed at competitors that can be successful, if communicated well, involves ensuring that the overarching strategy behind our pricing tactics is clear to them. In other words, it is important that the objectives of our actions be evident. For example: publicly stating that a significant price reduction is only applied to help clear our warehouse of a specific stock at risk of obsolescence (and as such it is also limited in time) could not only help competitors understand that ours is a temporary move, but also stimulate a reflection on our respective business strategies.

A third type of possible deterrent actions is based on communicating the risks associated with lower prices, for instance, a correspondingly lower output quality. The courier UPS is a good example of how to raise awareness: UPS repeatedly emphasizes in its communications how reliable and punctual it is in deliveries, citing ShipMatrix: UPS's on-time delivery rate is 99.3%, followed by FedEx at 97.0%.[5] UPS is the most punctual courier by far and leverages customers' aversion to risk, especially when they have an urgent need for timely delivery of documents. Customers of this kind are willing to pay a higher price in exchange for the certainty of a delivery within the specified time, and will not turn to cheaper but less punctual competitors.

A messenger who must reach the palace to warn that the enemy army is at the gates.

A quick change of horses.

The carrier, the best response to the unpredictability of war.

Showing one's strength can be used as a deterrent. And not being afraid, not even of being afraid.

The fourth deterrent, in fact, is to make competitors aware that we have an advantage. Sara Lee has low variable costs but positions its products in a relatively high price band compared to the competition. In the event of a price war, it would be able to lower its price to a level at which its competitors would incur significant losses. The mere knowledge of this fact proves to be an excellent deterrent. Sara Lee has no intention of competing on price; it wants to differentiate itself based on the value it provides. Its highly competitive cost base, however, is a threat to competitors and dissuades them from taking aggressive pricing actions against it.

The dawn over the valley, the crimson pink, and the passing clouds.

Is it really worth putting an equilibrium – life, our activities – at risk? This includes the life and activities of a business, which is itself a fully fledged living organism.

When to Fight

We have said it, and we will continue to repeat it. Price wars and counter-attacks should be avoided as much as possible. But sometimes, avoiding a price war is impossible.

That's what we observe in the consumer electronics sector, especially in the notebook category.

The growth in this market mainly occurs in the lower price segment, where the customer base is particularly price sensitive.

ASUS, the Taiwanese computer manufacturer, offers notebooks for as little as €139, such as the Chromebook CX 1400, a 14-inch laptop with an Intel Celeron N3350 processor and 8GB of RAM.[6] Brands positioned higher, such as HP or Fujitsu, are forced to reduce their prices if they want to access that segment.

In cases such as this, companies have to assess whether and when to respond with an equally low or even lower price than that of the competitor, rather than initiating pre-emptive attacks or, in this extreme case, a price war.

Just as we protect what we love, our heart, competing on price can make sense when a competitor becomes a threat to our core business. If that is the case, preventative strikes serve to signal our intention to fight fiercely, persistently, and tirelessly to defend our position.

The same applies when there is a cost advantage that makes us able to serve a price-sensitive customer segment. Or when greater market share leads to economies of scale. Or, further, when low prices can effectively push a rival out of the market: for example, if we are stronger (in terms of stability, expertise, or financial resources) and if there are high barriers that make access the market difficult, our defensive actions become walls that can make the return of an expelled competitor impossible.

Even in this case, however, the analysis of these actions should never overlook the risks in the medium and long term.

The first risk is educating customers to expect lower prices. Price-sensitive customers are the first to consider reduced prices as the new normal. Therefore, raising prices afterwards will be difficult. Additionally, customers may postpone purchases in anticipation of further price reductions.

The second risk is the reputational damage associated with lower prices. A low price level can raise doubts about the quality and image of an entire brand's offering and undermine the credibility of new products that will be launched.

The third risk is related to the loss of profits, which takes away resources for the development of new products and jeopardizes the company's future.

Considering these risks, if a pre-emptive attack is to be used for defence, it must be swift and targeted. This way, competitors will understand that their price reductions will be nullified, and the benefits of a price war will be short-lived. This will avoid further price cuts by adversaries.

How to Fight

It is the company's managers who deceive themselves into thinking that price cuts are easy, fast, and reversible; or believe that the price level is too high; or accept to sacrifice profits to increase sales volumes. However, actions of this kind, if opaque or misunderstood, lead to escalations as rapid as they are lethal.

We see it every day in wars of occupation. Amicable resolutions will be impossible because these situations reveal a conflict and can attract regulatory supervision and heavy sanctions. For example, Procter & Gamble and Unilever had to pay a fine of around

€315 million each imposed by European antitrust authorities for price collusion.[7]

Understanding the causes and characteristics of price wars, as well as the intentions of the competitors involved, always helps in deciding WHETHER and HOW (under what conditions) to fight.

Diagnosis and action

The first thing to do is to carry out a diagnosis of the situation.

Take the case of a small local lubricant producer that was attacked some time ago by a much larger and international competitor. The situation was dramatic: the large producer had cut prices by 60% – a price drop that the small producer would not be able to sustain. The initial reaction, however, was to respond with a price cut, although in the long run this would have put the company at risk, exposing it to significant losses. The management of the small company decided to look into the situation and discovered that the large competitor had not applied any price reduction in markets abroad: they had only lowered their prices in the local market, with the clear intent of gaining market share there – a classic case of price war with 'predatory' pricing. Once the reason of the attack was revealed – ghosts in the mist – the small producer hastened to inform distributors and customers that the large competitor was applying different prices in different countries. Foreign customers thus began to purchase at lower prices in the country of the small producer; foreign distributors did the same, and re-exported the products to their own countries, where they could charge the higher prices. This affected the competitor's profits in his domestic market.

Additionally, the small producer warned its customers that, if the price war triggered by the 'bigger fish' resulted in its elimination from the market, they would be left at the mercy of a monopolist who, freed from the constraints of competition, would inevitably raise prices.

These two moves led the large lubricant producer to back down, and the price war ended.

This case demonstrates that careful diagnosis – and a swift attack, as Sun Tzu would say – can lead to a rapid conflict resolution. In conducting an analysis of the situation, various aspects should be considered: the competitive and financial strength of competitors, the cost structure and one's own capabilities, the certain and potential reactions of customers, including their price elasticity of demand. Understanding why and where a price war occurs, and what options and resources are available to react, is crucial.

Selective price interventions

Another course of action is to reduce prices selectively, intervening only in those channels, countries, or market segments where there is pressure from competitors. The goal here is to change the parameters of customers' choice, and modify the competitive scenario that has caused the price war.

This is what McDonald's did in the 1980s, when it found itself under threat from the Mexican fast-food chain Taco Bell, which was offering tacos for only 59 cents compared to the $1.79 of a Big Mac.[8] McDonald's initial reaction was to reduce the price of their Big Mac by 80 cents, to just 99 cents. But they realized that a price cut only works in the short term but not beyond, and decided to change the terms of their customers' choice instead: no longer 'burger vs taco', but 'meal vs meal'. This is how the new formula of the *value meal* came to be, a package deal consisting of a burger, fries, and a drink.[9] The rest, it can be argued, is history.

Price bundles – like the value meal – are only one way a company can protect itself from price wars, or shrink the battlefield. Loyalty programmes or targeted price reductions are also feasible strategies.

The goal is always to avoid a generic price cut, and only intervene in the areas under attack.

By identifying the precise location where the price war is happening, we can stop it from spreading like a virus, like a plague that infects the entire offering or more market segments.

This was the strategy chosen by Northwest Airlines to defend itself against the price war initiated by low-cost competitor Sun Country Airlines.[10] Instead of lowering all prices, Northwest decided to maintain its fare level and only reduce it on routes also served by Sun Country Airlines. For example, a return flight from Minneapolis to Boston, offered by Sun at $308, was priced by Northwest at $310, with two restrictions: it had to be booked 7 days in advance, and the fare was only valid on the flight departing at 7.10 am and returning at 11.10 am (the Sun Country flights departed at 7.00 am with a return at 11.20 am).

It was a surgical price reduction intervention by Northwest, aimed exclusively at competing directly with the antagonist's flights. Conscious of the fact that Sun Country had a limited fleet, Northwest was able to keep prices unchanged on all the other routes where competition was not an issue.

Second brand

Another strategy to limit the impact of price wars is to use what is called a 'fighting brand'.

For example, Dow Corning, which produces silicone that retails at prices not affordable to many, decided to limit the damage from low-cost alternatives by developing the brand *Xiamater, silicones simplified by Dow Corning*.[11] Through this brand, customers can purchase standard Dow silicones online at lower prices, the only compromise being a more limited range of products.

Another example is the Lufthansa Group, which uses the brand Eurowings to offer a 'low-cost' solution without slashing prices on flights operated by the parent carrier, which, incidentally, in 2023 have risen significantly.

Having a second brand enables companies to keep the prices of the parent brand at the desired level, avoiding the risk of damaging the image of quality perceived by customers, and without incurring losses of profit. Instead, the second brand makes it possible for a company to access new customer segments.

New promotion or new channel

Sometimes, a second brand is unnecessary; a new promotion is all that is needed.

Procter & Gamble, for example, countered the move of a competitor in India to slash the price of its premium brand of washing powder by promoting a bulk package offer on its own product under the formula 'Buy 1 Get 1 Free'. The promotion, which was kept on for 6 months, managed to meet the demand for washing powder of price-sensitive customers for a whole 12 months, while simultaneously putting pressure on the competitor, who addressed this very same segment. The competitor realized that it would be a good idea to cease hostilities.

A further option is to offer more aggressive prices through alternative sales channels, as often happens in consumer goods.

For example, to increase sales volumes when there is ample production capacity, food manufacturers can sell their products through large retailers' own brand. This way, a substantial price reduction does not have a negative impact on the image of the manufacturer's brand.

All the above examples demonstrate that careful analysis of competitors' key features and motivations on the one hand, and of customers' needs on the other, makes it possible to determine an appropriate response that can make a company fight well and put a prompt end to the price war.

How to Get Out of Price Wars

Sometimes it's inevitable: you just find yourself in the middle of a war without knowing how you got there. The question is: how do you get out of it?

Experience shows that in business the following three measures have proven effective.

1. *Encouraging a cultural change that prioritizes value and profit, forgetting price and quantity as objectives to pursue*

This is easier said than done, especially for those businesses that have been accustomed to thinking in terms of volumes of sales. A recalibration of the incentive system that sets profit margin as objectives would support the cultural change.

2. *Establishing guidelines on how to react to competition*

Clearly predefined actions in response to moves from the competition can defuse the price war and pave the way to a 'ceasefire'. In other words, stopping any price retaliation is crucial.

3. *Outlining and sharing the company's strategic vision*

An action plan should be in place, which clearly communicates the company's *value narrative* and illustrates the direction of travel (for example, if the company is moving away from an aggressive stance to gain market share in favour of a position at the higher end of the market). The promotion of both existing and new products should focus on aspects of value and benefits rather than on prices, discounts, and promotions.

An example of how to win a price war using value as a weapon is the case of the Ritz-Carlton hotel in Kuala Lumpur, Malaysia.[12]

A period of strong economic instability combined with natural disasters (fires in large parts of the forest) triggered, in 1997, a price war in the hotel industry. Despite the devaluation of the local currency, the Malaysian *ringgit*, which made luxury hotel stays more affordable for foreign tourists, the limited demand forced all operators to constantly reduce prices, relentlessly damaging profit margins.

Within a short period of time, everyone in the hospitality industry was deeply immersed in a bloody price war, except for one hotel: the Ritz-Carlton.

The director of the Ritz-Carlton, James McBride, wisely decided not to get involved in the fray. His strategy was to focus on quality and value, coming up with creative responses to the price moves of others.

He decided that he would go in person to airport arrivals, to greet guests with floral gifts, music, and a 5-star hotel-style welcome and hospitality.

On seeing the reception that guests at McBride's hotel were receiving, some passengers with reservations in other establishments started cancelling their bookings to move to the Ritz instead.

Not only that: James McBride also had his personal mobile phone number printed on the hotel's flyers and advertised through local media – so that he could personally handle the reservations.

Guests who had purchased the all-inclusive offer had a 'technology butler' available 24 hours a day. For stays of more than five nights, guests received a special pillow. The menus were enriched with beverages and dishes, and served in an exclusive style.

The effect of this customer-focused approach based on quality, value, and service soon became apparent.

The occupancy rate was slightly higher than that of the competition, but with a significant difference: far higher profits!

If James McBride had joined the crowd and thrown himself into the price war, he would have reduced his profits and wouldn't have been able to offer all the attention that a luxury clientele expects, which costs money – from the staff required to maintain high service standards, to the floral gifts, to the lavish menus (all costs that can only be sustained with high hotel rates). Not to mention the damage to the brand's image if loyal customers of the Ritz-Carlton had found themselves next to the 'do-it-yourself tourists', happy to have secured a bargain price and landed in a facility otherwise well beyond their reach.

In short, actions should be planned according to the principle expressed in point 1 above. This means never react with price cuts with a view to obtaining increases in quantitative terms – more clients, or more products sold. If necessary, one should react with surgically precise actions: 'carefully compare the opposing army with your own, so that you may know where strength is superabundant and where it is deficient', *The Art of War* suggests, which means understanding on what fronts it is worth fighting.

Once it is established what the appropriate market share one can aspire to is, it is possible to decide what level of flexibility and compromise is acceptable.

The three measures help to regain a healthy level of competitiveness.

However, on rare occasions, a retreat can also make sense. One can decide not to engage in a price war but rather to relinquish a share of the market in order to avoid a long and costly (bloody) battle.

Examples of companies that have chosen this path are 3M and Intel.

These two companies are known for their high degree of innovation, and are constantly coming up with new product ranges. They also willingly give up market share rather than incur the losses caused by price wars.

3M registers an average of 4,000 patents every year and has placed innovation at the centre of its strategy.[13] It set itself the '30/4' rule: 30% of profits must come from new products launched in the last 4 years. The company aims to maximize profits by creating and selling value, and price wars are avoided as they do not fit with this strategy.

So, despite 3M having invented videotapes, when Asian competitors entered the market in the 1990s, causing prices to plummet and using price wars to conquer market share, 3M decided to withdraw.[14]

Intel applies a similar strategy: innovate, focus on value, and avoid price wars by withdrawing from the market if necessary. Just like 3M did with videotapes, Intel developed and then abandoned the Nand flash market in 2020, just as it had done with the Dram market in 1980, when Taiwanese competitors started another price war.[15]

Intel's orientation towards peaceful competitive contexts, which meant abandoning memory storage devices in favour of microprocessors, has proven to be a wise choice. Just look at their figures today, and at the products that have stood the test of time.

Summary

Price wars can damage an entire industry with a devastating and long-lasting impact.

Successful companies consciously avoid price wars for three main reasons: 1) customers expect the lower prices to become the new reference prices; 2) in a competitive context, reactions to price cuts by other players are swift; and 3) in a price war, everybody loses.

What are the main causes of a price war? Excess production capacity, high transparency with regard to pricing, a limited number of players, low or flat growth, recession, minimal differentiation between products, low cost of switching between suppliers, and a high price awareness among customers.

A price war needs to be stopped before it breaks out: to do so, the first thing to do is promote a corporate culture of value. This entails moving away from a culture of volumes or one driven by prices.

Several signals sent to the competition can help avert a price war. They include: a clear articulation of what our strategy is; a shared understanding of the risks associated with low prices and low quality; unequivocal evidence that we have a cost advantage over competitors, and that our lowering prices would not damage the quality of our output or our profits.

When to fight: sometimes avoiding a war is impossible. If this is the case, a pre-emptive move will manifest our intention to fight and make it clear that we are ready to defend ourselves with a swift and targeted response.

How to fight: understanding the reasons, the characteristics, and the possible intentions of competitors helps us decide whether and how to fight. The first thing to do is evaluate the situation and decide on the appropriate actions to take. We could reduce prices in a selective manner, choosing specific channels, or countries, or market segments where there is real competitive pressure. Or we could use a 'combat brand' without having to cut prices on the main brand – although sometimes a targeted promotion is enough.

An additional option is to offer more competitive prices through alternative sales channels.

How to exit price wars: a cultural shift must be encouraged, leaving behind targets linked to price and volumes of sales and prioritizing value and profit. The focus must be placed on selling value rather than offering discounts or low prices with the sole aim to increase volumes of sales. Once the 'right' market share has been established, acceptable levels of fluctuation can be considered. Ensure that actions implemented are coherent with the agreed plan, and, if necessary, respond to hostile moves with precise actions.

On rare occasions, a retreat may also make sense.

Whether you manage to avoid war, eliminate conflict, or defuse your rivals' intentions, take a deep breath! Make sure that everything you care about is safe. Now bask in the warmth of the sun, harbinger of the new day, safe in the knowledge that, whatever happens, it will rise again tomorrow.

RULE 7
CULTIVATE YOUR PRICE IMAGE

'We make to ourselves pictures of facts'

Ludwig Wittgenstein, philosopher

Introduction

Echoes of sirens at the harbour.

A vessel enters the channel, the city's drain, in the early morning fog.

The city's breath still sleeps, only the navigating hearts will succeed.

Roofs above puffing chimneys, it is the god of civilization and gangrene.

Who to follow? Follow the wake, the streaks in the sky. When everything is deceit.

The engine of the small boat puffs; it is only the forgetfulness of those we have lost during the journey, the opportunities we could have seized. What relationships, how many sails lowered or torn by the east winds. Yet here we are now. The buildings move at the entrance to the harbour, low white clouds, small whales, the harpoon drawn, what do we still believe in? Before throwing the anchor for the lapping wave.

It only takes a few seconds to understand the alchemy with those we do not know.

It only takes a few lines to imagine a place.

We base our entire existence on the images evoked by knowledge. All advertising is based on archetypes, elements, visions. A machine that opens not only car doors but also the doors of the future. A certain oil that is not heavy on our stomachs already weakened from the sedentary life of the metropolis, what happened to adventure? How much does our inner child get excited playing with Lego constructions with our children, watching Disney's *Pirates of the Caribbean* with them (a mega brand that we will also discuss when addressing the topic of the new frontier of pricing technologies)?

Our entire existence is a continuous reference to messages, images, doors that will open universes, whether parallel or potential. Not only because the worlds we have inside ourselves will increasingly resemble us and therefore we will like them more, but also because when we live, consciously or not, we act on the continuous reference of what we see, feel, love, perceive through our senses and through the tools we have accumulated so far. Then every journey is a movement, every experience a step forward with each person we will meet, with whom we will fall in love or with whom we will only share a part of the road, a port, a discovery.

We are all travellers of the present.

Yet now there is a piano playing somewhere, who could say otherwise? The experiment of Professor Umberto Eco, who, in his book *Six Walks in the Fictional Woods* in memory of his friend Italo Calvino, who died before being able to teach US students, recalled how the art of writing is the art of illusion. For if I were to say that

CULTIVATE YOUR PRICE IMAGE

at this moment, if we were together, a platypus has just entered our field of view, who, as a reader, could argue otherwise, precisely? What is true, what is false, in the era of fake news?

Meanwhile, our boat fixes its line to the pier, the rope is tight and worn, no longer elastic, belonging to someone who has travelled a lot, a pair of black boots, a buckle, and a wooden leg tapping on the deck. There will be lowly places and dead-end streets, questionable characters, and crates of rum (assuming it comes from English-speaking production areas, otherwise we would talk about *rhum* from French-speaking areas or *ron* from Spanish-speaking areas). Without even needing to say who he is, we have already been projected into an elsewhere, in another space, in another time. After all, words are like that, it's just the beginning, and they already lead us to the discovery of *Treasure Island*.

Cultivating the Price Image

This is why the image of our company is important.

This is why the sum of information that is encoded in the price is so important for our target market.

The price image, in this sense, denotes the customer's perception of a company's positioning.

It indicates whether a company's offering is more expensive than its competitors, comparable, or more affordable. It is an anchor, setting a base and a perimeter of action. It tells us within which range that customer will operate.

It is an essential element that needs to be defined, managed, and monitored, and it does not always reflect the actual price level but rather a feeling, a blurred image, formed consciously or unconsciously, of where the price level is positioned in the customer's mind.

For this reason, we need to refer to maps and boats, keep in mind the movements, and chart a course that is as consistent as possible with everything that can be part of the relationship between us and the customer.

The image of a price is a hybrid concept influenced by multiple elements. On the one hand, it derives from quantitative elements such as applied prices, price differences with competitors, and the price architecture of the offering, ranging from entry-level prices for basic products to higher prices for more advanced products. On the other hand, this image is also influenced by qualitative elements such as communication (even cinema: think about the comeback of the Sony Walkman after Marvel-Disney's *Guardians of the Galaxy* movie) or the coherence of pricing with the identity of a company or brand. All advertising relies on testimonials that embody, synthesize, and evoke that 'certain something' that I will have access to if I purchase. . . .

The price image reflects the impression the customer has regarding the overall level of a company.

An unfavourable image will reduce sales, resulting in a decrease in revenue and margin. Thus, it becomes a barrier that companies must overcome.

What if. What would happen if we accompanied a price increase with the release of a promotional video featuring the most popular singer of the moment? How would that price increase be perceived if our testimonial comes from someone whom we see as the embodiment of our dreams: a musician, or a famous Hollywood actor?

A typical approach to influencing the price image is the way the price point is presented. Price thresholds and the perception that comes from numbers come into play here. If you want to position a product currently priced at $10.00 as more competitive, numerous empirical studies have shown that by reducing it by just 1 cent to $9.99, customers perceive a price that is one whole dollar lower. By reading the price from left to right, they now see a 9 where there used to be a 10.

On the other hand, companies aiming for a higher-price image would do well to round their prices to whole numbers, in order not to emphasize the low price as an advantage but rather product quality attributes. Instead of offering $49.99, it would be better to switch to $50, and instead of $99, ask for $100.

Other companies maintain unchanged prices to preserve the price image but introduce new surcharges, decrease quantities in packaging without reducing the price, or charge for previously free services. The customer's overall expenditure increases, but since it is the sum of multiple components, companies hope that the actual price increase will be less visible, and the overall expenditure will be difficult to compare with others.

The Lettuce Entertain You chain of restaurants in Chicago has introduced a 3% surcharge called the 'processing fee' on receipts at its restaurants.[1] Haribo, the producer of bear-shaped sweets among other things, has kept the packaging and price but reduced the content from 200 g to 175 g, effectively resulting in a 15% price increase.[2] Peloton Interactive has started charging $250 for delivery and assembly of indoor bikes, previously provided for free.[3]

All this often happens quietly, much to the dismay of customers, and at the risk of jeopardizing the relationship with them.

Instead of trying to make a price seem lower or less significant than it actually is, companies should seek creative approaches that require customers to provide something in return for the product or service they receive.

There are various approaches to monetizing the value provided to the customer using the price while cultivating and safeguarding the company's image. These approaches, which we will now delve into, can also be applied to a specific part of the cargo hold, products, or for a certain period of time. What they will have in common, in any case, is the specific positioning of the company in the customer's perception through a well-defined price image.

Pricing as an Expression of One's Culture

Who has never bought a pirated good, or has been taken advantage of by paying a certain amount for a service only to end up spending much more than anticipated? The classic example is that of holidays at seemingly all-inclusive tourist resorts during the summer break by the sea with family, advertised at a certain price. Unfortunately, between payments for umbrellas and sunbeds not included, mandatory membership fees, car park, extra beach towels, beverages not included with meals, tourist taxes, and so on, the average spending ends up being 20% higher.

The same applies to flights: we are attracted by a reasonable ticket price, but then additional baggage fees, seat reservation costs, surcharges for card payments, onboard refreshments, make the flight cost much more than what we believed at the time of booking.

Is it possible to offer completely honest pricing without having to reach into our customers' wallets?

That's precisely the question the airline Southwest wanted to answer with a clear 'yes.' Southwest aimed to reflect its company culture centred around serving the customer in a transparent manner through a clear price image.

Over the years, Southwest has built a reputation as a company that puts the customer at the forefront. Transparency and honesty are of utmost importance in its culture, to the point where they have turned it into a philosophy and a neologism. They coined the term 'Transfarency', a wordplay combining 'transparency' with 'fare.'

Southwest describes the meaning of Transfarency as a philosophy where customers are treated honestly and fairly, where low fares remain low – without unexpected baggage surcharges, ticket changes, or hidden costs.[4]

Southwest's slogan, 'low fares and no hidden fees', further solidifies the price image centred around transparency, already supported by its excellent reputation.

Another example is Wise, a company that operates in international money transfers across more than 50 currencies. It was founded by two Estonian friends who, living abroad, regularly encountered unfavourable exchange rates and a range of high hidden costs for international transfers. Therefore, in 2011, they wanted to establish a company with a completely different approach and price image: 'There is only one fair exchange rate and, with Wise, that's what you'll get. We show you all our fees upfront. Why? Because profit margins and hidden fees are unfair, and the finance world has been unfair for too long.'[5]

Far from ill-gotten gains and deceit, here they gladly accept and appreciate the work of others, which, once demonstrated, should always be recognized, and therefore paid for.

THE 10 RULES OF HIGHLY EFFECTIVE PRICING

Other examples of pricing elevated to expression of company culture are Walmart in the United States and John Lewis in the United Kingdom. Walmart coined the slogan 'everyday low prices', indicating that there's no need to wait for the next promotion to save money. Savings are part of their culture and shape the price image.[6] Similarly, John Lewis, for almost 100 years, from 1925 to 2022, used the slogan 'never knowingly undersold' to indicate that anyone who found the same item at a lower price within 28 days of purchase would be refunded the difference.[7]

Both companies have thus created a price image that is centred and unequivocal in the minds of customers.

In this way, pricing becomes an expression of a company's ethics.

Thus, the price image of a company becomes a reflection of its culture and our values.

Exceeding Price to Attract Customers

A second approach to leveraging the price image on customers is to propose a significantly higher price. This does not necessarily apply to all products offered, but at least to a range of them, and the purpose is to make the brand appealing.

Let's suppose we are at an appliance retailer looking to buy a washing machine. What we find are several offers from various manufacturers, all priced around $400. Seeing these products and the price revolving around the same amount, we mentally prepare ourselves to pay approximately $400 for the purchase of a washing machine. However, as we head towards the checkout to pay for the chosen model, we discover a washing machine that costs $600.

What is the reaction to this 50% higher price?

Empirical studies indicate that a price of this kind is not immediately ruled out by customers. Quite the opposite: it captures their attention.

As a 'potential buyer', we wonder what justifies such a price.

We want to discover the characteristics of the product that lead to such an increase and whether these characteristics are also important for the product we already, in fact, selected (remember that we were ready to go to the checkout).

'Perhaps the product requires less maintenance?' our obsessive self will ask. 'Or maybe it has a longer lifespan?' the curious side within us will add. 'No, it certainly guarantees lower consumption!' our environmentalist self will propose. Or maybe it has more advanced washing programs (all elements that potentially matter for our purchase as well).

By exceeding the expected price, the manufacturer of this washing machine has managed to differentiate itself in a price-competitive market. If price was guiding the choice before the discovery of the 'new $600 washing machine', now the customer is contemplating the product attributes and its value in the choice of a washing machine. No longer just the price! It is a complete shift in perspective that occurs within the span of a walk along a neon-lit corridor of any retail store in any city.

Several companies successfully follow this approach. In the B2C field, Apple applies a premium price to its smartphones, sometimes exceeding 50% and more, while Smeg applies a premium of 40% and more to its appliances. Both companies are able to sustain this premium, grow profitably, and enjoy a large base of loyal customers.

Examples in the B2B field include machinery manufacturer Trumpf and one of the leading companies in bearings, SKF. Both position themselves with prices that are 40–50% above the market average.

Despite fierce competitors, some of whom come from low-cost countries, and an economic context that often puts pressure on customers to be mindful of how they spend their money, a moderate 'excess' in the requested price enhances the price image. Customers wonder why it is worth paying more than what they normally had in mind in these cases and evidently find the answer themselves.

Although the price excess usually does not apply to an entire company's product portfolio, offering these price points makes customers dedicate time and attention to both the product and the company, considering them for future purchases as well.

This leverages the created price image.

But what is the ideal premium price that attracts attention and motivates purchase before it becomes so high that it is no longer considered? It certainly varies from customer to customer, but it is possible to indicate price ranges.

In a study conducted some time ago, we presented a selection of products to a sample of buyers with a description of the product features. These products were organic and fair-trade tea and chocolate. We found that buyers were willing to pay a premium of an average of 25% compared to the same products that were neither organic nor fair trade.

However, when the organic and fair-trade tea and chocolate were priced at a 75% premium, the buyers in our sample were able to recall almost two-thirds of the features that justified the higher price.

When asked if they were willing to pay this price, a significant portion of the sample showed willingness to pay this much higher price, citing a range of product features. Evidently, the price exceeding the initial reference point had encouraged participants to dedicate more time and attention to the study of the products, much more than was done at the lower price point. This leads to a rather interesting finding: to increase a price, the customer's awareness must be increased simultaneously. Low prices correspond to little or no interest in exploring the composition and quality of the product.

At significantly higher prices (i.e. 200% higher) or prices close to the hypothesised price (higher by 5–10%), there was no greater willingness to pay.

A similar result was also found in a similar study conducted in the B2B field.

We can reasonably say that the ideal magnitude of the price premium to attract customer attention varies between 30% and 80%.

When a product exceeds the reference price within the 30–80% range, customers will question whether it is worth buying this product instead of a cheaper one.

The price difference prompts the customer to delve into and understand what additional benefits can be gained (rather than simply seeking the cheapest product).

However, the typical response to competitive moves is to reduce the price and emphasize the economic advantage, which leads customers to consider price as the guiding factor in choosing the product, disregarding its value attributes. Welcome to the vicious circle of *commoditization*!

In mature markets such as consumer electronics or tires, price wars have been observed. Companies like Sony and Samsung have found themselves competing on price, with factors such as resolution and backlighting taking a backseat. The same applies to Michelin and Continental, where grip and safety have had to make way for the 'usual suspects' of low prices as the selection criteria.

Yet, it is precisely in very mature and competitive markets, where the focus is on the lowest price, that deliberately setting an excessive price can capture customers' preferences. This is the case with Burt's Bees, a manufacturer of balms, creams, and natural lotions, which ignores the aggressive pricing positioning of competitors in personal care by applying an 80% premium.[8] In a market dominated by slashed prices and constant promotions, Burt's Bees has demonstrated that exceeding the price can draw attention to what makes the difference. In this case, products made with up to 99% natural and eco-friendly ingredients, like their lip balm, which sells at a rate of more than one per second, equivalent to over 86,400 per day.[9] Between 2020 and 2022, the company has further accelerated its growth, reaching a revenue of 270 million dollars, following a prolonged period of annual growth of over 25%.[10]

Who would have thought it possible to charge more than $4.50 for a latte and become the world's leading coffee chain present in 80 countries, with nearly 30,000 stores? Starbucks has consistently grown worldwide with a substantial premium, which has prompted its customers to reflect on the value of the coffee offered. Starbucks' choice was entirely deliberate and not based on a particularly affluent customer target. The intention was simply to draw attention to a significantly higher price and thereby signal an advantage over lower-priced products.

An excessive price is also the best option for pricing *real* innovations, as demonstrated by TKE, one of the world's leading elevator companies, whose headquarters are in Germany. TKE operates in a highly competitive context where several manufacturers have even resorted to selling their products with minimal or negative margins, hoping to earn money through post-sales services like maintenance and spare parts. Additionally, architects who previously were in charge of major building projects with a focus on innovation have been replaced by sales managers incentivized to minimize costs.

Despite such a challenging environment, in 2021, TKE presented its highly innovative solution: the Multi, the world's first ropeless elevator capable of moving vertically and horizontally, reducing the required operating space by 50% and returning more space to each floor.[11] It also reduces waiting times, between 15 and 20 seconds, with cabins capable of moving in a loop and consuming even less energy thanks to new lightweight materials used in its structure.[12]

In a market that struggles to grasp and appreciate so many benefits concentrated in a single solution, TKE had no choice but to propose a drastically higher price than the average. This was also a way to initiate discussions among sales managers, architects, and real-estate investors about the reasons behind such an excessive price, bringing TKE into the conversation to understand better the value of this solution. Being called upon to explain the value of the solution is the first step towards closing the next sale!

Uniform Pricing to Highlight Value

The story of Swatch is the story of a company that managed to turn around an entire industry and become the undisputed leader in its sector.

In 1983, Nicolas Hayek took over a company that was in a deep crisis and operated in the Swiss watchmaking industry, a sector that in turn was facing competition from Asian manufacturers of low-cost but equally accurate quartz watches.[13]

Hayek's vision was to respond to Asian competition, whose advantage was price, not deploying the same weapon – that is, lowering prices – but by using the weapon of value.

The new watches launched by Swatch were revolutionary in this regard: they were made of plastic, affordable, but of high quality, artistic, emotional, and *made in Switzerland*.

Those who wore a Swatch watch were fashionable and appreciated its value.

In just 5 years, 268 different models were launched, with estimated sales of 50 million watches.[14]

Swatch watches, which suddenly became synonymous with an object and status, became objects of cult, and marked the beginning of the Swiss watchmaking industry's revival.

Today, Swatch is the world's leading manufacturer of watches in its category.[15]

In addition to innovating the product, Hayek innovated the concept of pricing itself. In 1986, every Swatch watch had the same price, which was CHF 50. With uniform pricing, Hayek managed to shift attention away from price, an area dominated by competitors, and redirect it to value.

Customers who entered Swatch stores no longer had to worry about how much to spend, given the uniform price, but rather about which watch to choose among the enormous variety, and the sense of identification that each model suggested based on designs, colours, and style.

A similar strategy was followed by Apple to launch the music tracks offered on Apple Music in 2007 when it was called iTunes. Steve Jobs decided to adopt uniform pricing, which was considered counterintuitive by many: 99 cents for any music track without any price differentiation.[16]

Both major music publishers, like Sony, Warner, and Universal, and independents criticized Apple. The unanimous chorus lamented the fact that they were losing profits that differentiated pricing would have allowed them to capture. Recent music tracks would have withstood a higher price compared to older tracks, for which customers would have expected to pay less.

History proved the innovator from Cupertino right: pricing was one of the success factors for Apple Music. Thanks to uniform pricing, as indicated by Jobs, music enthusiasts no longer fixated on the price and asked themselves where to save money. Their attention was directed towards evaluating the vast choice of tracks as a 'clear source of value'.

Over time, it was seen that many users perceived the proposed pricing as fair, which further motivated them to listen to tracks through Apple Music.

In markets where customers do not perceive marginal differences in value between products, the primary criterion for choice becomes the price, more precisely, the lower price. In such contexts, differentiating the price becomes counterproductive. Provoking customers with the only factor that guides their choice – price – turns out to be a winning strategy. Their fixation becomes the solution: with uniform pricing, the question of value returns to guide the choice. Customers are forced to ask themselves what *really* drives their choice. They will then evaluate the offer more carefully to understand what satisfies their needs.

Provoke to Stimulate Willingness to Pay

A blatant provocation is also a way to create a well-defined price image. For example, with a coupon that normally entitles you to a discount, but in this case, it does not. It's not mean-spirited, it's a strategy. Let's see how, by worsening the initial data.

The coupon in question actually entitles you to *pay more* for the same product. It's entirely illogical, you might rightly say. A clear provocation!

Yet, that's exactly what the Belgian beer producer Stella Artois did when they offered coupons with the following message: 'Present this coupon and pay an extra 1.25 dollars.' This was part of a highly successful promotional campaign called 'reassuringly expensive', which accompanied the brand's growth for 25 years, until 2007.[17]

The purpose of this campaign, initiated by the giant AB Inbev, was to give a premium price image to the Belgian brand. The intention was to reposition it as a beer that was not only more expensive but also of higher quality. Prior to the campaign, Stella Artois had a higher positioning compared to other producers, but this was not supported by a correspondingly higher perceived quality of the product, and sales were poor.

The merit of that initiative, therefore, was to create a premium price image, which led to a surge in sales and revenue because consumers concluded that a higher price meant superior taste, justifying the higher price altogether.[18] A higher price, synonymous with quality, became the reason to purchase this beer and its competitive advantage.

Another case is that of IKEA in Saudi Arabia.

The intention here was to create an image of absolute affordability.

Instead of price tags on the products, they applied tags that expressed the price of other everyday items whose value corresponded to the price of the product in question. It was a kind of mental barter where a table cost the same as three cups of coffee. A bedside table was equivalent to six toothpaste tubes. A bookshelf corresponded to two pizzas.

At that point, if we adopt the perspective of converting not the price but the relative value of objects, buying cans of Orangeade or a lamp doesn't make a difference[19] (for example, I always convert the price of an item into books and ask myself how many books this item is worth; if the answer doesn't convince me, I don't buy it, but if I think, 'Okay, this item is worth my renunciation of X number of books', then it means that the product or service has truly convinced me. It's an enlightening exercise; you should try it with something you value . . . no, relationships are excluded!).

These associations help customers visualize and grasp how affordable an IKEA furnishing item is.

A third brilliant case of provocation aimed at increasing willingness to pay is when the entire management team, along with employees, publicly apologized for raising the price of a product by only 12 cents after 25 years without any increase. This is the case of the ice cream producer Akagi.[20]

The company specifically aired a television commercial to publicly apologize, with a deep bow, for such a modest increase of just a few cents after a quarter of a century. What an exaggeration! And what a brilliant move to strengthen their price image.

In all these cases, the blatant provocation stimulated willingness to pay, and strengthened the price image of the company.

Summary

The price image is the customer's perception of a company's positioning.

It is an essential element that needs to be defined, managed, and monitored. It doesn't necessarily reflect the actual price level but rather a conscious or subconscious feeling of where the price level is in the customer's mind.

A typical approach to influence the price image is the way the price point is presented. Thresholds and the perception derived from numbers come into play here. Alternatively, one can work with surcharges, which can work in certain cases but can also backfire on the price image.

Different approaches allow monetization of the value provided to the customer using the price itself while cultivating and protecting one's own image.

One way is to see pricing as an expression of company culture: Southwest, aiming for maximum transparency without hidden costs, or Walmart, offering low prices without having to wait for promotions, are examples of successful price image creation.

Another way is to exceed the price to attract the customer. When a product exceeds the reference price by 30–80%, customers will wonder if this product is worth purchasing compared to the cheaper one. The price difference encourages the customer to delve deeper and understand what additional benefits can be gained, as seen in cases like Burt's Bees and SKF. Even standardizing the price to emphasize the value is an option. By doing so, customers are encouraged to reflect not on 'how much' to spend but rather on which product provides the greatest value, as taught by Swatch and iTunes.

A blatant provocation is also a way to create a well-defined price image. The cases of Stella Artois and Akagi demonstrate how the price image has benefited from it.

These approaches can be applied to certain products or for a specific period of time. What they have in common is positioning the company in the customer's perception through a well-defined image. And as we all know, since the age of cave paintings, if image is not everything, it is not far off.

RULE 8
EMPLOY TECHNOLOGIES, DIRECTING ALGORITHMS

'A fool with a tool is still a fool'
> Abraham Verghese, American physician and professor

Introduction

The first Foundation will take place on *Terminus*, a planet on the edge of the galaxy. It is there that Hari Seldon will gather the best scientists and scholars of the time.

When Isaac Asimov wrote his *Foundation* series, he could not have known that one day humanity would face real epochal challenges: wars, populism, climate denial.

In his masterpiece, in many of his works, there are many who oppose change. Some because they cannot conceive it, others go along for convenience. Yet, if Asimov's protagonist chooses the revolutionary power of 'psychohistory', the art of knowledge guiding a great empire, shortly thereafter, it will fall under the blows of the mysterious figure of a horrible mutant who will destroy Seldon's dream. The arcane subjects of the new dictator will spread to the four corners of the Galaxy to exterminate the last sparks of resistance, while rumours circulate that, hidden from the dominion of the *Dark Side*, another has taken hold of what remains of the First Foundation: his name is Arkady Darell. Alongside him, a handful of survivors will attempt to assault the last empire of Evil.

Asimov was one of the greatest writers, not only in science fiction but of all time. It was 1951 when he published *Foundation*, and yet some themes are still disconcertingly relevant.

In his works, humanity always faces a crossroads: is the use of technology a good or an evil? And if psychohistory is the science of human behaviour reduced to mathematical equations, what will happen when Artificial Intelligence (AI) has assumed control of social relationships?

Between the first and the last book of the series, Asimov had the opportunity to witness over 30 years passing before his eyes (*Foundation's Edge*, the final book of the tetralogy, was published in 1982).

Today, 30 years seem like an impossible, infinite time. How much will technology change in 30 years? What devices will we have in 2050? Will the computer as we know it still exist? Furthermore, will we have solved the pollution problems in our cities and the global warming of the planet? Will our business still be present in the market?

Perhaps what needs to change is the point of view, Asimov would suggest. To understand change and be an active part of it, we cannot reason with a narrow short-term logic; we must learn that everything is in motion.

Leverage-Enabling Technologies

The most successful companies are those that leverage modern technologies for price management. The type of technology adopted depends on the size and characteristics of the business.

EMPLOY TECHNOLOGIES, DIRECTING ALGORITHMS

The process always starts with an initial company Foundation, let's say, a first version of oneself, consisting of a system of relationships and a specific organizational structure, which is then evolved.

One of the simplest paths in this regard starts with manual solutions or spreadsheets like Excel, and then progresses to more advanced tools like Tableau or business intelligence, eventually leading to customized, in-house-developed software, and finally to technologies offered by software companies specialized in pricing.

Every company has its specific needs, so it is essential that this uniqueness be reflected in the chosen technological solution.

The solution, the form, must be an integral part of the process from the beginning. Only in this way will the choices and decisions we make be consistent with our medium- to long-term objectives: our vision.

Modern technologies facilitate the transformation of pricing.

To be successful, it is important to ensure that they are integrated into the company's processes and supported organizationally by various departments, such as sales, information systems, and management control.

Companies that decide to revisit and optimize pricing processes with a cross-functional team before introducing a new technological system will obviously have an advantage.

Creating working groups also fosters essential team-building actions for the success of any project. In the team, each individual brings their own skills, shares them, and improves them through continuous interaction with others.

However, often overwhelmed by solving daily problems, the reality for many companies is different. We implement standard pricing systems without considering the company's processes or involving the sales force in the planning phase, thus losing their valuable support during implementation and future direction.

Adding a pricing optimization system to your Enterprise Resource Planning (ERP) system, for example, can become counterproductive. It will increase complexity without solving problems and, more importantly, without the necessary support from the organization. The result of the synthesis between interactions always generates something more than the simple sum of its parts.

Failure in this case is only a matter of time: significant investments of time and money to introduce new technology end up with a tool that does not produce the expected results or is not accepted and therefore not used.

Other problematic cases occur when different business units follow different technological paths.

In our case, you cannot think of colonizing a planet while everyone goes their own way. There must be a shared development idea. A fundamental logic, a shared vision, which will determine the success or failure of the mission.

In large organizations – and we are well aware of the danger of 'gigantism' and what it entails, just remember the old doomed adage 'TBTF' (too big to fail) from the 2008 crisis – you will end up with a series of disconnected technological solutions in different business units, unable to support an integrated price-management process for the entire company.

It often happens that some companies take one step at a time, perhaps adding new *ad hoc* tools without relying on integrated planning. In these cases, both an integrated pricing process and a robust system of data collection and analysis will be missing.

To avoid issues like the ones described earlier, it is advisable to follow a systematic approach when introducing a new technological solution.

The first step is to analyse the current state and then establish needs and solutions, in other words, determine the choices to adopt in order to best monetize the value offered. This will allow the identification of all the elements to be included in the planned technological solution. By coordinating all actions based on a future objective, we will have a clear course of action, since our choices will align with the envisioned future, including the remunerations, targets, and objectives.

Subsequently, the requirements that the pricing management tools should have and what they will be able to perform are articulated. These could be:

- price determination and updates,

- competitor price research through web crawling,

- discount management for customers or customer segments,

- price policy updates and mandates, and

- analysis and monitoring of performance from various viewpoints (e.g. by product, customer, channel, geographic area).

The type of business influences the choice of pricing software.

There may be improvements and extensions of the currently used solution or the introduction of a new one.

Companies engaged in project-based production will have the need to conduct historical analyses to gather information on demand, elasticity, and won and lost projects by comparing similar products and customers.

On the other hand, companies engaged in mass production will want to consider factors such as warehouse fill rate, market trends, the impact of push and pull actions, and price positioning across different channels. Once the requirements are determined, alternative options for implementing the technological solution are evaluated, such as purchasing a technology available on the market, offered by both larger pricing software vendors like Pricefx, Pros, Zilliant, and focussed/new players like 7Learnings, Buynomics, Competera, Ibbaka, or developing/extending software developed in-house.

In large companies, a customized external solution may require investments that quickly surpass *Mach 10*: $1 million (!) in addition to annual usage fees. However, they have the advantage of being continuously updated and managed by experts who also understand the specific needs of the various industries in which their clients operate. Based on the feedback received from users of these solutions, every dollar invested produces a return of between $4 and $8 in the software's lifecycle.

If the in-house solution option is chosen, costs for development and maintenance of the solution must be considered, and it is necessary to ensure the availability of the required skills to maintain and evolve the tool in the future. Hence, this option is often excluded *a priori* by companies that are less technologically advanced.

Once the most suitable option is selected, implementation takes place.

To be successful, detailed planning supported by adequate change management is required. A pilot project – to test the functioning of the solution, interfaces, and user experience – allows for verification that the expected benefits have materialized. This paves the way for the new system that will manage prices, supporting pricing processes and monetization of the (new) value created by the company.

Once operational, the system must never remain stagnant. As mentioned earlier, everything is in motion, and we must change accordingly. Therefore, it should be monitored, updated, and adapted based on the evolving needs of customers and the company.

UTI or: Undesired Technological Impact

A massive AI at the centre of a square. Robots moving everywhere, cybernetic nerves, stunted forms, hosts implanted under the synthetic skin. Humans on *Terminus* reduced to a meagre resistance. Metal panels, the central computer pulsating beneath the citadel. Neural networks, rebels, neuromancers, androids. The Machine civilization launches its final assault on what remains of humanity.

There is a part of science fiction authors who have imagined a subjugated world, shackled like Prometheus to the chains of the definitive replacement of mankind. A superhuman, transhuman body, the final monologue of Roy Batty in the science fiction film *Blade Runner*, directed by Ridley Scott in 1982 and inspired by Philip K. Dick's novel *Do Androids Dream of Electric Sheep?*: 'I've seen things you people wouldn't believe. Attack ships on fire off the shoulder of Orion. I watched C-beams glitter in the dark near the Tannhäuser Gate. All those moments will be lost in time, like tears in rain... Time to die.'

Some fear AI, the advent of an upheaval capable of dethroning man from the seat on which he has self-proclaimed himself the lord of the known world.

However, there is another way to understand technology: as a tool serving humanity, supporting and enhancing human intuition and creativity. As Brian Eno (who, among other things, created the start-up sound for Windows 95 that we have all heard at least once in our lives) says, 'Artificial intelligence (left to its own devices) is boring.' In music of our days we need emotions, feelings; they are what keeps us alive.

A growing number of companies rely on dynamic pricing systems or modern pricing algorithms to maximize profits.

The use of AI in pricing allows, for example, real-time price adjustments based on demand trends, competitor moves, market offers available at that moment, weather conditions, and many other factors. However, if pricing is left solely to the machine without human intervention, it can lead to an accelerated dynamic that can backfire and harm the company.

This was exemplified during the terrorist attack on London Bridge on 29 November 2019. In the heart of London, a man attacked pedestrians with a knife, causing death and panic. Thousands of people, including tourists and Londoners in the area, witnessed a significant deployment of law enforcement at 2.03 pm. Many of these individuals immediately sought to escape by calling an Uber for safety. However, for a staggering 55 minutes after the initial report of the attack at 1.58 pm, Uber's dynamic pricing algorithm had increased prices by over 150% in that neighbourhood.[1]

This is not an isolated case: during the 2017 terrorist attack in London, Uber's surge pricing increased prices by 200%. Uber faced harsh criticism for responding too slowly to the price surge during an emergency situation. To apologize, Uber decided to refund the fares for the rides taken.[2]

During the Seattle shooting in 2020, Uber and Lyft prices sky-rocketed, reaching an increase of +550%, sparking outrage among customers.[3]

In light of such evidence, both Uber and Lyft have pledged to deactivate surge pricing in emergency situations. However, so far, the dynamic pricing system has continued to function even in extreme situations.

Uber and Lyft are not the only companies facing this problem, which affects companies in all sectors that employ dynamic pricing technologies: from logistics to travel, from hospitality to retail, insurance, sports, energy, and entertainment. There is no boundary in the Great Artificial Mind.

A famous case is that of a low-value cabinet on Wayfair, which, through algorithms, ended up costing $14,500.[4] Or the failed attempt by Coca-Cola to charge different prices for cans based on outside temperature through vending machines equipped with software that increases prices when the weather was hot (an intention met with vehement protests from customers).[5] Another example is a book about flies that ended up costing around $24 million on Amazon.[6]

These are prices that no one would ever pay, created instead by out-of-control algorithms that process a large amount of real-time data. What is lacking in these cases is conscious management – or rather, human management – of prices. Although customers have become accustomed to interacting with (continuous) price fluctuations, excessive dynamism can backfire on the company implementing it.

A balance must be found between maximizing profits, leveraging modern technologies on one hand, and ensuring customer loyalty by making them feel they have paid a 'fair' price on the other. In other words, algorithms and pricing tools need to be directed in a way that fosters customer loyalty, applying a pricing strategy that can be accepted, or better still understood by customers.

IA (version 2) or: Directing the Algorithms

The key to success in implementing innovative technological solutions is to make customers understand the benefits of algorithm-driven pricing, where algorithms are directed, accompanied, and put to the service of humans.

Consequently, paying a fair price that is motivated and understandable will foster customer loyalty.

On the other hand, paying an excessive price, besides being perceived as 'unfair' and causing customer loss, may even inflict physical pain. Ofer Zellermayer from Carnegie Mellon University coined the term 'pain of paying' to refer to the negative emotions triggered by high prices:[7] some transactions bring joy, while others cause painful agony. Studies indicate that about 20% of the US population experiences chronic pain caused by high prices, directly impacting purchasing decisions.[8]

Companies must be able to avoid causing pain and prolonged agony to their customers. As Sun Tzu would say, it is better to have an immediate beheading.

The advent of new technologies, as seen in the examples above, can lead to significant price differentials: variations that catch customers off guard and give the impression of being generated arbitrarily and unjustifiably.

If intelligence (not the artificial kind) is about being able to look at things from another perspective, we must now put ourselves in the customer's shoes.

Before the introduction of algorithms, prices were stable and predictable, without personalized variations. Customers perceived greater fairness and an absence of discrimination because if price increases occurred, they were generalized and applied to everyone, not targeted at individual buyers. What can be done to control price dynamism and make the best use of pricing management technologies, overcoming the issues just described?

Let's delve deeper with some concrete examples of five business cases, illustrating how pricing algorithms can be directed to benefit the company without having negative repercussions on our relationship with customers.

Encouraging Purchases through Technology – the Case of IKEA

An innovative example of using modern technology to motivate customers to make purchases is offered by the Swedish furniture manufacturer IKEA, the first company in the world to 'reinvent the wheel'. IKEA lets customers pay using their time: How? The longer it takes to reach the store, the more you can buy.[9]

This initiative, introduced for a short period, called 'pay with your time', was launched by IKEA in Dubai. It allowed customers to convert time into spendable money. 'Before the birth of this campaign, we realised two things: time is precious today, and many loyal IKEA customers spend a significant chunk of it visiting our locations, which are sometimes away from the city centre', said an IKEA spokesperson, adding, 'We think it's only right to reward our customers' efforts by repaying them for the time spent reaching us.'[10]

In this case, the algorithm allows customers to manage dynamic pricing in an incentivizing and predictable manner. Here's how it works practically: after selecting items for purchase, customers at the checkout show the actual route they took using Google Maps, saved on their smartphones upon arrival at the store, along with the time it took. The cashier activates a pricing algorithm that takes into account the route and time, and determines an amount in local currency, which is used to pay for the selected items either in full or in part. Time becomes money. The longer the route and the more time it takes to reach IKEA, the greater the usable credit.

Despite the resulting price discrimination – each customer pays a different price for the same item, based on the distance travelled; or the same customer pays a different price for the same item based on the different distance travelled – the use of this technology has been completely transparent and well-received by customers.

For customers, it is more than understandable that IKEA wants to incentivize customers who are farther away.

Unlike the case of Uber, where prices skyrocketed unpredictably, here the pricing logic of the algorithm is clear. Additionally, the only possible variation is downwards, so in the worst-case scenario, the customer will pay at most (!) the list price.

The algorithm rewards without penalizing.

For IKEA, this implies a reduction in prices and therefore revenues. However, this loss is more than compensated by the increase in turnover resulting from a new customer base attracted by the pricing algorithm.

IKEA's dynamic pricing attracts customers who would not have visited the store without the algorithm and enhances the loyalty of regular customers.

This example demonstrates the importance of determining the objectives to pursue with technology and of managing pricing technology without leaving everything to data scientists. When this happens, there is a risk that dynamic pricing will solely focus on revenue and profit goals, neglecting the perception of the company by customers and the resulting price image. Excessive price dynamism disconnects from the customer, leaving them feeling isolated and estranged, which is the worst nightmare of contemporary times.

When setting up technological solutions, behavioural, psychological, and relational aspects must be kept in mind alongside scientific aspects. Only then can technology go beyond simply matching supply and demand.

Some time ago, a high-tech manufacturing company employed a pricing algorithm without realizing that it implicitly suggested to customers that the value of the product was not determined based on its ability to meet their needs with an innovative solution. Instead, it shifted the customer–product relationship to the mere availability of the product in the warehouse. This was a fatal mistake. This approach trains customers to buy the product when demand decreases, while also encouraging them to postpone the purchase in anticipation of a price drop.

The mistake to avoid is focusing the customer's attention on the price rather than the value.

In IKEA's case, no customer had the feeling of being penalized with increasing prices when demand rose or supply decreased. On the contrary, an incentive to purchase was provided even to distant customers, probably drawing in *non-customers*, people who would not otherwise have shopped there.

Creating Transparency with Technology – the Case of Root

A common complaint from customers is that companies employ algorithms that make such a high number of price changes that they lose their bearings.

This happens, for example, at petrol stations, to the point that people talk of 'fuel price roulette'.[11] The price sometimes changes even during refuelling, leading to an unpleasant surprise at the till when the per-litre price turns out to be higher than what was displayed at the pump.[12]

Other examples are platforms like Amazon, airlines, or tour operators, where the price of a product or a trip can increase, sometimes significantly, within a short period.

On the contrary, Root Insurance, founded in 2015 by Alex Timm and now operating in 33 US states, has made price transparency its mantra.

Root presents itself as 'a technology company revolutionizing personal insurance with a pricing model based upon fairness and a modern customer experience'.[13] The technological tool adopted in this case is a telematics pricing program that generates a specific rate for each customer. 'Through data and technology', as summarized by Root, 'we propose rates based on how people actually drive. The result is a fairer, more personal and much simpler experience – thanks to it all being in an app.'

Thus, while traditional insurers base rates on an 'old' world, using actuarial calculations and risk indicators related to anonymous demographic statistics, occupation, education, and so on, Root customizes pricing entirely based on an algorithm that accompanies the customer during all their car trips.

Root places driving ability at the centre of its pricing.

To be insured, one must pass a safe driving test.

'At-risk' individuals, who generate higher costs, are excluded from the start.

Once the test is passed, everything revolves around an app that constantly monitors the customer's driving style.

Those who adhere to speed limits, maintain a steady speed, brake gradually, and demonstrate overall careful and cautious driving are rewarded with advantageous rates. The philosophy is 'better driving = more savings', meaning that careful driving in line with road traffic regulations is rewarded with lower rates.

And the company prospers thanks to savings that sometimes reach up to 52% compared to competitors.[14]

Root is an exemplary case of how transparency applied to pricing algorithms can practically improve the relationship with the customer.

Customers understand how the insurance premium is determined and which levers are available to reduce them. Thus, different prices for different customers for the same insurance are sustainable and understandable.

Calibrating Technology with Human Intervention – the Case of Lyft, Inc.

Sometimes human intervention in technology is necessary to avoid harm to the company.

Modern pricing technologies are programmed to generate prices that maximize profits for each transaction. This potentially creates conflicts between revenue maximization and customer satisfaction and loyalty.

The old rule of 'set it and forget it' in pricing technologies, which means 'set the system and let it operate autonomously' – as used to happen in revenue management systems in the airline industry – is no longer feasible.

The power of dynamic pricing based on AI, together with other advanced technologies like ChatGPT, run the risk of going their own way, becoming not only boring, as Eno said, but also autonomous and uncontrollable.

That's why human intervention is necessary to calibrate or even stop the computer tool. As we have seen before, Lyft and Uber had to reimburse their customers affected by the exponentially increased surge pricing during human tragedies.

No company wants to be perceived as greedy, opportunistic, or unethical! This would result in a huge damage to the company's image, which can lead to the loss of customers.

If there had been a human operator governing the algorithm or, at the very least, a more timely alert mechanism, it would have been possible to intervene preventatively, calibrating or, better still, deactivating the algorithm to stop the price surge before it skyrocketed.

The price levels generated by algorithms must be governed and controlled. There must be constant oversight to ensure that the tech tool produces pricing in line with the company's strategy without negatively impacting the price image, the company in general, or compromising the relationship with customers. When necessary, immediate and direct intervention should be possible to protect the company's reputation and customer loyalty.

Increasing Customer Satisfaction with Technology – the Case of Walt Disney

In the theme park industry, the reference actor is undoubtedly Disney, which holds a true record with its Walt Disney World Resort, also known as Disney World, located in Orlando, Florida. With its approximately 60 million visitors per year, it is the most visited park in the world.

Until a few years ago, the park's pricing was traditionally manual and static. Then, in 2018, the company introduced new technology to change the pricing.

The pricing went from being static to algorithmic, and this change was presented by the global animation giant (currently also the owner of the Star Wars and Marvel Universe brands) with the promise that the change would make 'the "Happiest Place on Earth" a little more affordable' while at the same time 'trying to find ways to help spread out visitation'.[15]

With the new technology, the price now varies based on when and for what period the entrance tickets are purchased. Prices increase during peak periods but decrease during less busy periods, encouraging price-sensitive visitors to book when there is less demand and cheaper prices.

Previously, the price range started at $44 for low-season periods and went up to $184 during peak times.

The new technology allows for a calendar with different prices based on dates and duration of park access to be displayed.

Given the success of the new pricing algorithm, in 2022 Disney extended this technology to the Genie+ offering, a paid service that allows skipping queues at attractions in the park. Compared to the initial static price of $20, today the price varies between $15 and $25 depending on the day.[16]

The application of this algorithm has succeeded in increasing customer satisfaction, primarily by reducing demand peaks that congested the parks during peak periods (crowded weekends with endless queues for everything – from attractions to restaurants, toilets to parking – to the point where entrance gates had to be closed to contain the crowds). Part of the demand, especially price-sensitive demand, has shifted, for example, from weekends to weekdays to take advantage of more affordable prices.

The problem of overcrowding has been solved with a simple targeted price shift, and now it is possible to enjoy the attractions again, perhaps even making more stops, better utilizing time, having more fun, and spending more without long and exhausting waits.

The second merit of the algorithm is that it has shown that dynamic pricing provides benefits beyond increasing volumes and revenues: it allows for better utilization of the park's capacity. There has been a more linear (and manageable) redistribution of demand, with consistent revenues and number of visitors over time.

The algorithm has also reduced costs for Disney, as it no longer requires overtime or additional personnel to handle demand peaks during certain periods.

Managing Technology – the Cases of Delta and United Airlines

Frequent flyers are familiar with the typical mechanism of airline loyalty programs, which have been in place since 1979 when they were introduced in the United States: each flight allows you to accumulate a certain number of miles.[17] The incentive mechanism is clear.

Flight after flight, the quantity of accumulated miles increases, and once a certain threshold is reached, there is the opportunity to use the points to purchase a 'free' flight (actually paid with the loyalty of accumulated miles). The number of miles required for a flight is determined by the airline through conversion tables that indicate routes and required miles, which vary, for example, based on distance: a certain number of miles for a domestic flight, and an additional number of miles for an intercontinental flight.

First, Delta in 2015[18] and then United Airlines in 2019[19] replaced these static conversion tables, which customers relied on, with an algorithmic pricing tool.

Award flights are now offered based on supply and demand.

The advantage for customers is that for less popular flights, such as during the low season, fewer miles are required, as indicated in the Award Calendar, the dynamic interface of the technology used by Delta.[20]

The disadvantage arises for customers during peak periods: the miles equivalent for a flight increases with higher demand. Therefore, a New York to Bali flight can 'cost' anywhere from 100,000 miles to 1 million miles, depending on when you want to travel and when you book.

However, both airlines have successfully managed this change, which not all customers have appreciated, by communicating the new process in a simple and clear manner.

They have been able to motivate the majority of customers to remain loyal, avoiding a negative impact on the brand perception.

Another success factor shared by both airlines is having a dedicated team manage the algorithm, constantly monitoring the prices expressed in required miles, and being able to intervene immediately in case of software malfunctions.

Both airlines have thus managed to overcome the conflict between short-term profit maximization, through repeated changes in prices expressed in required miles, and customer loyalty based on a relationship built over the years.

A pricing algorithm does not take into account the company's strategy, how it seeks to strengthen its relationship with customers, or all the strategies the company implements to create a unique user experience and build loyalty. Instead, it focuses on the most profitable way to align supply and demand.

Moreover, a pricing algorithm is not even empathetic!

Some companies overlook these issues and give extensive autonomy to pricing technologies without realizing that, along with pricing, they are also entrusting the overall message of the company to technology. In today's era of social media and sharing, this is no longer acceptable. It is true that data analysts calibrate the tool, but they are not the ones who have to assess its impact on customers. Often, there is a lack of dedicated sections specifically focused on this aspect. By following the example of Delta and United Airlines, the overall situation can be fully managed, while simultaneously making a conscious use of technology.

Summary

Modern technologies allow us to explore new worlds . . . and also effectively manage pricing on Earth.

To succeed in implementing a suitable solution for a company, a structured process is followed: first, the current state is analysed, then the specific business needs are established. Next, the requirements are articulated, and the options to create the technological solution are evaluated. Once the most suitable option is chosen, the implementation phase begins, ideally starting with a pilot project to test its functionality.

Once operational, the system needs to be monitored, updated, and adapted based on the evolving needs of customers and the company.

However, be cautious of relying entirely on dynamic pricing systems or modern pricing algorithms to maximize profits. The key to success is to make customers understand the benefits of algorithm-based pricing. Five examples illustrate how this can be done:

1. *Incentivizing purchases with technology – the case of IKEA:* charging customers using their time. The more time it takes to reach the store, the lower the price at checkout. The logic of the

algorithm is clear and predictable. The only price variation is downward. The algorithm rewards without penalizing.

2. *Creating transparency with technology – the case of Root*: the insurance company employs an algorithm based on the customer's driving behaviour to determine the premium. The result is a fairer and more personalized price. Customers understand how the pricing is determined and what factors they have control over to reduce their insurance premiums.

3. *Calibrating technology with human intervention – the case of Lyft*: the power of dynamic pricing can sometimes be uncontrollable. This demonstrates why human intervention is necessary to calibrate or even halt the tech tool.

4. *Increasing customer satisfaction with technology – the case of Walt Disney*: customer satisfaction has increased while reducing peaks of demand, meaning fewer queues at attractions that used to congest the parks during peak periods. Now, entry prices are lower during periods of low demand.

5. *Managing technology – the cases of Delta and United Airlines*: reward flights are now offered based on supply and demand. By having a dedicated team manage the algorithm, it is possible to intervene and correct any software malfunctions.

RULE 9
SET THE PRICING GOVERNANCE

'I was everything the well-dressed private detective ought to be.
I was calling on four million dollars.'

Raymond Chandler, novelist, *The Big Sleep* (1939)

Introduction

There are at least two Chandlers.

Raise your hand if you have not seen or read at least one of the stories featuring Philip Marlowe – you know, the private detective played on screen by the fascinating Humphrey Bogart (in the adaptation of the best novel of the series, *The Big Sleep*) and Robert Mitchum (in *Farewell, My Lovely*). You can picture him: cigarette hanging from his lips; Borsalino hat on his head; tumbler of whisky in front of him as early as 11 in the morning; 'love' nothing more than a sad game of solitaire at the gambling table. This Chandler is considered by many as the father of the hard-boiled, a proper 'tough guy'.

Sadly, however, it is not Chandler the crime novelist that we will be talking about here!

Who is ultimately the true tough guy in the market?

Is it the one who can overpower competitors and wipe out others, or is it the one who, playing fair and wearing the best attire, aims to interact with their reference environment without causing chaos? Excluding trains or gangster cars. . . .

That's where pricing governance comes in – the system of rules, practices, processes, and organization through which pricing is managed in a company.

But since there is no freedom without music, no song without redemption, just as there is no detective without laws, we will endeavour to explore together the key elements such as organizational structure, positioning, roles and responsibilities, pricing processes, and incentives.

Organizational Structure

'Structure follows strategy' is the principle coined by 'the other Chandler' – Alfred Chandler – in 1962. It states that the organizational structure of a company should be designed in a way that supports the achievement of its strategy. By a similar token, Nobel laureate Mario Vargas Llosa believed that it is the form that creates the content – not by itself alone, but it shapes it, cocreates it.

Well, let's follow the white rabbit then!

Imagine what would have happened if the great painter Pablo Picasso, instead of painting *Guernica* on a canvas measuring approximately 3.5 m x 7.7 m – it is on display at the Museo Nacional Centro de Arte Reina Sofía, in Madrid – had opted for a smaller frame: no doubt *Guernica* would still be a masterpiece, yet I am certain that size, in this case, contributes to making a difference. And if you have not seen the painting yet, let's revisit my viewpoint after you have found yourself in front of what is, without a doubt, one of the most beautiful antiwar artworks in the history of humanity.

The same applies to the best pricing strategy: it will be the more effective the more the organization is sized 'in relation to' it. In other words, the way the company moves and is able to support the strategy will change, and the strategy will be all the more effective the more we are able to articulate the pricing mindset and roll it out across various departments.

Companies with above-average incomes are those that constantly review and update the process by which they create and monetize value, regulating it with a dedicated organizational structure equipped with all the necessary elements. This agility in pricing governance will become more important in a context where the way value is created, perceived, and captured is changing ever more rapidly.

It is also true that in recent years we have witnessed innovations in models across a growing number of industries: the proliferation of dynamic pricing, the introduction of AI-based pricing, and the increasing importance of sustainability reflected in price management.

A typical obstacle to the success of monetization strategies is the lack of an organizational structure that manages pricing. In various companies where it was difficult to introduce a function worthy of its name, the main resistance came from those departments or executives who did not want to lose the power to set prices independently or approve discretionary discounts and concessions to meet short-term objectives.

Having, in the organization, an adequate structure dedicated to pricing is therefore essential.

When considering how to set up such a structure, the degree of centralization to choose must be carefully evaluated. There are three possible models.

In short, this is a story disseminated with crossroads, where the ending will depend on the choices we make at each turn.

Perhaps our detective won't be there to help us identify the 'culprit' in the structure, in terms of the improper application of the pricing strategy, but we will have all the elements in our hands to discover it by ourselves.

As always, it will depend on our ability to identify the core of the problem, bring it back to an objective analysis model, and finally apply the right structures to the reference context. Even in novels, there is always a specific metric in the narratives. As Ian Fleming says in *Goldfinger*: 'Once is happenstance. Twice is coincidence. The third time it's an enemy action.'

Let's take a look at the three models, in order.

Centralized pricing

As the first 'archetype' of structure, centralized pricing stands out in that pricing strategies and tactics are decided at the central headquarters. The more similar the types of customers served, the competitive advantages that make the offering distinctive, and the competitors faced in different markets, the more important it is to coordinate decisions within the company. This type of pricing also has a strong symbolic character: it indicates that, given the importance of the matter, it is managed directly by the headquarters.

My personal experience of a centralized pricing approach was when I supported a leading lubricant company that sold the same products in different markets and needed to transform its pricing strategy. Until then, pricing decisions were decentralized and made from within the sales department in the various countries. This led to parallel imports and profit losses, as sales teams heavily discounted the lubricants to meet volume-based targets. Consequently, net prices varied significantly between countries, even neighbouring ones, and products were being re-imported between markets by distributors, damaging the company. The initial step was to centralize the pricing function under the direct supervision of the CEO for a transitional period of 1 year, making it clear to the entire organization that effective pricing management had become a top priority.

Centralizing pricing offers several other advantages: increased authority and control, reduced potential loss of margin at the local level due to inconsistencies across regions, easier standardization of tools and procedures for consistent and homogeneous management, and sharing intelligence on competition.

A centrally managed pricing structure is well-suited for companies with strong global brands that need consistent positioning across different markets, where prices are transparent, and there is a high risk of arbitrage. Apple is an example of such a company. Consistently managed pricing is crucial for Apple to ensure a uniform brand experience worldwide. Customers can easily compare and purchase Apple products in different markets, and centralized management helps mitigate risks associated with price discrepancies.

In the transport and energy sectors, pricing is often centralized. Consider the case of airlines or rail transport, where available capacity is centrally managed, and different prices are offered to various market segments. While there may be price differences between markets, these are intentional and strategically managed by the central team.

Regional pricing

In the second archetype, the regional or decentralized pricing, each business unit or country has its own dedicated pricing team and reports to the business-unit management or local country management. The relationship with the central pricing function, if it exists in this case, is limited, for example, to exchanging best practices or coordinating activities. In cases like this, we speak of a dotted line, rather than a direct line, between regional and central pricing.

When the corporate group has distinct customer types, numerous competitors in different markets, diversified business units with few commonalities or synergies, it makes sense to apply such a solution.

The market differences in this case are such that standardizing pricing is not feasible.

When there is significant heterogeneity, it becomes important to adapt fully to the local competitive context, in other words, to the rules adopted in that particular market. Equally, the more consistent we are with storytelling related to that market, the more we will be perceived as neighbours, 'friends', rather than rivals.

This approach brings us closer to the market and customers and provides greater flexibility in adapting pricing at the local level and reacting to local developments. In a decentralized company with different business areas, such as 3M, the central pricing team can develop principles, processes, and guidelines, but concrete price decisions are left to regional organizations or individual business areas.

Semi-centralized pricing

The third solution is a hybrid structure of semi-centralized pricing: on the one hand, the company feels the need to standardize processes to improve price quality; on the other, it is important to capture local willingness to pay. Thus, the central pricing team maintains a certain level of control over price decisions, tools to use, price corridors to respect, and processes to follow. Best practices are shared, and universal pricing strategies indicate the guidelines to follow.

Often, at the central level, there are experts who cooperate to perform activities such as advanced quantitative price analysis, market research management, development of pricing software for use throughout the group, and so on, which would be less cost-effective to manage and replicate at local level. To all intents and purposes, they act as internal consultants.

In retail or telecommunications, hybrid structures are often found, where different local elasticities need to be accommodated, whilst benefiting from all the support that the central team can provide.

In summary, just as there is not a single ending for our story or a single culprit for all mysteries worth their salt (except, for the butler of course!), there is no ideal solution for all companies in the whole wide world: based on how they operate, on how global or local their activities are, determining the best organizational structure for pricing needs to be decided on a case-by-case basis.

Location

One aspect related to organizational structure is 'where' to place the pricing function, which typically finds its natural habitat within the marketing function, whose task is to identify, satisfy, and retain customers by creating and delivering value. The marketing function is also responsible for product and service promotion, with pricing being an aspect of this activity. This is typical for product-based companies where there is no strong differentiation based on the customer, such as Bayer, Michelin, Alfa Romeo, or Apple.

However, the pricing function can be placed elsewhere depending on the type of company. It can be a separate department in companies where price management is particularly complex and requires a dedicated team of experts, as in the case of transport, travel, and tourism. Companies like MSC, British Airways, Hilton, Avis, DHL, or Alpitour have yield management departments, also known as revenue management, which handle pricing management by dynamically adjusting and differentiating prices based on specific segmentations.

What is discouraged is placing pricing responsibility within the sales function. The reason is that there is a natural conflict of interest. 'Cherchez la femme', the French advised when trying to find the culprit of a crime.

The sales function often has objectives in terms of sales volumes. It is therefore natural for a salesperson to tend to lower prices to meet sales targets.

That's why setting margin objectives in addition to quantity goals helps rebalance the incentives for the sales force. However, there are exceptions when there is a strong need to differentiate prices by customer. Examples of this are companies that sell projects, such as those operating in the field of infrastructure, companies like Webuild, HochTief, and Porr, or specialized logistics services for pharmacies, such as those provided by McKesson.

Another interesting case that I bring to your attention is that of trading companies specialized in buying and reselling goods. In this case, there are frequent changes in procurement costs, and the value-added to the product is limited.

I can already see the plot: the port of Marseille, or better still Singapore or Hong Kong, a group of Chinese workers unloading goods from a container just arrived at the port. Our investigator flicks the cigarette into the dirty waters, mist and vapours rise from the water's surface. Dressed in his inevitable beige trench coat, our hero will soon sneak unseen into the hangar where, in reality, not only beautiful antique objects are traded but ... to know the rest of the adventure and '[t]he stuff that dreams are made of', it is best to read *The Maltese Falcon*, a hard-boiled novel by Dashiell Hammett that was made into a film in 1941 directed by John Huston (which received four nominations at the 1942 Oscars) starring, of course, Humphrey Bogart.

In more everyday contexts like ours, price management is sometimes placed within category management or procurement. Examples of companies of this kind are Leroy Merlin and Metro, where there are also workers and containers travelling around the world (international trade is a fascinating subject). Finally, there are rare cases where pricing reports directly to the CEO or the Chief Financial Officer (CFO). This happens when there are critical levels of profitability, either too low or negative, and strict oversight is required.

We have seen that there are different options for where to place the pricing function. The most important aspect in making this decision is to ensure that those responsible for pricing are able to set optimal prices to monetize the value created for customers (we mentioned earlier the 'conflict of interest' related to achieving volume goals at the expense of profitability).

Roles and Responsibilities

After setting up the organizational structure, roles and responsibilities need to be defined. Depending on the size of the company, these roles can be full time, while others may be part time or covered by one person instead of a team.

In small companies, it may happen that there is a single dedicated resource who spends half of their time on pricing and the other half, for example, on marketing.

In large companies, such as airlines or pharmaceutical companies, there are often teams of dozens of full-time pricing managers and analysts. As a rough estimate, the following numbers can be considered:

For companies with a turnover of up to $500 million, the average size of the pricing team is five resources.

For every $1 billion turnover, there are approximately 10 resources dedicated to price management.

However, there are many companies that do not have any dedicated resources for pricing. Others, with higher profitability, typically have full-time pricing resources, which is certainly what every company should do to manage pricing effectively.

I know, you're thinking, it's your job, you would say that. Yes, and at the same time, in the case of part-time resources, it should at least be ensured that they have enough time to carry out pricing-related tasks and develop their skills through training. After all, isn't it studying the first lever taught in universities that allows us to 'move the world'?

After playing around with the sense of constructing the narrative for our business, following the pattern of a mystery where we need to discover who did what, let's now focus on the objectives we set for this chapter. That is, determining the three typical roles in pricing management.

The first role is the **pricing director**, also known as the *chief value officer, chief pricing officer, pricing champion, global pricing director,* or *pricing leader*. This person should be part of the company's leadership team and be involved in discussions on topics such as positioning, product launches, and business activities.

The responsibilities of this role can generally be divided into strategic and managerial.

Strategic

- Establishing the pricing strategy and model to monetize the value provided to customers effectively.

- Developing a vision for being at the forefront of pricing.

- Leading the development and adoption of processes, tools, skills, incentives, and IT systems.

- Setting priorities to optimize pricing and maximize profits.

- Supporting marketing in developing the *value proposition*.[1]

Managerial

- Coordinating and guiding pricing activities in business units or strategic areas of the company.

- Monitoring pricing management in these units and facilitating continuous improvement.

- Managing and coordinating resources involved in pricing.

- Promoting cultural change and inspiring the organization regarding monetization to ensure pricing remains a priority for the company and its importance is understood.

The second role is that of **pricing manager**. This is a professional role with strong marketing skills and analytical abilities, positioned at a more operational level than the Pricing Director.

The typical responsibilities of this role are tactical and operational.

Tactical

- Monitoring competition and drawing conclusions on how to react.

- Monitoring pricing management across channels, regions, and business units through KPIs (key performance indicators) and dashboards.

- Ensuring international price management to avoid the grey market.

- Market segmentation and differentiated pricing by segment.

- Implementing effective price communications.

Operational

- Proposing price changes and discounts based on analytical evidence.

- Quantifying product value and assessing willingness to pay.

- Producing price lists for business units, regions, or channels.

- Calibrating policies, processes, and tools for pricing management.

- Managing pricing analysts.

Finally, there is the role of **pricing analyst**, which is the most junior position and provides operational support to the pricing manager with strong analytical skills. Typical tasks include:

- analysing profitability and deviations to identify areas for improvement;

- calculating and preparing price lists;

- managing pricing processes, such as periodic reviews of price increases;

- conducting elasticity studies;

- coordinating market research when necessary;

- gathering data on competitors; and

- updating pricing tools with current data.

General Electric (GE) provides an example of a company that has introduced the role of Chief Pricing Officer in each business unit, directly reporting to the division head. Jeff Immelt, the CEO of GE, immediately noticed the positive impact that this new professional figure was bringing to the organization. Since the introduction of the Chief Pricing Officer role, pricing management discipline has significantly increased, enabling the company to achieve target pricing and desired profitability much faster and more effectively than before.

However, just like in any recipe, we shouldn't overlook the importance of the chef (which is why your cake or cookies can never be the same as your grandmother used to make). Hence, except in a few exemplary cases, to successfully replicate a winning pricing strategy, the people in the roles listed must not only possess quantitative skills, the so-called hard skills, which include the analytical abilities indispensable to interrogate complex data and translate analysis into understandable and implementable operational guidelines. They must also develop qualitative skills, the soft skills, to communicate clear instructions, guide and motivate teams, and maintain relationships at all levels of the organization, as pricing involves multiple functions such as research and development, product management, sales, finance, and IT systems.

Pricing Processes

Once roles and responsibilities are defined, the next aspect of pricing governance is establishing clear pricing processes. But what exactly is meant by a pricing process? A pricing process is a system of rules and methods for determining and introducing prices in order to monetize the value provided to customers.

These pricing processes can vary significantly depending on the company and industry. Each company must determine which processes are relevant in its case. For example, an oil company may heavily focus on industry supply and demand to keep prices aligned with market levels. An industrial machinery manufacturer may focus on the logic and policies governing discounts for different products and volumes. A consumer goods manufacturer may focus on customer value, using competitive analysis and elasticity analysis to set and adjust list prices.

In all these cases, processes with clearly defined phases, roles involved, inputs, and outcomes should govern the company's pricing decision making and activities. These processes lie at the core of price management. It is important not to limit pricing processes to merely defining prices and setting rules for granting discounts. The pricing process goes beyond that and encompasses everything related to commercial monetization. Companies need to determine which specific price decisions are critical to their success and then build robust processes around those decisions.

Negotiation with customers is an important aspect of the process, as are decisions related to revenue models and the recognition of ancillary services.[2] Another significant process is related to managing price exceptions, discounts, or special conditions.[3] Therefore, it is essential to have a broad perspective when identifying pricing processes. Furthermore, agility is required in updating processes or the timing of pricing processes. While in the pre-pandemic period it may have been sufficient to revisit and update pricing once a year in certain industries, today, due to increasingly strong and rapid fluctuations in raw material costs, it may be necessary to repeat the pricing update process multiple times a year.

Incentivization

A compelling cover and a catchy title, the promise of what we will find inside, are a good incentive to buy a book, choose a movie, or a Netflix series when we have only seen the trailer.

Similarly, every little thing we choose (or don't choose) every day must have, within itself, the broader and more general sense of what it represents. Let me explain. A sentence is good if it keeps me reading and turning the page. The taste of ice cream must surprise me; then I will try a new flavour, venture into something new.

This happens with any choice: it is the promise of something that so far we have only just tasted that makes us opt for one thing rather than another. It is a service that we had previously considered secondary or hadn't taken into consideration, which becomes necessary when we recognize a good reason to change our habits.

Likewise, in our companies – which provide goods and/or services – an optimal incentivization system motivates the sales force to structure their commercial policies in line with the broader company strategy. Ideally, we shouldn't even have to tell the salespeople what to do: the system should guide their behaviour in such a way that all actions taken will serve the company's interests. Calibrating an incentivization system to achieve these effects becomes a lever for growth, which also acts on individuals, motivating human resources to stay because they feel they are not just a number but rather part of a larger project.

The secret to success lies here, in the ability to balance two disparate forces, namely, balancing the individual stories that make up the company with the purpose of that company, ultimately the incentive for the sales force to contribute to the company's profitability. In this way, the financial interests of the company and those of the salespeople are aligned.

Instead of asking for extra discounts, salespeople will strive to sell value. Five steps allow for optimal incentivization of the sales force:

1. *Document the current incentive system* The first step should be to verify the metrics and incentives currently used in the company, and the extent that they are utilized. In addition to providing a clear starting point, this framework will allow understanding of how the corporate body functions and also determines the degree of similarity or dissimilarity in incentives between different business units, functions, or geographic areas.

2. *Align incentivization with the sales strategy* To achieve alignment among all decision makers involved in pricing, incentivization is aligned with the sales strategy. In other words, the company must determine and make clear which behaviours of the sales force promote profit growth and reward those behaviours with bonuses.

3. *Establish parameters* It is time to establish concrete parameters for measuring the success of salespeople. These values should be ambitious yet realistic. In addition to achieving indicators related to the quantity sold, it is important to clarify which

metrics measure the contribution to company profitability. This prevents penalizing value-driven salespeople who contribute to profits compared to quantity-driven salespeople who focus on volumes at the expense of profits.

4. *Clearly communicate how it works* To be effective, the incentivization system must be clear and understandable. After all, a story is not 'good' if I don't understand it, right? That's why the functioning and calculation of parameters should be explicitly explained. The more specific and concrete the examples and explanations are, the better the understanding of the logic behind the value, the rationale, the research comments, and more. Providing calculation examples such as, 'If you offer x percentage points less in discount, profit increases by y percentage points, and your bonus increases by z dollars', sheds light on the impact of discounts and rates on received commissions, helping understanding of how to influence various parameters to meet objectives.

5. *Implement and monitor incentivization* Once set, understood, and communicated, we are ready to implement the incentivization system. Regular monitoring of results and sharing information with the salespeople will allow us to assess how well we are achieving objectives, motivating the sales force to continue on the path indicated by the sales strategy. This also allows for corrective actions to be taken in case of deviations or discrepancies.

Throughout the implementation of these five steps, the success factors of this approach should be kept in mind: if people find the challenges ambitious yet realistic, stimulating, and understandable, they will be more inclined to take them on. By following these guidelines, the positive impact on profits will become noticeable in no time.

Summary

Establishing pricing governance, understood as a framework, a system of rules, practices, processes, and organization through which pricing is managed in a company, should be a must and a priority for any company aiming to increase its profitability. Moreover, if the pricing function positions itself as a strategic partner to other functions, facilitating the monetization of the value provided to customers, it will have the best conditions for success. Key elements include organizational structure, placement, roles and responsibilities, pricing processes, and incentivization.

The first element of pricing governance is the organizational structure dedicated to pricing. There are three possible archetypes.

1. In a **centralized pricing structure**, pricing strategies are decided at the headquarters, facilitating the standardization of tools and procedures to manage pricing consistently and uniformly.

2. In a **decentralized pricing structure**, each business unit or country has its dedicated team and reports to the local management. The relationship with the central function is limited to sharing best practices or coordination activities.

3. In a **semi-centralized pricing structure**, on the one hand, the company recognizes the need to standardize processes to improve price quality, while on the other, it recognizes the importance of keeping in mind the local willingness to pay.

The most appropriate organizational structure should be decided on a case-by-case basis, depending on how companies operate, and on the global or local nature of their activities.

A crucial aspect related to the organizational structure is where to place the pricing function. What its coordinates are in relation to external factors (the market, financial fluctuations, a war) and internal factors (structure, management, canvas size – 3.5 m × 7.7 m or 35 cm × 77 cm? – the outcome changes significantly!).

Normally, the pricing function finds its natural habitat within marketing. However, it can be placed elsewhere depending on the type of company. It can be a separate department in companies where price management is particularly complex and requires a dedicated team of experts (e.g. *yield management* departments). It is associated with the sales function in companies that sell projects, such as in the field of infrastructure. Another case is commercial enterprises, where price management is sometimes placed in category management or procurement. Finally, there are rare cases where pricing reports directly to the CEO or the CFO.

Several criteria should be applied to structure, manage, and deliver the pricing function.

The most important aspect is to ensure that the pricing managers are capable of setting optimal prices to monetize the value created for customers, without conflicts of interest related, for example, to achieving volume targets at the expense of profitability.

After establishing the organizational structure, roles and responsibilities need to be defined. Depending on the size of the company, these roles can be full or part time and can be covered by one or more individuals. Three typical roles are pricing director, pricing manager, and pricing analyst.

Once roles and responsibilities are established, pricing governance needs to define clear pricing processes, a system of rules and methods for determining and introducing prices in order to monetize the value provided to customers.

Finally, the incentive system should be set up to motivate the sales force to be consistent with the business strategy adopted. In this case, the incentive system will guide the individual's behaviours to cohere with the company's interests. Calibrating an incentive system to produce these effects means interpreting the (yet not fully articulated) mission of the company in the best possible way. In this sense, pricing is a lever for growth, for individuals and for the entire company.

And if, at the end of this chapter, you feel you have understood the difference between one Chandler and the other, and the difference between a company *with* a pricing function and one *without*, you can rest assured that you have. And besides you will have understood that it does not pay to apply the same model of behaviour whatever the context, that you must always take into account nuances, and local specificities – and that this principle applies to all life circumstances, including those related to work.

And there's one additional truth you will have learnt: that if your company is not managing to realize good profit margins, it is not the butler you should point your finger at!

And the truth, as we know, sets you free.

RULE 10
DEBUNK THE MYTHS
OF PRICING

'Myths which are believed in tend to become true.'

George Orwell, author

Introduction

A legend says that one day a puny young boy pulled a magical sword from a stone and became king of England. Another legend says that a man, who was king of an island far away in the Mediterranean Sea, fought a war that lasted for many years, he won it thanks to a wooden horse, returned to his kingdom and defeated his wife's rapacious suitors using only his bow and the favour of the goddess Athena. The poet Dante went through Hell so that he could meet Beatrice, and Hades came to Earth in person so that he could kidnap the beautiful Persephone.

Immaterial stories determine our choices much more than we believe.

Without the *Divine Comedy* Italy, would not have its national language; and without the adventurous journey undertaken by Ulysses to return to Ithaca, Western culture, which spans from Homer to Hollywood, wouldn't have begun.

This is the grammar of the stories that make up our cultural heritage, and shape our identity from childhood: from Romeo and Juliet to Batman, from Sherlock Holmes to Peter Parker AKA Spiderman. Myths make up our world, what we refer to as *reality*.

Without the Knights of the Round Table, King Arthur would not have built Camelot or created a kingdom inspired by the principles of heroism and loyalty.

In the narrative of Man on Earth – according to the latest theories, the first evidence of *Sapiens Sapiens* can be dated to roughly 300,000 years ago – the purpose of myth has always been to transmit acquired knowledge down the generations: to ensure that those who come after us can make use of skills that we have discovered and mastered, and be better equipped to deal with dangers that we had to learn to avoid.

Put more simply, myth has been used to foreground the *significance* of an event – the outcome of a hunt, an exchange (in the old days this would have been bartering) of a product, of an asset, of a service.

The Seven Myths of Pricing

As Yoda of *Star Wars* fame would say, there are 'positive' myths and just as many *dark myths*.

A few years ago, the fact that some people in the UK, gave the answer 'Jedi' to the question in the Census questionnaire 'what is your religion?' caused a stir and a smirk. Today it is a known fact that the myths portrayed in the world imagined by George Lucas – think of the Twin Suns, for example – have had a significant impact on the way we see 'the Other'. Think only of any marketplace in Jakku, where the protagonist Rey, to make ends meet, sells spare parts from old spaceships: what should she have charged for them? Does the currency exchanger give our friend – who isn't yet a Jedi – a price that is right?

We don't need to go this far out to the borders of the Universe. Although price management is known to be the most effective and fast-acting tool to increment profit margins even on planet Earth, it does cause anxiety and concern, associated as it is with many negative myths.

We will try to analyse what we can call the *false myths* in the era of fake news.

Having worked over the years with managers from thousands of companies worldwide, I have identified **seven myths of pricing** – seven, like the *7 Samurai* of Akira Kurosawa, like the *Magnificent 7*; seven as the number that in many cultures joins together heaven and earth. These myths (see Figure 10.1) – all of them negative – inhibit the profit-generating power of price management. Those companies that have had the courage to explode them, to challenge the scary mythological creature head on, have been successful and recorded higher than average profitability.

Myth 1 – There is Correlation between Market Share and Profit

Aiming for the highest market share and generating profit seem to be unreconcilable efforts. But why should aiming high come at the expense of profit?

An aggressive push to gain a larger share of the market usually has the consequence of driving prices down – so if on the one hand one ends up with higher volumes of sales, on the other the discounts offered on the products sold mean that profits diminish.

In an effort to pursue objectives linked to market shares, CEOs pay far too much attention to what competitors do, and lose sight of what

The seven myths of pricing, realities and rules

	Myth #1	Myth #2	Myth #3	Myth #4	Myth #5	Myth #6	Myth #7
	There is correlation between market share and profit.	The price of a commodity cannot be increased.	Small variations in price have a negligible impact on profits.	For B2B companies, dynamic pricing is as illegible as a black box.	Pricing is based on cost.	Price management means increasing or lowering prices.	Customers are after lowprices.
Fact	There is no correlation between market share and profitability.	It is possible to differentiate a commodity and increase the price.	Small variations, in price make a great difference to profit.	Dynamic pricing can be adopted both in B2C and B2B businesses, and because it is based on interaction with customers its logic is easy to understand.	Pricing must be based on value rather than cost.	Price management means setting out processes, systems, and a company culture that communicate value.	B2C customers hardly ever remember the price they have paid for a product. B2B customers rate Total Cost of Ownership higher than they do prices.
Rule	Aim to a leadership based on the value that is attributed to your product, not on market share.	Any product can be commodity?	Look after every cent: calculated over a large number of transactions, every single cent makes a difference to your overall profit margins.	Begin with applying it to specific use cases to test it against your products and see the advantages it generates. The more you use it, the more precise your data sets will become.	Understand what your customers need, and satisfy that need by creating value. Your pricing policy must be based on value.	To manage prices you must have established processes, systems, and a company culture that communicate value.	Segment your client base, and differentiate your offer according to what each segment values more. This will yield the highest returns for your company.

Figure 10.1 The seven myths of pricing.

really matters: making customers as happy as they can be. Instead of being masters of their own destiny – like Jason, *en route* to acquiring the golden fleece – companies that only focus on increasing their market share put themselves at the mercy of the waves – in other words, of the competition. Being distracted by what competitors do, they neglect their customers; neglecting customers inevitably means a crash in profits.

Market share is usually code for power and prestige. This clearly explains why managers want their companies to be market leaders.

The example of the automotive industry serves well to explain the obsession for market dominance.

For General Motors (GM), it became a mantra: expanding their position on the market was the primary objective of GM executives. Rumour has it that the then CEO Rick Wagoner had the number 29 engraved on his cufflinks – 29 being the market share he craved.

The same mantra explains why, still at GM, the then VP Bob Lutz pursued aggressive discount policies: to remain on course with their stated objectives, the plant had to keep working at full capacity and churn out vehicles which then had to be sold.[1]

Sergio Marchionne, then CEO of Fiat Chrysler Automobiles, another mass producer of cars, took a radically different view: 'Unprofitable volume is not volume I want', he said. 'We have a very good track record of how to destroy an industry – run the [plants] just for the hell of volume, and you're finished.'[2]

A pricing policy based on volumes was for a long time the philosophy at GM: sales staff were culturally inclined to offer hefty discounts so long as they could clinch a sale. Explaining the rationale behind promotions that offered discounts to the tune of $10,000 per client, a GM spokesperson admitted: 'It's to be competitive. You have to do something out there.' [3]

Understanding the meaning of that 'something' was key to unlocking one of the foundational myths of the commercial policy of the company: hold the sword and the shield at the same time. The underlying hypothesis at GM was that price was the main criterion customers used when choosing which car to buy. The consequence of this premise was that if a lower price was the main factor determining why a customer chose one car over another, then a car was simply a commodity.[4] This led to a reduction in investments in R&D, a curtailing of innovation, and a sole focus on cost containment. Discounted prices continued to be considered as the main drivers to sales. This was the reason why GM collapsed during the crisis of the year 2008, when cars were sold at cost or below cost so long as sales were made. All this because 'the monster' lurking behind management craved sales volumes. A fire-spitting dragon that the poor soldiers hopelessly attempted to fight from on board a tin jalopy, instead of a shining, sturdy metal armour. And customers understood the value that the soldiers gave to their vehicles – the value of tin, so to speak.

At the other end of the spectrum is the philosophy inspiring Porsche – the manufacturer with the rearing black horse and the colours of the German flag in its logo. Porsche believed in keeping prices as high as possible, and thus protect their used cars from depreciation. As CEO Wendelin Wiedeking put it, when demand fell, production had to slow down: Porsche kept prices high by having fewer cars available than orders in.

GM and Porsche believed in a different mythology about 'the Other', and this generated a different perception of themselves and of themselves vis-à-vis their customers.

GM went bankrupt due to a completely wrong pricing policy. Porsche was able to overcome the troubled waters of the year 2008, never surrendered to the sirens of the market share, and is today one of the most profitable actors in the automotive industry. Price management is disciplined to the point that the CEO is personally involved in setting the price for every new car.

But where does the myth of/obsession with market share come from?

Jack Welch – himself a somewhat mythical figure – was one of the main advocates of the importance of market share, when he was at the helm of GE. He insisted that every single one of his business units had to be number 1 (number 2, at a push) in the world, or else he would sell it.

The theory that underpinned this view is encapsulated in the acronym PIMS – profit impact of market strategy: the belief (derived from studies carried out in the 1970s) that there was a positive correlation between market share and profitability.[5]

Let's be clear: this might have been true back then, but it is no longer true.

In 2004, Robert Buzzel, who led the studies, admitted that there was 'no way that market share or relative quality could have "direct" effects on profitability'.[6] Nonetheless, the obsession with market shares is deeply rooted in the mindset of some senior managers. Think of the former heads of Polaroid, Blockbuster, or Suntech; or compare the likes of American Airlines or Dow with Ryan Air or DuPont, and you will understand the predicament that companies that focussed on market share found themselves in.

The issue of sacrificing market shares and increasing prices and profits was long debated in Sony. The Japanese giant evoked images of operational discipline against a background of cherry blossoms and invincible samurai warriors ready to fight for their loved one by moonlight. Until the sturdy construction collapsed, the losses revealed themselves to be unsustainable, and the company was forced to relinquish the dogma of market positioning in an effort to reclaim an acceptable level of profitability.

Companies like Apple, a market leader in numerous segments, never aimed for a specific share of the market, preferring – as Tim Cook put it – to create products that excited customers and thus enabled the company to keep price levels that guaranteed profitability.[7]

Kathryn Mikells, CFO at United Airlines, reflected on the company's decision to scale back their fleet and concentrate on the most profitable customer clusters with the goal of turning steady profits. 'There's a willingness not to be wedded to things that have not worked well – like market share', said Mikells, explaining a principle that can be applied to other manufacturing industries, where high fixed costs make a fixation with market share erode profits.[8] A forward-thinking leader knows that marked share is irrelevant.

As Jørgen Vig Knudstorp, CEO of Lego (another myth for many of us, young builders of dreams) put it, 'What matters to us is to be the best, not the biggest. We want to be the best playing experience for children, the best supplier to our retailers and the best employer.'[9] A view echoed by Verizon's CEO Hans Vestberg, who warned that no matter how competitive the company intended to be, it would never sacrifice profitability on the altar of market share.[10] And by Klaus Zellmer , CEO of Skoda, who stated: 'Before it was speculated about whether Skoda should aim for 1.5 or 2 million cars sold

DEBUNK THE MYTHS OF PRICING

a year. Our goal is and will be passing the 1 million mark, but in the current situation profitability is much more important than the volume itself.'[11]

In some cases companies willingly sacrifice profitability to maintain their market share. It is the case of Lyft, which consciously decided to lower prices and hence reduce their profit margins – as CEO Logan Green admitted – in order to remain competitive and not lose business to Uber.[12]

Now the question is: can a correlation between market share and profits ever be established?

It can. But only when there is *pricing power*, the power to set prices that correspond to the value of the product offered.

Pricing power is obtained when a company is capable of offering products or services that satisfy the needs and desires of customers – even when these are not yet explicitly expressed, when customers are not yet aware of them. Pricing power comes from the ability to interpret costumers' expectations, to translate them into an aspirational idea – which is much more than the simple product – that can be turned into a material object, and purchased.

It is those who can create value for customers – not those who occupy the largest space in the market – that are the most profitable.

A profound knowledge of one's customers promotes innovativeness, and innovation confers pricing power. In these conditions, a high market share is positive: it favours healthy profits, it is justified and sustainable. But to obtain and maintain a market share by setting sale prices below costs is a losing strategy, it shows an absence of vision: profits will be eroded, before long losses will be incurred, not to mention the risk of causing a price war. Altogether an unsustainable situation.

Myth 2 – Any Product and Commodity Can Be Differentiated

The term 'commodity' refers to a raw material or a primary agricultural product that can be bought and sold. In business parlance, the term is synonymous with products or services that are interchangeable with other goods of the same types, and whose only defining feature is the price.

So, if in a company the sales team resist requests from their senior managers to increase the price of their products for fear of losing volumes of sales (on the grounds that 'the market determines price'), then they see what they are selling as a commodity.

But is this objection legitimate, or is it just an excuse to keep prices at the current level?

An example taken from the automotive sector can help us understand what happens when a company regards their product as a commodity.

The reason why Chrysler went bankrupt is precisely this: their top management was convinced that the only way to convince customers to buy their cars was the price difference. Hence a low price, be it in the form of a discount or cashback – we all remember the film scenes where, upon signing the contract, customers would receive a cash sum from car salespersons – resulted from a flawed but engrained argument: cars are all the same; customers buy a car if it is economical; customers will be incentivized to buy our cars if there are financial advantages – discounts or cashback.

Unable to produce sufficiently distinctive cars, Chrysler could only rely on low prices to attract customers, effectively reducing their cars to nothing more than commodities. Sales became locked and subordinate to price, making the adage 'the market determines price' a self-fulfilling prophecy.

Yet, it is possible to make any product – any commodity, even – distinctive in some respects. This should the core function and the objective of marketing teams in a company.

But if YOU yourself believe that what you are selling is a commodity, why should your customers think any differently? It is not a mere question of self-perception, right or wrong as it may be. It is the root cause of price wars, loss of innovativeness, of dynamism, of creativity, and ultimately of profitability.

When we were students – young, enterprising, and attractive – we learnt that it is always hard to sell something that is already available for free. But if this is true, how can we explain why we pay for water?

Three-quarters of the earth surface is covered by water, and yet the world market for bottled water is worth €283 billion.[13]

Water from the kitchen tap costs 1 cent per litre. If I buy it bottled, I pay 25 times as much. If the bottle is branded – say Perrier, for example – I will pay €4. If I order it in a Michelin-starred restaurant, and it happens to be branded Ferrarelle Gucci, I could be charged as much as €30. I wonder if this is the reason why Evian reads like naïve backwards.

Is it possible that the myths, the narratives constructed around a product, have the power to manipulate customers' perceptions and have such a portentous effect on price?

Innovation is the main key to get out of the blind alley that is commodification. But there are other aspects that merit attention.

A possible option would be to concentrate on the ancillary elements of the deal – for instance, attractive payment plans, practical aspects linked to the sale (terms of delivery, prompt availability), after-sales support, warranties, official certifications.

Let's consider cement, by way of an example: I could sell 1 ton a cement at a set price – purely for ease of calculation I will call it €400. If I am asked to deliver it to a site located at some distance from my premises, I could raise the charge to €500, to cover transport costs plus a margin. If the delivery has specific requirements – say it is to be made to the construction site for a special infrastructure and at incovenient hours – the total price could go up to €800. If I am asked to deliver at the weekend, after 6.00 pm, and in winter, when temperatures drop, meaning that the cement needs to be kept at a specific temperature to keep it from freezing, the price could rise to €1,200 a ton. The example shows that even with an apparent commodity such as cement we can find distinctive elements that can treble the price at which I sell it.

In essence: a glass of water is a glass of water, but if you found yourself in the desert you would probably think of it differently (and by the way: the oasis you think you saw was not real or free. It was a mirage).

Market leaders with higher-than-average profits do not rate any of their products as commodities. They believe that any product can be differentiated.

Fuel is another example. While clearly a commodity – fuel is fuel, it is initially undifferentiated and sold as such to various retailers – it is differentiated in exemplary ways.

Lab tests have confirmed that, in terms of quality, fuel is the same wherever you buy it – be it branded or unbranded stations – because it often comes from the same stockists or distributors.[14] Then Shell introduced *V-Power*, Esso *Synergy*, BP *Ultimate*, and Total *Excellium*. The names allude to additional desirable qualities that are unlikely to be real and are questionable, particularly considering that we should be aiming towards cleaner forms of energy.

Let's examine the case of Shell's *V-Power*, a high-octane fuel that promised motorists the performance levels of Formula 1 cars. As Shell was the sponsor of Ferrari, the promise gained some traction with motorists. Notwithstanding the higher-than-average price at the pump, the marketing campaigns magnifying the impact on car performance, paralleled by a reduction in fuel consumption, succeeded in promoting *V-Power*, whose sales grew steadily.

In 2023, 22 years after it was launched on the market, *V-Power* and the other high-octane fuels represent 25% of the sales of petrol. *V-Power* helped Shell increase its market share at the expense of competitors: with a price at the pump up to 20 cents higher per litre than conventional petrol, and with minimal incremental costs, *V-Power* is extremely profitable.[15]

The question to ask if one wanted to appraise the advantages of buying *V-Power* as opposed to normal fuel should have been: does it really improve performance and reduce fuel consumption? The verdict came as the result of several tests conducted on a range of car models – including Porsche, BMW, Audi, and Volkswagen: using the more expensive petrol brought no significant advantage.[16] Car manufacturers themselves state that their engines are optimized for the traditional fuel, and that no additive is needed to improve their health or performance.[17] Surprisingly, a study from the University of Nuremberg demonstrated that premium fuel can result in under-performance, meaning that normal fuel is not only cheaper but also better for our cars.[18]

The lesson from the case of Shell and *V-Power* is that no matter how irrelevant a differentiation is, it creates value for customers and increases their willingness to pay more money.

Customers are irrational, and differentiation is grounded in perceptions.

If a customer perceives a product as differentiated, then the product becomes differentiated. It is the customer's point of view that makes the differentiation real and relevant, even if technically this is minimal.

The case above demonstrates that a) differentiation is always possible, even in cases where products are pure commodities, and b) differentiation makes profits grow. Company managers must stop being afraid of undifferentiated commodities, and must learn the words to 'narrate' their products. After all, as Ludwig Wittgenstein said, it is language that creates the world.

Myth 3 – Small Variations in Price Have a Negligible Impact on Profits

Most business managers are under the impression that small price increases have no positive impact on profits. Nothing could be more wrong.

An improvement by 1% of net sale prices – that is a price increment by 1% or a reduction by 1% of the discount, increases profitability even by 10% or more. I will illustrate this with an example.

A company with a 10% operating profit margin would improve this to 11% simply by raising prices – that is, increasing list prices or reducing discounts. In companies with lower operating profit margins the impact of price variation on profitability is even more pronounced. Take the case of Volkswagen, whose operating profit margin from the 2021 sales was 7.6%: by increasing sales prices by 1% it would increase its profitability by 13.1%.

This goes to show that small price increases generate a significant effect.

One of our clients – a manufacturer of chewing gum – was astonished to discover the difference a few cents can make. A typical packet of chewing gum is priced at 90 cents. The results of market research that we conducted for one of our pricing projects revealed that €1 was an important price threshold – which meant that we could increase the price of the chewing gum to 99 cents without risking perceptible losses in terms of market share, and that the risk would present itself only if the €1 threshold was crossed. Our predictions were confirmed, the volume of sales remained stable, and the additional 9 cents, multiplied by the very high number of items sold, brought in a higher revenue – which was in fact net profit, because our costs had remained the same.

If we applied the same logic to discounts, we would realize how small improvements make a big difference.

The CEO of a well-known multinational involved me in a pricing project in an attempt to increase the company's profitability, which had been lower than anticipated. We started by looking at their discount policies.

We noticed that their discounts were offered in multiples of 5: 15%, 10%, 5% (could it be because subconsciously we associate the number five with love, health, empathy?). We sought an explanation from the sales team. 'Well, you know, when a client asks for a discount I start off with 5%, then advance with another 5% to show commitment, and eventually I offer another 5%, just to close the deal', was what we heard. The team acted in good faith, confident that what they were doing was to the company's advantage: they were closing a deal after all. But if even for George Orwell 2 +2 can = 5 (as we read in the wonderful *1984*, which incidentally Orwell wrote in 1948), it was obvious that the sales team had forgotten that other numbers exist beyond five and its multiples, say one, or two, or three; but even six or seven or eight. But joking aside, sometimes habit trumps common sense.

The CEO and I organized training sessions on selling value, for the entire sales team. In one of the modules, we discussed how to manage the discounts – starting off at 5% and offering further decreasing increments, for example an additional 3% and a final 2% – in any case avoiding multiples of 5!

We did not want the sales team to feel that we were blaming them, nor did we want to completely revolutionize their sales practices, and these easily applicable adjustments made an enormous difference to the profitability of the company.

When prices are set, they must be optimized. When haggling begins, discounts must be kept to a minimum. You are working on perception; you are selling the value of a product or service. What is at stake is not simply the name, but the appeal of the company – what the French would call *allure*.

Myth 4 – Dynamic Pricing Is a Black Box

Dynamic pricing is fundamental for businesses regardless of the sector in which they operate, and its significance is destined to grow. If it was originally applied in the air industry, to balance supply and demand, it has become a great opportunity for B2C and B2B companies.

Dynamic pricing enables businesses to set flexible prices for products or services based on current market demands or on specific customers.[19] Despite the flexibility it offers, it is met with scepticism, especially from B2B companies, that consider it a disincentive, or a process that requires special technology for its application. We will debunk this myth.

The mechanisms behind dynamic pricing are indeed governed by a system of rules, formulae, and algorithms. However, to consider the tool as an impenetrable black box managed by a computer means to miss the opportunities that a dynamic management of prices can offer. While there may be some metaphysical, sci-fi elements to it – cue images of gigantic machines that manoeuvre society unbeknownst to humans – we must come to terms with the principles of this technology, especially the aspects that relate to AI.

It is not a question of choosing whether the setting of prices should be left to a computer or to a human being, but rather of finding a solution that combines the strengths of both artificial and human intelligence, whilst not forgetting that even the most advanced quantum computers are programmed using human language, and not the machine language magnified by tech experts.

It is the human brain that establishes the rules and parameters to feed into the dynamic pricing engine. The engine learns, elaborates, and churns out results, but the responsibility for evaluating them and making decisions about pricing level rests solely with people.

Therefore, those who use AI tools should have some level of understanding of their mechanisms, they must be able to read the engine's *white box* – where the adjective 'white' emphasises its transparency, legibility: when the calculation criteria and the parameters to be used are clear, the results are appropriate and can either be adopted or tweaked by senior managers if the circumstances require.[20]

A positive factor of dynamic pricing is that it entails automation whilst also needing user (that is, human) engagement in the planning process, proving that it can be a useful and easy to understand tool, an added bonus that augments the power of the human brain alone by generating supplementary data, and not an impenetrable or senseless black box.

A word of warning: dynamic pricing is not miraculously going to turn salespeople into data scientists. However, if the teams in charge of setting prices are able to provide a general explanation of how the dynamic pricing engine works to the teams in charge of sales, possibly with practical demonstrations, the logic behind prices thus set will make sense to all.

A second myth to debunk is that dynamic pricing is only applicable in a B2C context, that is to say with private customers.

I have personally introduced dynamic pricing to a number of B2B companies, with very positive outcomes, and a substantial and sustainable increase in profitability.

I remember the case of a B2B outfit selling spare parts, whose EBIT (earnings before interest and taxes) margin shot up by 180 basis points thanks to the positive synergy realized between people and machines. Technology provided an invaluable support to the business, helping it deal with hundreds of thousands of products being sold to tens of thousands of customers worldwide. To help us set and constantly update billions of single price points, we implemented an algorithm based on a series of historical data sourced internally and externally – for example, customer types, transactions – as well as data on competitors' prices mined using webcrawlers.

Through machine learning we calculated the specific willingness to pay for each individual customer and product. Then we invited each sales team to review the draft proposed prices and suggest adjustments for specific situations or specific customers. The feedback was fed back into the machine, which learnt the required recalibration criteria.

The constant interaction between users, sales teams, and machines has led to significant improvements: an increase in net prices and in profitability with no loss of volume of sales.

The further myth to debunk is that dynamic pricing is a lengthy and convoluted process that requires complete sets of data to be considered and implemented. In over 20 years of experience as a management advisor, I can state that it would probably be easier to find the proverbial needle in the haystack, or the Graal (Holy Grail), or the philosopher's stone, than to find a company with impeccable data.

No company adopts dynamic pricing having perfect records or infrastructures. If they did, they wouldn't need anything more than they already have!

Imperfect data sets should not discourage a business from considering dynamic pricing, nor make its implementation difficult until data are in order. Quite the opposite, in fact: dynamic pricing eventually improves a company's ability to collect and analyse data at a granular level.

What we did in many companies was start with a limited number of use cases, observed manageable sets of life cycles, and identified exactly the type of data that the customer needed. Use cases give the possibility of introducing external data in the engine, for example, data linked to the per capita income by region, or data on seasonal/ temperature variations.

Dynamic pricing is not solely a technical, tactical, and data-driven tool, but it marks a process of evolution and transformation in the ethos of a company, affecting its internal processes and the perception of its value from outside.

It took a large distributor of building materials less than 8 months to move from manual price setting to a dynamic pricing engine that also returned real-time information on competitors' prices and promotions. The result was an increase in short-term profits by €52 million and a concomitant growth in volumes of sales: 12% in the first year alone, with no attendant negative impact on market or price positioning.

B2B businesses that successfully implemented dynamic pricing started off from a single use case and progressively expanded until – using a reasonable mix of human wisdom and technological capability – they found the perfect format: prices that were sound but also could be modified at relevant times and personalized by customer.

Myth 5 – Pricing Is Based on Cost

It is custom and practice in a business to define prices based on cost.

The concept of *cost plus* pricing is based on the premise that a company should first and foremost cover costs. Hence, once costs have been established, the desired profit margin is added and price is thus obtained.

When costs are fixed and stable, the calculation is simple. However, the application of the formula above implies that whenever costs go down prices correspondingly go down. The customer is the only one to benefit, and the business misses out on the opportunity to increase its profit margins. In addition, the price obtained from this calculation does not necessarily reflect what the client is prepared to pay, the value that the client attributes to the product. The higher the value customers sense a product to have, the more money they will be willing to pay to buy it – but with this pricing approach is willingness to pay won't be captured.

Another problem with the *cost plus* pricing method is that in many businesses it is impossible to determine the unit cost before deciding a price, because unit costs vary according to the levels of production. This happens, for example, in cases where the majority of the costs are fixed and the unit cost is given by the ratio of total costs and quantities or number of items produced. Establishing a unit cost in these conditions and with so many variables is *mission impossible* worthy perhaps only of Tom Cruise as Ethan Matthew Hunt.

The *cost plus* system will set prices too high if the market position is weak and fixed costs are distributed along smaller unit numbers. In case of strong demand, products will be sold at very low prices, due to high quantities.

If this sounds a bit complicated, let's try to cut the Gordian knot using the conviction and stamina that, as the legend goes, enabled Alexander the Great to become the emperor of the Phrygians.

We estimate that roughly 20–25% of businesses set their prices based on the value that their customers attach to their products. The overwhelming majority of businesses set prices based on costs or on the competition, even though this reduces profitability compared to a more mature value-based pricing.

To do something stupid once is stupid. To do it twice is the onset of a philosophy of stupidity.

The value of the book you are holding in your hands now is not the mere sum of the costs of paper, ink, glue, binding, and so on, but (one would hope) it is the value of the content it delivers.

Never be guided by accountants in setting prices. Same as with feelings, you cannot put a figure on something that has a strong irrational dimension simply by doing sums. Purchases are driven by some element of reason, but also by passion, desires, wants. When you buy a house, size is only one thing to consider; there are innumerable imponderables that make you fall in love or not, and determine your decision.

Only if we take into account all the costs incurred in making them, can we be sure that our products will be profitable. But given that these details are held in the accounting department, it is normally the accountants that make pricing decisions – except that they can only focus on *internal* factors.

We know today that the environment in which we live, work, fall in love – the *external* context – matters a lot. By a similar token, the value of our product is affected also by external factors, by the consideration that our customers have of it, and of us. Whilst company accountants can account for internal cost to the last cent, when setting a price that is supposed to represent the value of our product to the outside world we need to consider and include all the intangibles.

It is not true that only small businesses, or businesses that have no direct contact with final users, set prices based on costs. Many companies, whatever their size, follow the same pricing policy. Until 2010, Nike, one of the largest clothing companies in the world with a volume of business of over €44 billion, used to apply a *cost plus* model, simply adding a margin on production costs.[21] Recently, however, the company moved to a pricing model based on value. Don Blair, former CFO at Nike, explained that 'with the strength of our brand and the flow of innovation we have into the marketplace, we have been essentially trading the consumer up to premium product. . . . So what this is is that long-term trend to building [a] product that's premium for the consumer and can carry that price premium.'[22] A substantial part of Nike's spectacular growth – in 2022 the gross profit margin was 46% – can be attributed to this change of pricing strategy and the offer of a product that the consumer views as premium.

In 2022, the German luxury clothing company Hugo Boss recorded global sales for €3.7 billion, moving from a cost plus to a value pricing strategy.[23]

A classic example used to debunk the myth of *cost plus* pricing refers to the price of the bright yellow or red tinted brakes that can be seen in the wheel rims of supercars. What is the cost of producing them? About €1000. What would the *cost plus* pricing strategy suggest? That adding 30% to the cost would yield a reasonable margin, and take the price to €1,300.

Now guess what Porsche charges for this braking system. The list price is around €9,000 for what they call Porsche Ceramic Composite Brakes.[24] Fair do's, some might say: if I spend €130,000 on a Porsche Cayenne, I certainly don't want to miss out on my bright red brakes. And do you know what Ferrari charges for the same product? €16,000. Some *cost plus* this is!

The same principle applies if you opt for metallic paint for your new car: the price tag will go up by something between €800 and €2,000. And the price of metallic paint? Less than €90 per coat. All cars must be painted anyway. The only difference in your case is that the need to add an additional coat that contains metallic pigments.

The examples above prove that willingness to pay goes beyond real production costs, but it is a factor of the value that customers attach to the product.

Creating in customers the perception of a high value enables companies to set high prices against low or non-existent additional costs.

This is the fundamental principle of pricing: there is no link between clients' willingness to pay and cost to the company. Hence prices must be based on the perceived value of items, not the cost to the company of making them.

Myth 6 – Price Management Means Increasing or Lowering Prices

When asked how they manage prices, many company managers explain how they have raised or lowered them.

But managing prices is not a simple question of moving them up or down a certain axis. When price management focuses on perceived value, sales are generated without touching prices at all.

Here is an example of how prices can be managed without the need to change them.

The CEO of a company producing forklift trucks hired me to help them improve their price management, as their level of profitability was below what had been forecasted. One of the first things I did was interview the sales staff, in order to work out the issues they had with pricing. 'We sell our forklift trucks to logistics providers and to the manufacturing industry. We deal with purchasing managers who are determined to get the lowest price possible. Our forklift trucks are the same as those of our competitors: they have 4 wheels and are made of metal', they all would say, all concluding that 'in order not to lose a sale to the competition we have to give larger and larger discounts'. Totally predictable.

Buyers were aggressive negotiators, who intimated that they were ready to take their business elsewhere, unless they got the price they wanted. My client was at a crossroads.

Imagine going into a forest – a place that has its rules, that can be dangerous, and that is populated by creatures competing for the same thing. Imagine the market to be like a forest. You have to decide something at the outset: either you plan your itinerary carefully, or you take is as it comes, changing course, or stride, or stance in response to what you find there. For many businesses, discounts are one form of adaptative response to the context: they prefer to lower their prices (which means securing a sale, although with reduced profit margins) to holding the original price (which potentially means missing out on sale and profit). *Give discounts or lose the sale? That is the question.*

But not surprisingly, there is a third option, which nobody can see.

A company should illustrate – with tangible data – the virtues of their product, and demonstrate that the added value customers would get is worth much more than the price they are paying to get it.

For my forklift truck producing clients we decided to equip the sales team with sheets providing extensive information about the trucks and illustrations of the advantages of using them. We ensured that we provided evidence of the direct and indirect impact that our trucks would make on the users' business in terms of profitability. Essentially before we even considered making any changes to prices, we had applied a price philosophy. We had articulated the story of the company, its experience and standing in that field of work. We had taken the company history as testimony of product value. This made the sales team aware of features of the trucks they were selling that they had neglectfully taken for granted: having understood them from the inside (within the company) they could competently and enthusiastically exalt them to the outside world (their clients). And so, potential customers were told about aspects that had never before been mentioned – like the quality and robustness of the forklifts, meaning less risk of breakages and of costly repair, which in turn meant no interruption of activity and more productivity for their business. Or like the ergonomic seats that supported the operator's back – meaning less risk of back pain, and fewer days off sick. Imagine what this meant for somebody who spent their entire working day sitting on one of those trucks. And more: the integrated software that communicated with the warehouse was yet another way to improve productivity. And finally: the after-sales support, offering prompt intervention with spares delivered the same day.

What this proved is that you can quantify value even in a product that offers little or no potential for differentiation. The information sheets had provided many suggestions to the sales team to illustrate, quantify, and sell value to their customers.

The salesperson who had been lost for words when a customer threatened to take their business elsewhere now could say: 'True, our forklift truck costs 20% more than your low-price model from Asia. However, I can show you that that difference translates into benefits worth €20,000, and precisely: a) you don't have to stop using it while you wait for spare parts or ordinary maintenance; b) a sophisticated software that increases efficiency; c) higher quality of chassis and parts; d) higher level of comfort for the operator, and so on.'

Imagine describing a trip that has impressed you. You would enthusiastically talk about what you have seen and done; perhaps you would omit specific details but would convey the beauty of your experience and the joy you felt. After you describe the pleasure of eating at a vegan place in Copenhagen, your interlocutor will want to book a place straight away!

The message for the purchasing managers was unequivocal: you may spend more now, but you will have a higher return on your investment than with any other seller of forklift trucks. If you pay more now, you will pay less later.

The profitability of the company and the satisfaction levels of its customers have increased exponentially. This goes to show that it is possible to manage prices without changing them: identifying, quantifying, and communicating the value of your product to your customers will make them more willing to buy from you, and reduce your need to offer discounts (which is good for your profitability!).

Analysing the value that customers attribute to a product enables the identification of the aspects of that product where there is a misalignment between perceived value and price. Whenever the value perceived by the buyer is higher than the item price, price can comfortably be raised without the risk of losing sales.

Myth 7 – Customers Are After Low Prices

'The market is global. It is transparent. Customers' main concern is to spend as little as possible.' This is something that we hear often, in different contexts and parts of the world. Is it true, though?

Let's take this step by step. A customer who is mainly concerned with price has low expectations in terms of the quality of the product. For this reason, the customer is mindful of price variations. The customer will not justify a higher price tag if a product appears to be similar to another, because the customer is unable to see that different characteristics translate into tangibly different value.

Are customers really price aware? In the consumer goods market, customers often state that price is a core criterion in their choice. And yet their behaviour would suggest otherwise.

There are studies that analyse the level of price awareness in customers, and all reach the conclusion that this is limited. One study shows that customers generally under- or overestimate prices by 6 to 20%.[25] Another shows that 50% of customers in a supermarket were unable to tell the price of the item they had just put in their trolley, and that over 50% of those who had picked up something at a reduced price had not been aware that it had been reduced.[26]

In one of our projects for the energy sector, we interviewed thousands of residential customers about their latest electricity or gas bill. Only 3% could remember the correct amount they had to pay.

The findings of tens of academic studies published subsequently were along the same lines. Over 50% of consumers are unable to recall the price of items they buy frequently, and find it easier to remember unfamiliar prices than familiar ones.[27]

And yet, if questioned directly on the criteria they apply to make decisions about purchases – which is what we often ask in our consultancy projects – many respond that price matters, a lot, if not most. This is the first paradox of price response: in theory, consumers are very sensitive to price; in practice, evidence shows, they are not.

The second paradox, as emerges in many studies, is that companies are convinced that consumers' price sensitivity is high, when in reality it is very low. They believe costumers instinctively haggle and are willing to move over to a better deal whenever they have the chance. In reality, consumers are mythological creatures of habit, their behaviour often shows much less sensitivity to and awareness of price than they care to admit.

There are of course customers who look for cheap deals and remember the price they have paid for their purchases. These are not the majority, and it is essential to identify what their defining features are. To find the answer to this question, we must segment the market, identify the characteristics and the different requirements of the individual segments, and customize our offer accordingly.

I have conducted hundreds of segmentation projects for businesses in many sectors, and I have concluded that the consumer segment that is most focussed on price is 25% or less of the total. The other 75% look for quality, cost effectiveness, after-sales care, availability, speed, personalization, certification, exclusivity, and so on. For clients whose main concern is price, the offer can be disaggregated, so that what is presented is a more basic product configuration, which is consequently cheaper. This means that there should be a series of different product configurations, with correspondingly different prices.

So far, we have discussed private customers. We can now discuss business customers and their sensitivity to price.

One of our recent studies examined the factors that make an industrial client choose one key-account supplier over its competitors. An interesting fact is that B2B clients are more sensitive to benefits than they are to cost. Besides, for many business purchases, the initial purchase price accounts only for 15–30% of the expenditure incurred during the life cycle of that product. The majority of expenditures comes after the purchase – for example, for the installation, ordinary and extraordinary maintenance, spare parts, energy consumption, and disposal.

So, what business buyers tend to assess is not the purchase price, but the TCO (the total cost of ownership). In many cases this is the most important criterion, way more important that the price.

Those who sell to B2B clients can secure the sale if they are able to quantify the total value that the product offers, outlining the sum of the measurable benefits – for example, increase in performance, a more efficient use of raw materials, reduction in production costs, energy savings – and of the qualitative benefits (prompt intervention post-sale, reputation of the brand, problem-solving support, and so on). With all this in place, a premium price can be set.

To sum up, differentiation of the offer is possible in both B2B and B2C contexts. Only very few customers make a purchase based solely on price, and the approach that offers the highest returns is one that foregrounds the value of the product, showing how this exceeds its price tag.

Summary

7 myths crush the potential of the pricing lever

Business who debunked the myths record higher than average profitability. Perseus frees Andromeda from the chains, and from the monster. Think pricing, act pricing.

Myth 1 – there is correlation between market share and profit

In fact, this is not true. Rather than aiming for large volumes of sold quantities and market shares, businesses should have a clear view of what their customers need and what it is that they value, and set their prices based on the perceived value of their product.

A market share is sustainable if sales come from products of high perceived value, sold at prices that guarantee reasonable profit margins.

A market share is unsustainable if it relies on prices below costs or with insufficient margins. These erode profits, trigger price wars, and may lead to company failure.

Myth 2 – any product and commodity can be differentiated

Any product and any service can be differentiated, which means that its price can be increased. Market leaders, with higher-than-average profits, do not consider any of their products to be commodities. Some elements of what they offer may be more difficult to differentiate compared to what competitors do, but there is a wide range of aspects where differentiation could make an important difference – for instance, after-sales services, warranties, terms of payment, delivery times, or product certification.

Myth 3 – small variations in price have a negligible impact on profits

The sum of many small variations in price has a substantial impact. For this reason, listed prices must be adhered to as much as possible, and discounts kept to a minimum. The pricing lever impacts earnings, and the sum of small variations in several different price levers makes a difference to profitability.

Myth 4 – dynamic pricing is a black box

The most effective form of dynamic pricing is planned starting from a set of rules determined by human intelligence, it produces clear and understandable proposals, and can be likened to a white box. It is not necessary to have perfect data sets to implement it, and a good start would be to test it against specific use cases. Dynamic pricing is applicable both to B2B and to B2C businesses, to which it brings substantial benefits.

Myth 5 – pricing is based on cost

It is value, not cost, that should determine price. Setting the price of a product on its cost has the advantage of being an easy thing to do, but it fails to consider external factors, such as what customers are effectively willing to pay.

Myth 6 – price management means increasing or lowering prices

Managing prices means identifying and quantifying the value that customers receive. When this principle is followed, the desired volume of sales can be achieved without the need to reduce prices. The value associated with a product justifies its price.

Myth 7 – customers are after low prices

While some customers may consider prices as a deal clincher, this is not a universal attitude. Private customers are often unaware of the prices they pay, and business customers are more concerned about other factors beyond price. It is therefore essential to segment the market and to design sales policies that are customized to each segment, for example, in some cases low price instead of high quality, in others affordability, after-sales care, availability, speed of delivery, personalization, exclusivity, for example.

PART III
HOW TO WIN

HOW TO WIN

SUCCESS WITH THE PRICING TRANSFORMATION

'Men learn while they teach.'

Lucius Annaeus Seneca, philosopher

Introduction

On that morning, the skies of Paris were the colour of powdered sugar. He left the house in May, or was it perhaps October? He couldn't remember anything. Nothing else mattered except his experiments: breakfast, lunch, dinner – days quickly passing by with more or less important, more or less different events. Distillation kits, Bunsen burners, wide pants, and frock coats – what was the music people listened to in the eighteenth century? And all those people in Paris, what was going on?, in the air the smell of snow and apple pie. Only his experiments, while around him owls hooted in the night, and young people addressed the crowds in the days. But Antoine – oh, no – all Antoine cared about was his experiments. The laboratory and his ideas that turned into numbers. Things that turned into other things, in the infinite chain of centuries. How many experiments had he performed in the last 2 months? He couldn't even recall that. Nor was he able to say if he had eaten yesterday, or what colour Martine's eyes were.

'Quantities', the boy thought, 'It is the quantities that can reveal the true essence of objects.'

After all, he had studied this since he was a young chemist – 'Nothing comes from nothing,' the ancient Greeks said – that's why he had started weighing substances, observing reactions. He wanted to know the true meaning of life. Death. The colours in between. The demon of obsession had captured him only to make him, one day, one of the greatest names in history.

It was precisely that morning that Antoine, after months of work, had one of the most important insights that humanity would remember: it was clear before his bewildered eyes, the scales gleaming in the sunlight, that if the reaction of an object occurred within a closed container, without the contents coming into contact with the out-side, the masses of the reactants were equal to those of the products, a process still far from being clarified, except that Antoine had the gift of synthesis on his side: 'In a chemical reaction, nothing is cre-ated, nothing is destroyed, but everything is transformed', the words slipped from his mouth in a breath. Nothing comes from nothing, it was true. In between, everything was taking shape, kneading life into what was around, dissolved, and began again.

It was 1789, and Antoine de Lavoisier didn't know it yet, but he had just grasped one of the most important principles of physics: the Law of Conservation of Mass. It was 1789, the year of the French Revolution, and an unknown chemist would forever change the course of history.

Nothing is created, nothing is destroyed, everything is transformed: this applies to everything, including us, our insights, our projects, our ideas about the world; even to economic theories, to political ones too. And yes, even to pricing.

Preparing the Pricing Transformation

This book does not aim to be a miraculous synthesis of all the transformations required to achieve 'The' solution that we all desire. Lavoisier knew full well that you cannot explain the entire world, the meaning of life, with one theory alone. A theory, however, can help systematize things, it can implement a process of synthesis, in the case in point here, of economic chemistry.

In this chapter, we will focus on the 10 rules to follow to transform price management, if not in a chemical manner, at least in an economic one.

Transformation is a necessity. Everything must undergo transformations if it doesn't want to perish. The first thing to understand is that evolution is natural – it is a feature of simple and complex organisms alike, of individuals as well as of communities. Everything must evolve, transform, or risk remaining stuck. Those who fail to grasp the necessity of transformation do not understand the significance of change, the value of being able to respond by adapting to what new situations, contexts, and techniques require. In short, to move with Time, the great sculptor.

This also applies to the concept of transforming value into price, especially because prices change with varying contexts. Today, I assign a certain value to a glass of natural water. But what value would I give it if I found myself in the desert? Or if instead of being here, reading a book, I happened to be in ancient Roman times, like General Maximus, the Spaniard from *Gladiator*? Or in the near future as hypothesized by the World Bank, which suggests that by 2050, due to climate change, many of us and our grandchildren will have to relocate due to drought or rising sea levels (which is why the Indonesian government is having to move the capital, Jakarta, now submerged by water, with all the implications this decision has for people, businesses, and services).

Based on my experience, embarking on a path of change will allow a company to monetize its value to the fullest. This outcome will be a tangible increase in profits, usually between 2% and 8% of revenue return, depending on the maturity of the current price management. However, first and foremost, let's explore the methods of implementing this transformation.

Firstly, integrating the 10 rules of this highly efficient new pricing approach into the company's context will require rigour and discipline. It is a known fact that people are resistant to change. Additionally, it will be important to regularly promote change in order to keep the transformative force of the programme alive, while monitoring its progress.

However, we must remain realistic throughout. Nothing is created, nothing is destroyed, but above all, not everything happens instantaneously. It takes time and perseverance. Often, a shift in mindset within the organization is necessary. Furthermore, consensus must be earned. Some will follow us because of our reputation or simply because of our track record of achieving results. However, there will be individuals who, rightfully so, may oppose us –dissenting voices, whispers, handshakes. They will demand evidence and proof of the expected benefits. They will argue that what works for other companies may not work here. After all, we know that every company is different, unique, and increasingly green, just like the grass on the other side.

The reasons of others are the lifeblood of healthy competition. Democracy forms the basis for a debate between divergent yet equally valid positions. There is no singular truth, but there are choices. And decisions.

Resistance can be overcome. Dissenters can be sounding boards, mirrors, and if we can bring them to our side, if we can make them see things from our perspective, this will add value to what we propose – having persuaded those who were holding tight to their own viewpoint because they had never considered alternative possibilities. They had never thought that transformation was possible. Why? Because it is easier to continue with what is familiar, it is easier to let the days pass by doing what is tried and tested. In the belief that, by doing so, what we have accomplished will remain, forever. Unfortunately, forever doesn't exist or, at least, it seems rather elusive, according to those who have written about love and death, such as Homer or Shakespeare.

The many success stories presented in the various chapters should provide the foundation for demonstrating the importance and benefits of transformation.

Now, after many words, let's see what concrete actions need to be taken.

Firstly, I recommend that you create a short list of questions to aid in the preparatory phase of the transformation, which can also help define priorities.

One fairly simple assessment question, for example, is to rate the company on a scale of 1 to 7, where '7' represents the best rating and '1' represents its negative counterpart:

Questions

- Are monetization and price leverage management a priority for the company's top executives?
- Is a profit-driven culture deeply ingrained in the company?

- Does an effective pricing governance structure exist?

- Is there a full understanding of the value created, and a corresponding marketing of that value?

- Is pricing effectively differentiated?

- Is technology being used proactively to manage pricing?

- Does the company succeed in increasing prices to the point where they capture the value provided?

- Is there consensus that price wars are detrimental and should always be avoided?

- Is there awareness, both in words and actions, that pricing myths need to be debunked?

- Is the appropriate attention given to maintaining the price image?

The further away from a score of 70, the greater the potential to be realized through a pricing transformation. If only some of the themes covered in the questions receive particularly low scores, these are the areas to prioritize for improvement. On the other hand, the closer the score is to 70, the more aligned the organization will be with the '10 principles' outlined in the book. As a result, achieving a significant increase in return on sales and having above-average pricing maturity will be more likely. This will translate into an additional profit increase, maintaining the same resources and organization. The mindset will have changed, and at that point the transformation will not only be absorbed but actively implemented in all economic processes and business relationships.

Elements of Success in Pricing Transformation

Over the past 20 years, I have supported a large number of transformations in various industries and geographical areas. There are several elements that contribute to the success of revenue-focused transformations. Five of these have consistently proven to be particularly relevant in the various programmes conducted.

1. Establish a specific plan for your company's transformation

'No wind is favourable for the sailor who doesn't know which port he wants to reach', said the Roman philosopher Lucius Annaeus Seneca. Indeed, the first factor for success in transforming pricing is knowing which port you want to reach, that is, having a clear idea of the type of pricing you aim for and setting a plan to achieve those objectives.

This plan should be tailored to your company, based on the level of maturity you want to achieve, starting from a lower level. It should consider the competitive context in which you operate, the changing needs of customers, the internal corporate culture, your competitive advantages, and all the elements that impact the achievement of the set goal. The coveted destination, the Golden Fleece for us Argonauts of the *Mare Monstrum* that is the global market. Undoubtedly, you can draw inspiration from best practices, observing how other companies have successfully completed pricing transformations. However, a specific plan is still necessary, customized to your specific needs. Every ship has its own cargo, its specific waterline, its crew, and its captain, in good and bad times.

When I have supported companies in formulating this plan over the years, I have often created a brief vision or target picture to give an image of how monetization would be managed in the future. This helps make the objective verifiable because the most important thing for humans (from cave paintings to today) is to see, materially, what the risks are, how to overcome them, to envision the ideal world, the reason we are fighting that battle: the broader sense of purpose.

'What is Rome?' Caesar would ask. Therefore, touching, being able to visualize what we previously only imagined often motivates us even more. The whiteboard is there, concrete, made up of formulas and numbers, vision, and milestones that bring us closer to our promised land.

2. Let a champion lead the transformation, involving a team

What would have become of Menelaus's army without Achilles? The Trojan War would have unfolded differently: true, Ilium would not have mourned its princes; on the other hand, the West would not have had one of the most important works of human intellect, the *Iliad*.

As in the case of the wooden horse, once the plan for pricing transformation is in place, action must be taken to initiate the work. However, before doing so, another critical factor for success must be established: who will lead this project? The person's name! Ideally, the individual leading the pricing transformation should have both commercial and pricing experience and be well-established within the company. Their experience and existing relationships lend them credibility and practical guidance on how to proceed.

The champion of the pricing transformation, the leader of this project, must be supported by all the top executives of the company. It could be the CEO directly, or the head of marketing or finance, who act as true 'transformation sponsors' serving as mentors to the champion. Often, executives are uncertain whether to appoint a seasoned, experienced but weary professional or instead a younger, ambitious but impulsive one. Over the years, I have seen several companies that have had excellent experiences with veteran profiles. These individuals, thanks to their seniority, have often experienced disruptive change phases, crisis situations, and shifts in direction caused by competitive turbulence. These situations have forced them to abandon established practices to facilitate transformation, which, as we know, is not always delicate and peaceful. Sometimes, the transition from one phase to another for a company happens abruptly and unexpectedly. The ability to navigate through change is, therefore, a fundamental quality required for this role. In the absence of such a figure, a person with solid experience on the commercial front, who knows the customers and the market, and enjoys a good reputation among marketing and sales colleagues, can be recruited.

Once the champion is nominated, the team must be built around them. If the team, the crew, in other words, the members brought on board, come from diverse areas (one from marketing, another from sales, one from controlling, another from information systems, and so on), it ensures both support and buy-in from the key intra-company functions.

That being said, due to its heterogeneity and size, the team does not dedicate itself full time to this initiative but simultaneously attends to all critical phases of the transformation.

3. Transformation is a marathon, not a sprint

Two-thirds of change projects fail due to difficulties in accepting change. Transforming the way a company monetizes its activities presents various risks and complexities. It is important to be aware of this even when we are convinced and conscious that it is the only thing to do. Pushing the accelerator, however, can become counterproductive. Instead, we need to learn to wait for the right moment, as if we were witnessing the cherry blossom, practicing the art of waiting like a Zen monk sitting by the river, waiting for the mortal remains of the enemy to pass. Inhale and focus. Especially when tackling multiple projects simultaneously: from strategy to processes, from tools to culture. Exhale and strike.

Like all initiatives that require change, pricing transformation also requires support and constant attention. It is a marathon, not a sprint. A marathon takes time and effort that should not be underestimated. However, the result, in the form of increased profits and better focus on the value offered to customers, will not be delayed.

After starting the transformation marathon, continuous motion towards achieving one milestone after another should be facilitated with regular progress updates: work, internal communication, coaching aimed at changing culture and mindset, training interventions to assimilate the new way of operating.

Here is where, after the shift in mindset, logic comes into play – the counting, the analysis of data. To implement it, we need indicators and metrics that can reveal progress. These indicators should create transparency regarding our objectives. They should be able to transform mere numbers into the ability to understand, analyse, and ultimately make choices.

Certain metrics can be qualitative, as is the case when, for example, we have a series of notes that highlight how the company culture is oriented towards value and profits rather than volume generation (strong, moderate, or low value orientation). Other metrics will instead be quantitative, allowing for immediate comparison, such as the increase in average prices (current average prices compared to the previous year).

Competing in a marathon also means that we need to shift our orientation in decision making. Transformation is a medium- to long-term process: the benefits of pricing will not manifest in a single fiscal year; they are an investment in the future. A change in paradigm, after all, does just that. It changes our habits and short-term vision – we see the tip of our nose but not the moon – and it teaches us to think in a dual manner. This is why a higher level of pricing maturity, the introduction of a new tool or process, once implemented, yields benefits not only in the first year but also in the subsequent years.

We live in an increasingly dynamic world: the competitive landscape is constantly evolving, customer needs change, the macroeconomic situation fluctuates, crises alternate with periods of strong growth. When we reach the end of the transformation, we set ourselves in motion again: the marathon continues.

4. Do not retreat in the face of difficulties

Change is not always welcomed with open arms, at least not by everyone. Those who oppose or are more sceptical eagerly await the first signs of difficulties – such as losing a customer due to a new pricing strategy – to produce evidence solely to prove that their doubts were justified.

In this regard, it is advisable to identify the main possible barriers and risks that may be encountered along the transformation journey and define proactive actions to mitigate their consequences and, if possible, overcome them.

An example of a risk could be losing the support of the sales team when they are asked to adopt sales practices that are more profitable for the company before changing their own incentive system. If the sales team has been given specific objectives at the beginning of the year, a programme that changes the rules of the game during the fiscal period – as the accountants would call it – inevitably creates difficulties and resistance. For example, it may conflict with goals that favoured other actions (such as focussing on operating margins) or previously agreed upon objectives (perhaps centred around achieving certain sales quantities).

Although unfortunate, such a situation can occur when a pricing transformation is launched part way through the fiscal year for which objectives and incentives have already been agreed upon. Therefore, difficulties of this nature need to be anticipated in order to propose solutions that allow for overcoming such obstacles. In the aforementioned example, efforts should be made to explain the logic of the new incentive system to the sales team in an understandable and clear manner, and to propose a transitional solution for the current year that does not penalize them but rather uncovers further potential. Transformations sometimes happen in this way, one step at a time.

5. Share and celebrate successes

When we achieve the goal, and only at that point, we should take a moment to share and communicate the milestones reached; it is the best way to support the pricing transformation. Everyone is invited to the grand celebration after the battle, just as in ancient times with the celebrations of Dionysus, or when the team captain lifts the cup in present times.

While the evidence of success is missing, the power of storytelling, the narrative – which is the vehicle for the transmission of skills, of lessons to learn, and a moment of celebration – will be missing too. This applies to both individual business units and to all levels of an organization that wants to be successful. When they discover the value of sharing, they will be the first ones to want to implement the changes resulting from the pricing transformation.

The narrative of that success will be like an icebreaker along the path to the next collective adventure. Every transformation is, in fact, nothing more than a new journey or another way to chart a course. But this can happen only if we are able to recognize the dangers, consider the structure and weight we carry, what needs to be acquired, and what, like ballast, should be left behind, of what we were before. We must do this before the new course, as the US President Franklin Delano Roosevelt would have said.

But what can be done to break the ice? For example, start a large transformation programme with a small pilot project first. The goal of the pilot episode (as they are also called in communications) is to generate evidence that there is potential and that the company can seize that potential through a renewal, resulting in a benefit.

Drawing from my own experiences, I proposed a gradual approach at one point to a well-known furniture manufacturer who wanted to revolutionize their pricing, which was of the cost-plus type. The objective was to demonstrate the existence of concrete benefits that the group, consisting of several business units, could achieve.

The work began by analysing the pricing within just one unit, not the main one but not an insignificant one either, let's say an 'average' one, through a targeted pricing health check, which is a diagnosis of the pricing management approach, lasting a few weeks.

The results were immediate and evident to everyone: the screening was able to identify a whole series of pricing management improve-ments that could be implemented, some in the medium term and others immediately. The latter, known as quick wins, included price rounding. The price list containing all the furniture in that division had never been optimized, and due to multiple cost-based price increases, it was not calibrated according to psychological price thresholds.

This lever alone was able to generate several hundred thousand Euros in increased profits without losing volumes. Furthermore, it was put into action immediately. The business unit that initiated the initial pilot was celebrated for believing in the initiative and supporting the work. They became ambassadors for the benefits in a subsequent targeted pricing programme. The success story was shared within the company, generating significant interest.

Seeing this success in terms of increased profits in the pilot unit, the leaders of all the other business units in the group immediately wanted to be involved in the transformation. They understood how optimized pricing would help them achieve their goals.

Sharing and celebrating the successes of a pricing transformation become a catalyst for a change project, especially when there is resistance to change. The credibility and attention gained after sharing a success like that of the furniture manufacturer becomes a driving force for transformation. Moreover, celebrating the success and attributing it to the colleagues involved (from management control to sales) serves as a catalyst to strengthen trust and carry the initiative forward.

Launching the Pricing Transformation

We have gone through the 10 rules together to transform the way we monetize, with various real-life cases from different industries operating in diverse geographies. Then we have seen the questions we need to ask ourselves to determine where to start and what success factors to keep in mind.

Now it's time to draw conclusions.

Based on the developed plan, the first thing to do – with low costs and immediate results – is to start a pilot project. At that point, after sharing the results, the pricing transformation can be initiated throughout the entire company!

As we have seen, the term 'pricing transformation' may sound limiting. The scope of the concept is much broader. It involves implementing a business strategy that impacts all functions of the company, in every part of the organization. It is a long-term change where the concept of value creation and extraction becomes the common factor driving the efforts of the entire company.

In this way, the fate of the company is changed. By generating and capturing value, the company will have many more resources to continue evolving and prospering.

Becoming a company with above-average profits is not a random event. Just as the ability to capture value is not an innate talent that one either has or doesn't have. To achieve higher margins and effectively monetize customers' willingness to pay, a systematic approach deeply rooted in the company's culture and processes is needed.

The ability to capture value needs to be developed, evolved, and institutionalized. Companies that follow the 10 rules in this book can distinguish themselves for their higher profitability.

For companies that have differentiated themselves in their industries with above-average profits by adhering to the 10 rules and placing the concept of value at the centre of their operations, the reasoning presented in the book seems entirely logical, natural, and obvious. However, it is not always the case.

Let's not forget that such companies are the exception. The majority of companies – at least 75% in every industry sector – suffer from reduced margins and are unaware of or neglect the 10 rules.

Clearly, for many, these 10 rules are not logical, natural, and obvious at all. Otherwise, there would be a significantly higher percentage of companies with superior profits. And in turn, we would be out of work. So, it's all for the best!

To excel in monetization, one must strive and apply the 10 rules better than their competitors. There is no one-size-fits-all formula. It takes perseverance, dedication, teamwork, and a lot of practice.

Just as there is no absolute and general timeframe for everyone, each individual company knows its own timing, that is, when it is time to take the first step towards pricing transformation.

The 10 rules explored in this book aim to be a facilitation platform for the journey of a harmonious and complex transformation that will elevate the level of pricing maturity and, with it, the profits.

If, after reading this book, you are inspired to implement the 10 rules in your company, I would be very curious to know how they will be applied. Who knows, thanks to your efforts, the company you work for may become a success story that could be included in the next edition of this book. That's why I have provided my LinkedIn profile and an email at the end of this book. I would be pleased to stay updated on your progress.

In any case, I wish you all the very best of luck,

Dan
zatta.danilo@gmail.com
www.linkedin.com/in/danilo-zatta/

Summary

This book illustrates 10 concrete rules that will help you transform the way prices are managed within your company, unlocking profitable growth. A few preliminary rating scale questions help prepare for the transformation while also defining the priorities to follow. The further the results deviate from the full score, the greater the potential to be seized with a pricing transformation. However, if only some of the issues encoded in the questions receive particularly low scores, these may be the vectors on which to immediately trigger change.

There are five elements that favour the success of a pricing transformation:

1. Establish a specific plan to be followed. 'No wind is favourable for the sailor who does not know which port he wants to reach.' In fact, the first key to success in increasing the maturity of your monetization approach is to have a clear idea of the type of pricing to strive for, setting a plan to achieve the objectives.

2. Let the transformation be guided by a champion, involving a team. Once the plan is ready, action can be taken. To start the work, it is necessary to determine who will lead the expedition and who will be in the crew.

3. Transformation is a marathon, not a sprint. Like all initiatives that require change, a pricing transformation also takes time and attention. Being 'marathon-minded' means that the orientation must be long-term, just like the benefits that derive from it.

4. Not backing down in the face of difficulties. In a pricing transformation, obstacles and difficulties will be encountered.

Identifying the main possible barriers and risks and defining actions capable of mitigating the consequences in advance proves to be the best way to overcome them.

5. Sharing and celebrating successes. Communicating the positive outcomes is the best way to support pricing transformation: everyone will want to be part of a successful programme, which also strengthens confidence in the initiative.

We have gone through the 10 principles to transform the way companies monetize value, using various business cases from different industries operating in different geographical locations. Then, we looked at what questions should be asked in advance of any action plan, so that the appropriate starting point can be established. Finally, we considered success factors that need to be kept in mind.

Now is the time to draw conclusions for your company and start your own journey.

I wish you all a successful pricing transformation!

ACKNOWLEDGEMENTS

I feel extremely lucky to have worked for more than 20 years on pricing and monetization topics that are innovative and of strategic relevance. I also feel privileged that I am able to work with companies and investors across all industries and geographies to help them prepare for the future and create strategies that will enable them to grow profitably.

This management advisory work allows me to learn every day, and a book like this wouldn't have been possible without it. I would like to acknowledge the many managers who have helped me get to where I am today – all the great people in the companies I have worked with who put their trust in me to help them and in return gave me so much new knowledge and experience. I must also thank everyone who has shared their thinking with me and has allowed me to collect and quote case studies and secret success recipes as well as concrete examples of successful pricing transformations. I would like to express my most sincere gratitude to them. I am also lucky to personally know many of the key thinkers, pricing experts, and thought leaders in business, and I hope you all know how much I value your inputs and our exchanges.

I would also like to thank monetization passionates, practitioners, CEOs, advisors, and sparring partners for the enriching discussions and deep dives on all aspects of pricing transformations.

ACKNOWLEDGEMENTS

I was humbled by the amazing endorsements received by scholars, C-levels, corporate leaders and journalists. I am so grateful for the time dedicated to review this book and provide such great statements by all these great persons. I am so honored and still overwhelmed.

A special person that I am also very grateful for is Mauro Garofalo. Thank you for your sparring, friendship and professionalism in all the interactions we have.

I would like to thank my editorial and publishing team for all your help and support. Taking any book from idea to publication is a team effort and I really appreciate your input and help – thank you, Annie Knight, Laura Cooksley, Julie Attrill, Vithusha Rameshan, Suganya Selvaraj, Susan Cerra, Nicoletta Di Ciolla, and Alice Hadaway for having supported with enthusiasm this editorial project right from the beginning and for their support in the previous editorial project.

My biggest acknowledgment goes to my wife, Babette, and our three children, Natalie, Sebastian, and Marilena, for giving me the inspiration, motivation, and space to do what I love: learning and sharing ideas that will help companies growing and prospering.

ABOUT THE AUTHOR

Danilo Zatta is one of the world's leading advisors and thought leaders in the field of Pricing and TopLine Excellence. As a management consultant for more than 25 years, he advises and coaches many of the world's best-known organizations. He has led hundreds of projects at both national and global level for multinationals, small and medium-sized companies as well as investment funds in numerous industries, generating substantial profit increases. His advisory work typically focuses on programmes of excellence in pricing and sales, revenue growth, corporate strategies, TopLine transformations, and redesign of business and revenue models.

He has acted as CEO, Partner and Managing Director at some of the world's leading consulting firms, building up international subsidiaries, entire pricing and sales practices, and fostering growth. Dan has also written 20 books including the international best seller *The Pricing Model Revolution* (Wiley, 2022), translated into 10 languages, *At the Heart of Leadership* (Routledge, 2023) and *Revenue Management in Manufacturing* (Springer, 2016). He has also published hundreds of articles in different languages and regularly acts as a keynote speaker at conferences, events, associations and at leading universities. He also supports as a personal TopLine coach several CEOs of leading companies.

Dan graduated with honours in economics and commerce from Luiss in Rome and University College Dublin in Ireland. He got an MBA from INSEAD in Fontainebleau, France and Singapore. Finally, he completed a PhD in revenue management and pricing at the Technical University of Munich in Germany.

Dan has been recognized amongst the Top 5 Pricing Thought Leaders on LinkedIn, in the list of the most engaging and impactful pricing thought leaders globally. The Financial Times defined him as 'one of the world's leading pricing minds'.

Connect with Dan on LinkedIn at www.linkedin.com/in/danilo-zatta

If you would like to talk to Dan about any advisory work or speaking engagements, please contact him via email at:
zatta.danilo@gmail.com

PREVIOUS WILEY BOOK OF DAN ZATTA

THE PRICING MODEL REVOLUTION

International Pricing best seller, translated into 10+ languages

An incisive and accessible blueprint to pricing your company's products and services

In *The Pricing Model Revolution: How Pricing Will Change the Way We Sell and Buy On and Offline*, world-renowned pricing expert Danilo Zatta delivers an essential and engaging blueprint to building an enduring competitive advantage with insightful pricing models. In the book, you'll learn to identify the best monetization approaches for your products and how to execute the one that makes the most sense for your business. From freemium to subscription, pay-per-use, and even neuropricing, the author discusses every available option and shows you how to choose.

Although it's rigorous and evidence backed, *The Pricing Model Revolution* avoids an overly academic perspective in favour of providing you with concrete, practical guidance you can apply immediately to start generating more revenue. You'll learn things like:

* How to make smart and innovative pricing a core component of your next product offering.

* How to distinguish between every new, future-oriented monetization approach.

* The factors to consider when you are choosing on a new pricing model for your most popular products.

An essential read for C-level executives, managers, entrepreneurs, and sales team leaders, *The Pricing Model Revolution* belongs on the bookshelves of every business leader seeking to learn more about one of the foundational topics driving top-line revenue and bottom-line profitability today.

'There are many books on pricing. This is the best read for managers wanting a review of several innovative pricing methods.'
Philip Kotler, Professor of International Marketing, Kellogg School of Management

'A useful handbook that offers a fresh perspective on pricing models. Not only will these models help you increase your profits, but they also give you a simple and practical tool to better understand your business.'

Stephan Winkelmann, Chairman and CEO, Automobili Lamborghini

'This book is a must read: it will help you calibrate your corporate strategy through innovative revenue models. Dan Zatta, leading strategy and monetization thought leader, brings new perspectives, relevant for every company.'

Peter Brabeck-Letmathe, Group CEO Nestlé a.d.

"If you want to understand why price is becoming the most important strategic lever for any business, read The Pricing Model Revolution."

The New York Times

"Zatta's book is a must-read for anyone who wants to price successfully in the future: It offers many insights and concrete ideas on a subject that is fundamental to corporate profitability."

Thomas Ingelfinger, Member of the Executive Board, Beiersdorf

"The best book on pricing: practical, concrete, enlightening. A must-read for all managers written by a leading pricing expert."

Giovanni B. Vacchi, Group CEO, Colombini Group

NOTES

Why Pricing Is Key But Seldom Effective

1. Discussion on pricing between the author and Peter Brabeck-Letmathe, November 2022, Rome, Italy.

Rule 1: Make Pricing a CEO Priority

1. Petro, Greg. (2014, 6 August). Why pricing power is the real secret to value investing. *Forbes*. https://www.forbes.com/sites/gregpetro/2014/08/06/why-pricing-power-is-the-real-secret-to-value-investing/?sh=22bf57c12565 (accessed 21 July 2023).

2. See for example Zatta, Danilo. (2022). *The Pricing Model Revolution*. Hoboken, NJ: Wiley.

3. Stewart, Thomas A. (2006, June). Growth as a process (Interview with Jeffrey R. Immelt). *Harvard Business Review*. https://hbr.org/2006/06/growth-as-a-process (accessed 21 July 2023).

4. Liozu, Stephan. (2019). Penetration of the pricing function among global Fortune 500 firms. *Journal of Revenue and Pricing Management* 18: 421–428.

5. See Konzernbereiche: Porsche. (nd). https://geschaeftsbericht2022.volkswagenag.com/konzernbereiche/porsche.html (accessed 23 July 2023).

6. Wittich, Holger. (2022, April). Stärkster Handschalt-Elfer im Edel-Design. *AutoMotorSport*. https://www.auto-motor-und-sport.de/neuheiten/porsche-911-sport-classic-2022/ (accessed 21 July 2023).

7. My translation. Aldi erhöht die Preise – Weitere Händler dürften folgen (2022, 17 March). *Münchener Merkur.* merkur.de/wirtschaft/aldi-erhoeht-die-preise-weitere-haendler-duerften-folgen-zr-91417480.html (accessed 21 July 2023).

8. *The Wall Street Journal Europe*, 1 February 2013.

9. Hyundai seeks solution on the high end. (2013, 19 February). *The Wall Street Journal Europe.*

10. Glover, George and Nolan, Beatrice. (2023, 9 March). Tesla has declared a price war on electric-vehicle and traditional automakers alike. There are signs Elon Musk's company is making early gains. *Yahoo News.* https://uk.news.yahoo.com/tesla-declared-price-war-electric-083132430.html?guccounter=1&guce_referrer=aHR0cHM6Ly93d3cuZ29vZ2xlLmNvbS88&guce_referrer_sig=AQAAAKxTB-5u8gRZQ1nDzgn4ikIX8yFO5WLdB2YIWeOTwKDQUqPk8xxeY5rfxxrKnBhMLja41EBX-5eLAB7yD_ERm2AurnvBKVCy48W3dMy1l6S4TZFaJsv9RmcmCk659UmJ3N_bG01b6UidiX1J3MafaTEla-5EdLHQnNaYNcjDm2zy (accessed 21 July 2023).

11. Raval, Anjli, Sheppard, David, and Brower, Derek. (2020, 8 March). Saudi Arabia launches oil price war after Russia deal collapse. *Financial Times.* https://www.ft.com/content/d700b71a-6122-11ea-b3f3-fe4680ea68b5 (accessed 21 July 2023).

12. Olvide, Shira. (2014, 17 April). A price war erupts in cloud services. *The Wall Street Journal Europe.* https://www.wsj.com/articles/a-price-war-erupts-in-cloud-services-1397604953 (accessed 21 July 2023).

13. Sapsford, Jathon. (2005, 27 April). Toyota sends mixed messages on Detroit woes. *The Wall Street Journal.* https://www.wsj.com/articles/SB111447831655116719 (accessed 21 July 2023).

Rule 2: Disseminate the Culture of Profit

1. Patel, N. (2015, 16 January). 90% of startups fail. https://www.forbes.com/sites/neilpatel/2015/01/16/90-of-startups-will-fail-heres-what-

you-need-to-know-about-the-10/?sh=70902d926679 (accessed 25 June 2023).

2. Bryant, S. (2022, 26 November). How many startups fail and why? https://www.investopedia.com/articles/personal-finance/040915/how-many-startups-fail-and-why.asp (accessed 25 June 2023).

3. An extended discussion of monetization strategies and pricing models can be found in Zatta, Danilo (2022). *The Pricing Model Revolution*. Hoboken, NJ: Wiley.

4. Drucker, Peter F. (1954). *The Practice of Management*. New York: Harper-Collins.

5. Adapted from Zatta, Danilo, et al. (2009). *Battere la crisi*. Milan: Il Sole 24Ore.

6. See Laricchia, F. (2023, 13 April). Apple's revenue worldwide. Statista. https://www.statista.com/statistics/265125/total-net-sales-of-apple-since-2004/ (accessed 11 June 2023).

7. This section is taken from Zatta, Danilo. *Le basi del pricing*. Milan: Hoepli, 2021; Zatta, Danilo et al. (2013). *Price Management*. Vol. I. Milan: Franco Angeli.

8. See Ritter, Johannes Von. (2015, 13 November). Erfolg ist ein guter Leim. *Frankfurter Allgemeine Zeitung*. https://www.faz.net/aktuell/wirtschaft/unternehmen/im-gespraech-miele-gesellschafter-erfolg-ist-ein-sehr-guter-leim-11958429.html (accessed 21 July 2023).

9. Ritter, Johannes Von. (2015, 13 November). Erfolg ist ein guter Leim. *Frankfurter Allgemeine Zeitung*. https://www.faz.net/aktuell/wirtschaft/unternehmen/im-gespraech-miele-gesellschafter-erfolg-ist-ein-sehr-guter-leim-11958429.html (accessed 21 July 2023).

Rule 3: Understand and Sell Value

1. In these cases, it is imperative to abide by the rules and legislation in the countries where this is done.

Rule 4: Differentiate Prices

1. See Zatta, Danilo. (2016). *Revenue Management in Manufacturing.* Cham, Switzerland: Springer.

2. The price enquiry was done on 19 March 2023 and it relates to the night of 17 May 2023.

3. Smallwood, K. (2018, 27 February). That time Coca-Cola tried to introduce vending machines that charged more on hot days. Today I Found Out. https://www.todayifoundout.com/index.php/2018/02/time-coca-cola-tried-introduce-vending-machines-charged-hot-days (accessed 21 July 2023).

4. Ellson, A. (2016, 19 January). Women charged more on 'sexist' high street. https://www.thetimes.co.uk/article/women-charged-more-on-sexist-high-street-3gpwv2ck3qd (accessed 23 July 2023).

5. Hughes, T. (2016, 19 January). Women are being fleeced by 'sexist' high street stores. *Daily Mail.* https://www.dailymail.co.uk/news/article-3405875/The-sexist-high-street.html (accessed 21 July 2023).

6. Haslam, K. (2023, 19 July). When is the best time to buy an iPhone? Macworld. https://www.macworld.com/article/672505/when-is-the-best-time-to-buy-an-iphone.html (accessed 21 July 2023).

7. 4 New York (2022, 21 September). Wanna watch Aaron Judge tonight? https://www.nbcnewyork.com/news/sports/yankees-ticket-prices-soar-with-aaron-judge-on-home-run-brink-heres-how-much (accessed 21 July 2023).

8. Van Gerven, G., Colin-Dubuisson, Ostrovsky, S., and Prompers, L. (2020, 22 April). Parallel trade and export restrictions are back in the spotlight. https://www.linklaters.com/en/insights/publications/2020/april/parallel-trade-and-export-restrictions-are-back-in-the-spotlight (accessed 21 July 2023).

9. EURACTIV. (2001, 21 November/2010, 29 January). Levi Strauss wins European trademark case. https://www.euractiv.com/section/

social-europe-jobs/news/levi-strauss-wins-european-trademark-case/ (accessed 25 July 2023).

10. Kohlpharma. (nd). Kohlpharma – pointing the way. https://www.kohlpharma.com/en/about-us (accessed 21 July 2023).

11. Lattwein, R. (2021, 12 March). Wie Kohlpharma und Co. mit Unterstützung von Wirtschaftsminister Altmaier abkassieren. Saarlandinside. https://www.saarlandinside.de/wie-kohlpharma-und-co-mit-unterstuetzung-von-wirtschaftsminister-altmaier-abkassieren/ (accessed 21 July 2023).

12. Stoldt, Moritz von. (2018, 21 May). Lohnt sich die DB bahnCard 25? Reisetopia Hotels. https://www.reisetopia.de/guides/lohnt-sich-die-db-bahncard-25/#Wann_lohnt_sich_eine_DB_BahnCard_25 (accessed 21 July 2023).

13. MSC Cruises. (nd). Early booking fares. https://www.msccruises.fi/cruise-deals/early-booking-type-of-fares (accessed 21 July 2023).

14. Apple Trade In. (nd). Trade in. Upgrade. Save. It's a win-win-win. https://www.apple.com/shop/trade-in (accessed 21 July 2023).

15. Dell. (nd). Dell price guarantee. https://www.dell.com/de-de/lp/price-match-guarantee (accessed 21 July 2023).

16. Mediamarkt. (nd). Jetzt als myMediaMarkt-Kunde dein Wunschprodukt zum Top-Preis sichern. https://www.mediamarkt.de/de/campaign/preisversprechen (accessed 21 July 2023).

17. Iberia. (nd). Miglior prezzo garantito. https://www.iberia.com/it/miglior-prezzo-garantito (accessed 21 July 2023).

18. Der Spiegel. (nd). Douglas Rabattcodes. https://www.spiegel.de/gutscheine/douglas (accessed 21 July 2023).

19. NIKE. (nd). Studenten erhalten 10% Rabatt Auf Nike.com. https://www.nike.com/de/student-discount (accessed 25 July 2023).

20. Gutschein.PRO. (nd). Shell.de Clubsmart promotional codes and vouchers. https://www.shell.gutschein.pro (accessed 25 July 2023).

Rule 5: Consolidate Profits by Increasing Prices

1. Seal, Dean. (2023). Caterpillar's sales jump 17% on higher equipment prices. *The Wall Street Journal.* https://www.pressreader.com/usa/the-wall-street-journal/20230428/282067691251807 (accessed 21 July 2023).

2. Spiegel Reise. (2010, 14 September). Bahn-Tickets dürfen am Schalter teurer sein. www.spiegel.de/reise/aktuell/gerichtsbeschluss-bahn-tickets-duerfen-am-schalter-teurer-sein-a-717481.html (accessed 21 July 2023).

3. Welt. (2008, 29 August). Bedienzuschlag treibt Bahnkunden auf die Palme. Wirtschaft. www.welt.de/wirtschaft/article2369820/Bedienzuschlag-treibt-Bahnkunden-auf-die-Palme.html (accessed 21 July 2023).

4. Frankfurter Allgemeine Zeitung. (2023, 21 July). Sparkasse München rudert nach Protesten zurück. www.faz.net/agenturmeldungen/dpa/sparkasse-muenchen-rudert-nach-protesten-zurueck-19049611.html (accessed 23 July 2023).

5. Forbes. (nd). Gilette. www.forbes.com/companies/gillette/?sh=2b07e71410a0 (accessed 21 July 2023).

6. Ryan, Frances. (2019, 22 January). Shrinkflation. *The Guardian.* https://www.theguardian.com/commentisfree/2019/jan/22/shrinkflation-for-those-struggling-its-about-more-than-just-chocolate-bars (accessed 21 July 2023).

7. verbraucherzentrale. (2022, 6 January). Mogelpackungen. www.verbraucherzentrale.de/wissen/lebensmittel/kennzeichnung-und-inhaltsstoffe/mogelpackungen-tricks-mit-luft-und-doppeltem-boden-11707 (accessed 21 July 2023).

8. Meisenzahl, Mary and Dean, Grace. (2022, 25 August). From toilet paper to candy bars, companies hide rising costs by shrinking the size of everyday products. *Insider.* www.businessinsider.com/shrinkflation-grocery-stores-pringles-cereal-candy-bars-chocolate-toilet-paper-cadbury-2021-7 (accessed 21 July 2023).

9. $8 up to 24 hours for medium-sized bags, or $2 per hour (prices obtained in a telephone call to the Berlin hotel on 27 March 2023).

10. Ryanair. (2023). Fees. www.ryanair.com/gb/en/useful-info/help-centre/fees#! (accessed 21 July 2023).

11. www.faq.europcar.de/buchungen/wie-kann-ich-meine-buchung-stornieren.html (last accessed 25 June 2023).

12. www.finder.com/nz/credit-card-surcharges (last accessed 25 June 2023).

13. reistopia. (2022, 16 December). Lufthansa hält an Preiserhöhungen auch im nächsten Jahr fest. Reistopia Hotels. www.reisetopia.de/news/lufthansa-preiserhoehungen-2023/ (accessed 21 July 2023).

14. RedaktionsNetzwerk Deutschland. (2023, 3 March). Lufthansa kündigt höhere Preise an. www.rnd.de/reise/lufthansa-kuendigt-hoehere-ticket-preise-an-X4PC7AAJ675K3VJOVFX6LAK5XA.html (accessed 21 July 2023).

15. Zatta, Danilo. (2022). *The Pricing Model Revolution*. Hoboken, NJ: Wiley.

Rule 6: Avoid Price Wars

1. Sun Tzu. (1962). *The Art of War*. Trans. Samuel B. Griffith (1963). New York: Oxford University Press. Ch.3.

2. Jin, Hyunjoo and Sriram, Akash. (2023, 31 March). Tesla's price war. https://www.reuters.com/business/autos-transportation/teslas-price-war-cheaper-cars-expected-drive-record-sales-2023-03-31/ (accessed 21 July 2023).

3. Harloff, Thomas. (2023, 4 May). Tesla startet Preiskreig, Ford macht mit. *AutoMotorSport*. https://www.auto-motor-und-sport.de/verkehr/preiskampf-rabattschlacht-elektroauto-hersteller-tesla/ (accessed 21 July 2023).

4. For more details see Zatta, Danilo, et al. (2013). *Price Management. II*. Milan: Franco Angeli Edizioni.

5. UPS. (2021, 16 December). UPS is leading the industry in on-time performance. www.about.ups.com/us/en/our-stories/people-led/ups-on-time-performance.html (accessed 21 July 2023).

6. Offer available in Europe in April 2023.

7. Tait, Nikki and Wilson, James. (2011, 13 April). P&G and Unilever fined for price-fixing. *Financial Times*. www.ft.com/content/e0e21f9a-65b3-11e0-baee-00144feab49a (accessed 21 July 2023).

8. Lev, Michael. (1990, 17 December). Taco Bell finds price of success. *The New York Times*. www.nytimes.com/1990/12/17/business/taco-bell-finds-price-of-success-59.html (accessed 21 July 2023).

9. Collins, Glenn. (1997, 4 April). McDonald's reinvents a promotion in fast-food frenzy. *The New York Times*. www.nytimes.com/1997/04/04/business/mcdonald-s-reinvents-a-promotion-in-fast-food-frenzy.html (accessed 21 July 2023).

10. www.apnews.com/article/14d759033fac0823f9c8418e29f5feba (last accessed 20 June 2023).

11. www.apnews.com/article/14d759033fac0823f9c8418e29f5feba (last accessed 20 June 2023).

12. PriceBeam. (2017, 5 April). How the Ritz won a pricing war without lowering prices. https://blog.pricebeam.com/how-the-ritz-won-a-pricing-war-without-lowering-prices (accessed 21 July 2023).

13. Trivedi, Suryakant. (2021, 27 May). The strategy that makes 3M an innovation powerhouse. The Strategy Story. www.thestrategystory.com/2021/05/27/3m-innovation-strategy/ (accessed 21 July 2023).

14. Warren, R. (1987, 20 November). Improved recording tape by 3M was born in the USA. *Chicago Tribune*. www.chicagotribune.com/news/ct-xpm-1987-11-20-8703270587-story.html (accessed 21 July 2023).

15. Ahmad, Majeed. (2020, 9 November). A brief history of Intel's memory business. www.ednasia.com/a-brief-history-of-intels-memory-business/ (accessed 21 July 2023).

Rule 7: Cultivate Your Price Image

1. Gasparro, Annie. and Rubin, Gabriel T. (2022, 12 February). The hidden ways companies raise prices. *The Wall Street Journal* www .wsj.com/articles/companies-hidden-inflation-consumer-price-index-11644549254 (accessed 20 July 2023).

2. Guboff, Marcel. (2022, 19 August). Weniger darin bei gleichem Preis: Haribo reduziert Inhalt bei Produkten. www.wa.de/verbraucher/haribo-goldbaeren-inhalt-reduziert-preis-erhoehung-pico-balla-kleinere-verpackung-kunden-91730348.html (accessed 23 July 2023).

3. Gasparro, Annie and Rubin, Gabriel T. (2022, 12 February). The hidden ways companies raise prices. *The Wall Street Journal* www .wsj.com/articles/companies-hidden-inflation-consumer-price-index-11644549254 (accessed 20 July 2023).

4. Southwest. (nd). Reward seats only on days ending in 'y'. www.south west.com/html/air/transfarency/ (accessed 21 July 2023).

5. La storia di wise. (nd). *wise.* www.wise.com/it/about/our-story (accessed 21 July 2023).

6. Walmart. (2020, 26 March). We mean it when we say it. www .corporate.walmart.com/newsroom/2020/03/26/we-mean-it-when-we-say-it-every-day-low-prices-anytime-anywhere (accessed 21 July 2023).

7. Butler, Sarah. (2022, 25 February). John Lewis drops 'never knowingly undersold' pledge. *The Guardian.* www.theguardian.com/business/2022/feb/25/john-lewis-drops-never-knowingly-undersold-pledge (accessed 21 July 2023).

8. ACaseStudy.Com. (nd). Burt's Bees case study. www.acasestudy.com/burts-bees-case-study/ (accessed 21 July 2023).

9. Mackenzie, Macaela. (2018, 15 December). Burt's Bees beeswax lip balm has more than 1,00 five-star ratings on target's website. www .allure.com/story/burts-bees-beeswax-lip-balm-sold-every-second (accessed 21 July 2023).

10. ZIPPIA. (nd). Burt's Bees revenue. www.zippia.com/burt-s-bees-careers-17650/revenue/

11. TKE. (nd). Geschäftsjahr 2020/2021. www.tkelevator.com/global-de/newsroom/pressemitteilungen/geschaeftsjahr-2020-2021-tk-elevator-erreicht-umsatzwachstum-margensteigerung-und-wichtige-strategische-meilensteine-132160.html (accessed 21 July 2023).

12. TKE. (nd). Multi. https://www.tkelevator.com/de-de/produkte/multi/ (accessed 25 July 2023).

13. Swatch Group. (nd). Geschicichte der Swatch Group. www.swatch group.com/de/swatch-group/geschichte-der-swatch-group (accessed 21 July 2023).

14. De Burton, Simon. (2015, 4 March). Diese Swatch-Sammlung könnte Millionen einbringen. www.classicdriver.com/de/article/uhren/diese-swatch-sammlung-koennte-millionen-einbringen (accessed 21 July 2023).

15. Swatch Group. (nd). Geschicichte der Swatch Group. www.swatch group.com/de/swatch-group/geschichte-der-swatch-group (accessed 21 July 2023).

16. Apple Inc. (2007, 17 October). iTunes plus now offers over two million tracks at just 79p. www.apple.com/de/newsroom/2007/10/17iTunes-Plus-Now-Offers-Over-Two-Million-Tracks-at-Just-99-Cents/ (accessed 21 July 2023).

17. Hill, Lee. (n.d). 'Reassuringly expensive'. Insightful. www.insightfulux .co.uk/blog/customer-experience-beat-price/ (accessed 21 July 2023).

18. Rogers, Charlotte. (2022, 13 April). From flower sellers to ice skating priests, the two-decade long campaign propelled Belgian beer brand Stella Artois from sluggish sales into a market leader with a place in advertising folklore. www.marketingweek.com/frank-lowe-stella-reassuringly-expensive/ (accessed 21 July 2023).

19. Digital Synopsis. (nd). IKEA comes up with a brilliant way to show how affordable their products are. www.digitalsynopsis.com/

advertising/ikea-affordable-products-saudi-arabia-ogilvy/ (accessed 21 July 2023).

20. *The Straits Times*. (2016, 5 April). Japan dessert firm Akagi Nyugyo offers apology for 12-cent ice cream price hike. www.straitstimes.com/asia/japan-dessert-firm-akagi-nyugyo-offers-apology-for-12-cent-ice-cream-price-hike (accessed 21 July 2023).

Rule 8: Employ Technologies, Directing Algorithms

1. Author's interview with Uber drivers in London

2. Shead, Sam. (2017, 5 June). Uber has refunded customers caught up in London terror attack. Insider. www.businessinsider.com/uber-refunds-customers-surge-pricing-london-terror-attack-2017-6 (accessed 21 July 2023).

3. Soper, Taylor. (2020, 22 January). Uber and Lyft criticized for automated surge pricing after Seattle shooting. www.geekwire.com/2020/uber-lyft-criticized-automated-surge-pricing-seattle-shooting/ (accessed 21 July 2023).

4. Morris, David Z. (2020, 14 July). What causes crazy-high prices on Wayfair and Amazon? www.fortune.com/2020/07/14/wayfair-cabinet-conspiracy-algorithm-amazon-pricing-ecommerce/ (accessed 21 July 2023).

5. Leonhart, David. (2005, 27 June). Why variable pricing fails at the vending machine. *The New York Times*. www.nytimes.com/2005/06/27/business/why-variable-pricing-fails-at-the-vending-machine.html (accessed 21 July 2023).

6. Solon, Olivia. (2011, 27 April). How a book about flies came to be priced $24 million on Amazon. www.wired.com/2011/04/amazon-flies-24-million/ (accessed 21 July 2023).

7. Zellermayer, Ofer. (1996). The pain of paying. PhD Thesis. Department of Social and Decision Sciences, Carnegie Mellon University, Pittsburgh, PA.

8. Chan, Eugene Y. (2021). The consumer in physical pain: Implications for the pain-of-paying and pricing. *Behavioral Pricing* 6 (1): 10–20.

9. Chandler, Simon. (2020, 17 February). IKEA becomes first retailer to let customers pay using time. Forbes. www.forbes.com/sites/simon chandler/2020/02/17/ikea-becomes-first-retailer-to-let-customers-pay-using-time/?sh=76170b95557b (accessed 21 July 2023).

10. Chandler, Simon. (2020, 17 February). www.forbes.com/sites/simon chandler/2020/02/17/ikea-becomes-first-retailer-to-let-customers-pay-using-time/?sh=76170b95557b (accessed 21 July 2023).

11. Munsberg, Von Hendrik. (2021, 23 April). Neue Regeln beim Spritpreis-Roulette an der Tankstelle. *Süddeutsche Zeitung.* www .sueddeutsche.de/wirtschaft/benzinpreis-spritpreise-entwicklung-tankstellen-1.5273156 (accessed 21 July 2023).

12. Motor talk. (2018, 13 April). Tankstelle ändert während des Tankvor-ganges den Betrag de Liter Preises an der Zapfsäule. www.motor-talk .de/forum/tankstelle-aendert-waehrend-des-tankvorganges-den-betrag-des-liter-preises-an-der-zapfsaeule-t2461075.html (accessed 21 July 2023).

13. Root®. (nd). About Root Inc. https://inc.joinroot.com/company/ (accessed 25 July 2023).

14. Thimou, Theo. (2019, 3 December). 6 things to know about Root insurance. Clark.com. www.clark.com/insurance/car-insurance/root-insurance/ (accessed 21 July 2023).

15. Catalate. (2022, 11 October). Is there any magic behind Disney's varia-ble pricing strategy? www.catalate.com/blog/disney-magic/ (accessed 21 July 2023).

16. Rosen, E. (2021, 20 May). 40 years of miles. www.thepointsguy.com/ guide/evolution-frequent-flyer-programs/ (accessed 21 July 2023).

17. DizN with the Donohues. (2022, 11 October). Disney announces variable pricing for Genie+. www.destinationdizn.com/2022/10/11/ disney-announces-variable-pricing-for-genie/(accessed 21 July 2023).

18. Olse, Kyle. (2023, 17 July). Your complete guide to the Delta SkyMiles program. Delta vacations. www.thepointsguy.com/guide/ultimate-guide-delta-skymiles/ (accessed 21 July 2023).

19. Gollan, Doug. (2109, 5 April). United Airlines' move to stop publishing mileage plus award levels is unfriendly but not surprising. Forbes. www.forbes.com/sites/douggollan/2019/04/05/united-airlines-move-to-stop-publishing-award-levels-is-unfriendly/?sh=4b72171e17fa (accessed 21 July 2023).

20. Delta. (nd). Get to know your SkyMiles®. www.delta.com/us/en/skymiles/how-to-use-miles/travel-with-miles (accessed 21 July 2023).

Rule 9: Set the Pricing Governance

1. This refers to everything that makes a product or service unique to that company.

2. Examples of processes include: defining/revising pricing strategy; price determination and revision; pricing for new products; channel-specific pricing; discount monitoring; and margin analysis.

3. In an extreme case, a company did not have a regular price list but only 'exception prices' or 'non-exception prices'.

Rule 10: Debunk the Myths of Pricing

1. Simon, Bernard. (2007, 15 November). GM launches its last-chance saloon in family car market. *Financial Times*, 22.

2. Linebaugh, Kate and Bennett, Jeff. (2010, 12 January). Marchionne upends Chrysler's ways. *The Wall Street Journal*, B1. https://www.wsj.com/articles/SB10001424052748703652104574652364158366106 (accessed 20 July 2023).

3. Simon, Bernard and Reed, John. (2008, 20 August). GM makes a U-turn over sales incentives. *Financial Times*, 17. https://www.ft.com/content/bcd3009c-6e0d-11dd-b5df-0000779fd18c (accessed 20 July 2023).

4. A commodity is a basic good that has no intrinsic value, and it is interchangeable with goods of the same type. Being only valued in relation to its price, the lower the price is, the more appealing the good.

5. Buzzell, Robert D., Gale, Bradley T., and Sultan, Ralph G. (1975). Market share: A key to profitability. *Harvard Business Review* 53 (1): 97–106.

6. Buzzell, Robert D. (2004). The PIMS program of strategy research: a retrospective appraisal. *Journal of Business Research* 57 (5): 478–483. Available at https://www.sciencedirect.com/science/article/abs/pii/S0148296302003144 (accessed 20 July 2023).

7. Bradshaw, Tim. (2013, 27 August). Cheaper iPhone seeks to retain core values. *Financial Times*, 15.

8. Baer, Justin. (2009, 15 April). United Airlines sets ambitions at lower altitude. *Financial Times*. https://www.ft.com/content/251e76ee-2917-11de-bc5e-00144feabdc0 (accessed 20 July 2023).

9. Milne, Richard. (2013, 22 February). Lego brushes off toy sector gloom. *Financial Times*, 14. https://www.ft.com/content/adefc266-7c15-11e2-bf52-00144feabdc0 (accessed 20 July 2023).

10. Edited Transcript. (2023, 24 January). Q4 2022 Verizon Communications Inc. Earnings Call.

11. Reuters. (2022, 11 November). Skoda focused on profitability over volumes, CEO tells E15. *Euronews*. https://www.euronews.com/next/2022/11/07/volkswagen-skoda (accessed 20 July 2023).

12. Lee, Dave. (2023, 10 February). Uber surges further ahead of rival Lyft in ride-share race. *Financial Times*, 16.

13. Grand View Research (nd). Bottled water market size & share report, 2022–2030. Available at www.grandviewresearch.com/industry-analysis/bottled-water-market (accessed 20 July 2023).

14. This is what emerged from a study commissioned by the Italian consumers' association Altroconsumo (2014, 7 February). Benzina senza

marca conviene. www.altroconsumo.it/auto-e-moto/automobili/news/benzina-senza-marca-conviene (accessed 20 July 2023).

15. Kroher, Thomas. (2023, 27 January). *Premiumkraftstoffe: Was können V-Power, Ultimate & Co.?*, https://www.adac.de/verkehr/tanken-kraftstoff-antrieb/benzin-und-diesel/premiumkraftstoffe/ (accessed 25 July 2023).

16. Paschek, L. (2003, 27 July). *Shell: 100-Oktan-Kraftstoff fällt durch im ADAC-Test durch*, ATZ online, Springer Professional.

17. Kroher, Thomas. (2023, 27 January). *Premiumkraftstoffe: Was können V-Power, Ultimate & Co.?*, https://www.adac.de/verkehr/tanken-kraftstoff-antrieb/benzin-und-diesel/premiumkraftstoffe/ (accessed 25 July 2023).

18. Weclas, Miroslaw. (2004). *Hochoktan ottokraftstoffe für Hochleistungs-motoren*. Nuremberg: Institut für Fahrzeugtechnik der Georg-Simon-Ohm Fachhochschule.

19. Zatta, Danilo. (2022). *The Pricing Model Revolution*. Hoboken, NJ: Wiley.

20. The colour white as code for positivity and clarity is also used in other fields connected to ICT – in hacking, for example, a difference is made between white and black hats: the former hack for good reasons, the latter instead use hacking for criminal purposes. On the concept of social engineering, see Mitnick, K. (2003). *The Art of Deception*. Hoboken, NJ: Wiley.

21. Barrie, Leonie. (2014, 24 July). New pricing strategy pays off for Nike. Just-Style. http://www.just-style.com/analysis/ (accessed 2 March 2023).

22. See O'Reilly, Lara. (2014). Nike is becoming a luxury brand. *Insider*. https://www.businessinsider.com/nike-q2-2015-earnings-beat-analysts-estimates-but-demand-has-slowed-2014-12?r=US&IR=T (accessed 20 July 2023).

23. Hake, B. (2009). Hugo Boss: the use of analytical tools to supplement pricing decisions. Presentation at the 8th Strategic Pricing Conference, Marcus Evans, 10–11 September, London.

24. Porsche Car Configurator. (nd). https://www.porsche.com/uk/modelstart/ (accessed 20 July 2023).

25. Kohli, Chiranjeev and Suri, Rajneesh. (2011). The price is right? Guidelines for pricing to enhance profitability. *Business Horizons* 54: 563–573.

26. Dickson, Peter. and Sawyer, Alan. (1990). The price knowledge and search of supermarket shoppers. *Journal of Marketing* 54 (3): 42–53.

27. Gaston-Breton, Charlotte and Raghubir, Priya. (2014). *The Price Knowledge Paradox: Why Consumers Have Lower Confidence in, but Better Recall of Unfamiliar Prices.* New York: Springer Science+Business Media. This effect is due to the fact that unfamiliar prices tend to be processed more intentionally, codified, and therefore remembered. Conversely, with familiar prices consumers feel confident in their memory and do not feel they require an intentional effort.